Tin Pan Alley Gi

Tin Pan Alley Girl

A Biography of Ann Ronell

TIGHE E. ZIMMERS

McFarland & Company, Inc., Publishers
Jefferson, North Carolina, and London

"Love Happy" lyrics reprinted by permission. Words by Ann Ronell.
©1949 Jewel Music Publishing Company, Inc. (ASCAP)

LIBRARY OF CONGRESS CATALOGUING-IN-PUBLICATION DATA

Zimmers, Tighe E., 1949–
Tin Pan Alley girl : a biography of Ann Ronell /
Tighe E. Zimmers.
p.   cm.
Includes bibliographical references and index.

ISBN 978-0-7864-3905-8
softcover : 50# alkaline paper ∞

1. Ronell, Ann.   2. Composers— United States— Biography.
3. Lyricists— United States— Biography.   I. Title.
ML410.R63296Z56   2009   782.42164092 — dc22   [B]   2008055747

British Library cataloguing data are available

On the cover: Ann Ronell, age 18 (Nebraska Jewish Historical Society)

Manufactured in the United States of America

*McFarland & Company, Inc., Publishers
Box 611, Jefferson, North Carolina 28640
www.mcfarlandpub.com*

To the many cabaret singers and musicians
who are keeping the American Popular Songbook alive

Acknowledgments

Special thanks to the following: Robert Cowan, Ann Ronell's brother-in-law and the executor of her estate, who died during the writing of this book, and his son-in-law, Douglas Brotz, who was especially helpful in the later stages of the book; George Bozwick and the staff of the New York Public Library for the Performing Arts, Special Collections and Billy Rose Theatre Collection; Renee Corcoran, executive director, Kathy Weiner, and Dottie Rosenblum of the Nebraska Jewish Historical Society, Omaha, home of the Ann Ronell Papers collection; Patrick Donahue, my computer wizard.

Thanks to the personnel of libraries, collections, and various institutions: Frank Driggs, Frank Driggs Collection of photographs, New York; David Stein and David Farneth at the Kurt Weill Foundation and Weill-Lenya Research Center, New York; Sam Fein of the Songwriters' Guild of America in Nashville, Tennessee; Penn Genthner, archivist for the Pasadena Playhouse, Pasadena, California; Bob Grimes, sheet music archivist and historian, San Francisco; Barbara Hall and the staff of the Margaret Herrick Library of the Academy of Motion Picture Arts and Sciences, Beverly Hills; Katherine Kraft, archivist, Radcliffe Institute for Advanced Study, Radcliffe Archives; E. A. Kral, historian of famous Nebraskans, Wilber, Nebraska; Thomas Lisanti and Stephen Saks of the Permissions Department of the New York Public Library; Staff of the Harry Ransom Center for the Humanities Research Center, University of Texas, Austin; Staff of the Newberry Library, Chicago; Staff of the Park Ridge (Illinois) Public Library; Robert C. Ray, Special Collections Librarian, Miller Nichols Library, University of Missouri–Kansas City; David Schulson of David Schulson Autographs, New York; Amanda L. Green of Serendipity Books, Berkeley, California.

Thanks to members of Ann Ronell's extended family, her friends and acquaintances and others involved and interested in the world of music: Adele French, New York; Marni Nixon, the first "Susanna"; Joan Peyser, George Gershwin biographer, New York; Lali Ray, Great Neck, New York; Liza Redfield, New York; Robert Russell, Helena, Montana; Benjamin Sears, pianist and musical historian, Boston; Beatrice Sommers, Omaha, Nebraska; Julia Tucker, Boston, daughter of photographer Richard Tucker.

Thanks to family, friends and others who helped out in various ways: readers and critics of my various drafts of the book: my sister Malilee Elis, my wife Noreen, and cabaret singers Joan Curto, Justin Hayford, and Cory Jamison; my children, Colin and Therese Zimmers, especially in the early stages of the book when they had to keep moving the Ann Ronell boxes from one place to another; Dan Stetzel, piano accompanist, cabaret professor and expert on the American Popular Songbook, Roosevelt University, Chicago; the friendly staffs at the Starbucks Coffee shops where I did much of my work.

Contents

Preface

Ann Ronell couldn't help herself. She kept writing songs. She wrote the class song for her public high school graduation and the convention song for the Hai Resh Fraternity in Des Moines, Iowa. She wrote the class song for Wheaton College in Norton, Massachusetts. At Radcliffe College, she wrote "College Is the Place for Me," which won a songwriting prize and was published in the *Radcliffe Songbook*. Then she got serious about her composing.

Ronell was educated and worked during a period in America of great musical creativity. The publishers of Tin Pan Alley and the producers of Broadway musicals and Hollywood provided artistic outlets for myriad composers and lyricists. From the turn of the century through 1960, this group of artists, almost exclusively male, created a body of music known as American Popular Song, songs that have endured, not confined to one performer, arrangement, or style. Ronell was active in all of these arenas—Tin Pan Alley, Broadway, and Hollywood—often breaking the gender barrier. Among her accomplishments, she was the first woman to:

- write both words and music for a Broadway musical
- compose the score for a Hollywood movie
- conduct the score for a Hollywood movie
- earn an Academy Award nomination for a song and musical score.

But Ronell just wasn't first, she was good. Her Broadway songs from *Count Me In* were critically praised. Her early songs were legitimate hits, including "Rain on the Roof" and "Baby's Birthday Party." Another, "Willow Weep for Me," lives on in the pantheon of American Popular Song and jazz standards. One of her songs, "Who's Afraid of the Big Bad Wolf?," written for a Disney cartoon, is still heard around the world. Ronell's movie work as composer, arranger and conductor was successful. She collaborated with several of the leading composers of the era, including Vincent Youmans, Kurt Weill, and Werner Janssen. She worked hard to promote a movement towards "opera in English," translating the librettos and reworking orchestrations of several classical operas and writing special material for opera singers based on the classics.

Ronell did all of this in an era when female musicians, with few exceptions, were confined to roles as rehearsal pianists, transcriptionists, and personal assistants. Usually juggling numerous projects, she was immersed in the artistic worlds of New York and Hollywood, never confined to one genre.

I discovered all of these things after I purchased a large collection of her professional papers around 1999. As an autograph collector and amateur historian in the area of American Popular Song, I was aware of Ann Ronell. I knew she had written "Willow Weep for Me," but that was about all. Her name became more prominent to me when I purchased a few notes that had been written to her by stage actress Lotte Lenya, Kurt Weill's widow. The autograph dealer who sold me these pieces was surprised that I knew of Ann Ronell. He told me that he had access to a large collection of her papers that a book dealer in California was trying to sell. I didn't know quite what this would entail, but I was sure that such a collection would have great letters, references, etc., to American Popular Song. After a few months, the deal was closed, and I received twenty-six boxes of Ann Ronell materials, delivered by UPS into my dining room.

Storage alone was a problem, as the boxes did not look good in the dining room. Eventually, they were stored in the basement, and I started to go through them. Everything I came across was new to me, especially her Broadway musical *Count Me In* and her extensive work in opera in English. The letters I had anticipated started to show up, interesting early finds including notes from Irving Caesar, Hugh Martin, Harpo Marx, Mary Pickford, Kay Swift and several long Aerograms from harmonica virtuoso Larry Adler.

After two years of organizing and discovering what a varied life in the arts Ann Ronell had lived, I decided to write a biography. I had much writing experience in the field of emergency medicine, all in journals, but I had never written any history or biography. Over the next five years, I took a box at a time, and forged a biography, one project of hers at a time — songs, movies, musicals, operas. The book focuses on her professional work with occasional forays into her personal life, mostly regarding her marriage to independent Hollywood producer Lester Cowan.

In addition to my collection, the New York Public Library for the Performing Arts was of invaluable help in my research, as that collection has strengths in areas mine did not have. Also of great help in research were the collections and especially the staffs of the Nebraska Jewish Historical Society in Omaha, Ronell's hometown, and the Margaret Herrick Library of the Academy of Motion Picture Arts and Sciences in Beverly Hills.

Except for occasional magazine articles over the years, little has been written about Ann Ronell. The most extensive article focusing exclusively on her was written by Edward Jablonski for *Nebraska Life* in 1997. No biographies have been devoted to her. When Ronell's name does appear, it is in music encyclopedias or articles about women composers of American Popular Song. Her story was prominent in a PBS show, *Yours for a Song: The Women of Tin Pan Alley*, first aired in 1998. Almost all references to Ronell focus on her popular songs, especially "Willow Weep for Me" and "Who's Afraid of the Big Bad Wolf?," and some of her movie work. Except for brief mentions, usually overlooked are her years of work in opera in English, particularly translations and revisions of *Martha* and *The Gypsy Baron*, her creation of an art form, the "ballet-sing," compositions for two musicals (*Count Me In* and *Oh! Susanna*) and years of work in Hollywood film circles including Academy Award nominations for Best Score and Best Song ("Linda" from *The Story of G.I. Joe*).

Readers may be drawn to this book out of interest in a particular area — Tin Pan Alley, Broadway, opera, film music — and certain chapters should pique their interest. Some may be doing research on women in the arts. Others may look at Ann Ronell's career in its entirety, one of work and interest in music and musicians, one which could not be pigeonholed, forged by a young woman in fields dominated by men.

1

Omaha and New England, 1905–1929

"You never think of Ann without music or dancing."

Ann Ronell always had a birthday cake, no matter what her age. She insisted on it.[1] As she was born on December 25, it was the only way she could make family and friends remember her day.

She had grown up in a modest section of Omaha, Nebraska. Her parents and their families had been part of the Jewish emigration from Russia in the late 19th century, drawn to the Midwest by family and available work. Months after the assassination of Czar Alexander II in 1881, widespread pogroms against Russian Jews had occurred, tacitly approved by the government. Frequent between 1882 and 1905, pogroms eventually ended with the Bolshevik revolution.[2] To escape this persecution and to avoid service in the czar's army, Ann Ronell's father, Morris Rosenblatt, emigrated to the United States in 1895 at age seventeen. His parents, Chaym Rosenblatt and Chana Gerstein, had married in 1874 in the Russian town of Kinif in the province of Volhynia (Appendix B). Morris had been born to them in 1878.[3]

Before settling in Omaha, Morris, called Rosey from youth, had worked on the railroad in Chicago, then Davenport, Iowa. In the latter town, he was a boarder with the family of Rabbi and Bertha Rabinowitz. They had twelve children, the youngest of whom was Mollie. She and Morris developed a friendship over the years and eventually married, in 1899, when she was sixteen and he was twenty-one.[4]

They had four children: Sol Ariah (born 1900), Anya (1905), Leah Gussie (1910), and Herman Samuel (1914). Mollie ran the household and was a practical woman. She had had some musical training and taught Ann to play the piano with crossed arms.[5] Both parents were quick to notice when Ann began to play by ear as a child. Morris, who ran a local coal business, Consumers' Coal & Supply, was more the dreamer with a strong interest in the arts that carried over to Ann. He had taken her to concerts and other entertainments in her early years. She said of her father in a letter to a nephew later in her life:

> He took me to dancing school when I was 5, and taught me to dance the kazatsky with him in our living room, always encouraging me to enter the musical field. I've always wondered from whom Dad obtained his exquisite taste in living, his special comprehension of color combinations in clothes, the delicacy of food he preferred, and of feelings more importantly.[6]

Ann attended public elementary school in Omaha and also Temple Israel School for her Jewish faith from which she graduated in 1914. Her earliest piano lessons were with a well-

known pianist-teacher in Omaha, Jean Duffield, and her early dance teachers were Adelaide
Fogg and Carol Marhoff Pitts.[7]

Ann showed interest in music and composition early. As she told an interviewer years
later, "Well, I think as long as I remember, I've been writing words and music."[8] She wrote
her high school class song as well as a few high school shows. She played the songs from one
of these productions for a noted band leader whose group came through Omaha. He liked
the songs and advised her to study harmony and continue her composing. That she did,
involving herself in numerous projects, usually as leader. She appeared on a local radio vari-

Ann (left) with two unidentified friends in an Omaha, Nebraska, neighborhood, circa 1918 (Nebraska
Jewish Historical Society).

ety show on Omaha's WNAL and was most favorably reviewed by the *Daily News:*

> Miss Ann Rosenblatt, 16, chalked up her name among the elite of WNAL's entertainers on Thursday night. Miss Rosenblatt arranged a program of piano and vocal solos, including the heaviest classic to the lightest jazz, and that it pleased tremendously was proven in flattering reports of listening fans....
>
> She is a pupil of Jean Duffield, and her deft touch and perfect technique mark her as one of the leaders of Omaha's young musical set.[9]

She graduated from Central High in 1923, with yearbook entries from friends that included: "You never think of Ann without music or dancing."[10]

That fall found Ann at Wheaton College, a small liberal arts college in Norton, Massachusetts, south of Boston. She studied religion, languages and the arts. Essays and notebooks from that time show that she demonstrated some proficiency in German, no doubt helpful in her later translations of the German operas *The Gypsy Baron* and *Martha.* She wrote and sang a song, "Love's Like a Rose," which won an award as best athletic song and was published in the College Songbook of the year.[11] But the ever-busy Ann's activities were not confined to music, as a scrapbook from the period shows that she was in the Wheaton Dramatic Club and on the hockey team, and a sophomore class officer and assistant editor of the *Wheaton Record,* the campus daily.[12]

However, Wheaton College had no music department, so Ann transferred to Radcliffe College in Boston in 1927. But she gave credit to a Wheaton drama teacher, Violet Robinson, for convincing her to pursue music composition:

> I should never have begun this sort of career if it hadn't been for her. Gershwin, Youmans, Berlin are all said to have "discovered" me, but she was my real discoverer. She was the first to realize—before I did myself—that I had a flair for composing, and it was she who insisted that I study along those lines.[13]

At Radcliffe, music and composition dominated her life, both academically and socially. Her music courses included harmony, vocal composition, and instrumentation, though she continued her major in English literature. Her Harvard-based teachers included Edward Ballantine, Archibald Davison, and Walter Spalding. She was an exceptionally good student at Radcliffe and was excused from her final exams in music.

She was in the Radcliffe Choral Society, president of the

Top: In dance outfit, circa 1920. *Bottom:* Ann Ronell, age 18. Both from the Nebraska Jewish Historical Society.

Music Club, and music editor of the *Radcliffe News* from 1925 to 1927. The Choral Society, along with the Harvard Glee Club, performed at concerts in Boston's Symphony Hall under conductor Serge Koussevitsky. As president of the Radcliffe Music Club, Ronell organized programs and concerts, playing piano in many of them, often in duet with other Radcliffe students.

Late in her senior year, she played with a Radcliffe classmate, Lola Wilson, their duet entitled *A Study in Cross Relations*.[14] That same year, she composed a short score for a show back at Wheaton College, *Trojan Women*, and wrote a composition, "College Is the Place for Me," which was performed by the Choral Society in a New York City concert and published in the *Radcliffe Songbook* at the time.

The Radcliffe College yearbook, *The Yardstick*, summed up her years there with these words:

> Anne is a composer. Need we say more! Sometimes we fear that she is only lent to us for a short time — as any genius, merely passing by. But again she seems quite human, saved from the ethereal by the very earthly characteristics of a profound love of jazz and a wholesale and very ardent hero-worship.[15]

So encompassing was music in her life that her dormitory mother was prompted to say of her years at Radcliffe:

> Ann was very temperamental but popular and big-hearted and always means well. Goes out a great deal in the evenings, but mostly to musical things or dancing until 12 at some hotel. Very depressed and moody if she does not get out to dance or a musical evening five times a week.[16]

Ronell's artistic interests were broad and a "musical evening" might include a ballet or modern dance performance, a musical revue or pre–Broadway show, a classical concert or presentation of the music of one of the new modern composers— Aaron Copland, Darius Milhaud, Arnold Schoenberg, Igor Stravinsky, and Anton Webern. In Boston especially, Serge Koussevitsky with the Boston Symphony Orchestra was a champion of the new music. Ronell even exposed George Gershwin to a few of the modern European composers.

In the first issue of the *Radcliffe Magazine*, January 1927, she attempted to explain the modern movement in the arts in an essay entitled "A Dissertation on What's It All About" (Appendix I). Dealing with a topic not discussed by the average college senior, Ronell was able to educate but with a light comic tone. She ended her two-page essay with the following:

> That's *what it is all about*! It's all about a growing tree, proverbially called Progress, that is decked out by foresters with all the artificialities of the Xmas spirit to appear as unfamiliar as possible to the old woods birds, who keep to their haunts only to see their offspring pecking at the fascinating tinsel to find out what's underneath.
>
> And what *is* there? New shoots and strong branches, —just a bit silvery from star-dust.
>
> Anne Rosenblatt[17]

Late in college career, circa 1927 (Nebraska Jewish Historical Society).

In early childhood, Anya had become Anne, Americanizing her Russian name. Her professional name, Ann Ronell, was created during her early songwriting years in New York, at the suggestion of George Gershwin. He often encouraged artists to modify their names, usually making them less Jewish sounding, as anti–Semitism was much in existence in America between the wars. Of the new names Gershwin helped create, Vladimir Dukelsky a.k.a. Vernon Duke was the most famous as a composer of American Popular Song and classical music as well.

But as Anne Rosenblatt, she did interviews for *Radcliffe Magazine*, speaking with various artists performing in Boston, including Copland, Koussevitsky, and Sigmund Romberg. In the summer of 1926, George Gershwin was in town and became the subject of a Ronell interview. As she explained in an *American Illustrated* interview in 1963, her first professional break came during her meeting with him:

> Mr. Gershwin turned the tables and started asking *me* questions — about my studies and my wish to continue composition — and I played some of my songs for him. He liked my songs and later arranged to have me play them for his brother, lyricist Ira Gershwin, and for his publisher in New York.[18]

To meet with George Gershwin was no small feat, as friends and family, especially his brother and lyricist Ira, guarded his time and exposure carefully. By 1926, Gershwin had been a composer for ten years, with his first hit in 1919, "Swanee." He had contributed songs to several of the *George White's Scandals* in the early twenties and had done several shows, including *Lady, Be Good!*, *Tip-Toes*, and *Oh, Kay!* Among his hits by then were "Somebody Loves Me," "Fascinating Rhythm," and "Someone to Watch Over Me." As if popular songs and shows weren't enough, he had moved over to classical music cum jazz with his historical *Rhapsody in Blue* in 1924.[19] He was the "real deal." The songwriting business being what it was, an interview and audition with the smallest publisher of Tin Pan Alley was an accomplishment; to get a hearing with George Gershwin was extraordinary.

When the interview finished, Gershwin explicitly told her to look him up in New York when she had completed her studies at Radcliffe. Toward the end of their senior year at Radcliffe, Ann and Elizabeth Hayes, a friend and fellow pianist, visited New York. They met briefly with Gershwin and, at his behest, with H.S. Kraft, a press agent. The young women auditioned with their two-piano act. Gershwin thought Kraft should book them at the Roxy Theater in New York and call the act "Black & White Keys."[20] Apparently Kraft did not share Gershwin's enthusiasm, or perhaps the young ladies were not ready, but nothing came of it.

Graduation in 1927 found Ronell back in Omaha for several weeks, but New York and music beckoned. To her, the decision was a simple one: "It seemed to me to be the thing that I did best. I liked it, and decided to go into it as a business. That's why I went to New York and established myself there."[21] At the time, her parents were divided as to her choice:

> My mother was quite upset as she did not want me to go East again. On the other hand, my father, who had heard the record of *Rhapsody in Blue* when one of my boyfriends had brought it home during one of my vacations from college, liked *Rhapsody in Blue* very much and was greatly impressed by my having made a friend of its composer.[22]

Always the businessman and looking out for his daughter, Morris Rosenblatt reasoned, "If you have a contact you say is good, maybe he will get your songs published."[23]

Taking Gershwin up on his offer, she visited him when she got to New York and was warmly received. He took her under his wing and taught her "about the musical intricacies of rhythm and arrangement."[24] He stressed that the only way to write for the theatre was to become involved in it. In that 1963 interview for *American Illustrated*, she explained that she was then faced with two choices:

So he suggested I either join a Broadway dance chorus—I believe he was impressed with the way I danced the Charleston at the time — or get a job as a rehearsal pianist. I chose the latter, thinking it easier. I found out later, much to my chagrin, that the long hours of playing piano for rehearsal can be just as arduous as chorus work.[25]

Ronell had always made dance a part of her arts education. She knew tap and ballet dancing, both of which meshed well with her musicality to make her a good dancer. Nonetheless, early on she knew her musical future would be on the other side of the footlights.

She played rehearsal piano for several Broadway shows, including *Whoopee* (1928) by Walter Donaldson and Gus Kahn, *The New Moon* (1928) by another of her mentors, Sigmund Romberg, *Show Girl* (1929) by the Gershwins and Vincent Youmans, and *Great Day!* (1929), also by Youmans. On *Rosalie*, a collaboration of Romberg, P.G. Wodehouse, and the Gershwins, Ronell was personal accompanist to the star of the show, Marilyn Miller. She also rehearsed Eddie Cantor, Ruth Etting, Evelyn Herbert, and Dorothy Stone.[26]

When not busy on the rehearsal stage, she worked as a vocal coach, writing special materials for established and upcoming stars of the various revues which flooded Broadway through the mid-thirties. Her clients included Helen Morgan, Tamara Geva, The Tiller Girls, and Imogene Coca. When working with singers, Ronell tried "to develop a 'trademark'—an individuality,"[27] and realized early on that arranging for singers was more complex than one might think. As she detailed in a deposition over 25 years later: "Why a vocal arrangement for a radio performance is based on the singer's own key, the singer's own range, the style of that particular singer's personality, vocal personality."[28]

Her education continued in Manhattan at the New School for Social Research, as she attended Aaron Copland's "Modern Music" lectures. Ever resourceful, she avoided tuition by agreeing to take extensive notes on Copland's lectures which were then kept on file by the New School, a practice done for many of their famous lecturers.

Also, because of her petite stature—five feet, one inch and one hundred pounds[29]—Ronell was able to earn money modeling adolescent clothing. Her weight was understandable, as Ronell only ate to live and her inexhaustible activity would no doubt burn up those calories. In addition to this, she was described by one journalist as "an outdoors-walking type of girl, preferring her own easy gait to street cars or taxis...."[30]

Her low weight was to bother her future husband, Lester Cowan, who once convinced her to have a full checkup. When those results came back all normal, he was relieved, and her lawyer at the time, William Hinckle, reassured Ronell: "[A] symposium of the most learned medicos in the west have reached the startling conclusion that you don't devote enough of your time to eating. This to me means that either Lester hasn't been feeding you or you are trying to live on the royalties you are getting from Schirmer. My only suggestion for gaining weight is to go on two diets at the same time."[31] Her stature was a vital aspect of her persona, as she was called "The Little Lady of Song" later in her career.

To summarize her early days in New York, she told an interviewer from her home town of Omaha: "Work, more work, and don't weaken, is a good formula for anyone."[32] But for a young woman in New York in the late twenties, no matter how hard one worked, finances could be tight. In a letter to a young adult member of her extended family, she recalled those leaner years:

I once had a room with no private bath at 61st and Lex. for $9 a week. George Gershwin came to take me home one night after rehearsal and saw the nook. He was so disquieted by my poverty, evidently, that having just bought his sister a leopard coat he vowed he'd buy me one, but it wasn't so cold a winter and I was able to move out of there soon after.[33]

How close Ronell became with Gershwin is unclear. Though Gershwin was well known as a ladies' man, he was no cad, and he was also viewed as a mentor by many songwriters of the era. Among those who recognized Gershwin's contributions to their careers—advice, encouragement, money, and thoughtfulness— were Harold Arlen, Vernon Duke, Jay Gorney, and Burton Lane.[34] In a humorous anecdote regarding the great composer-mentor, Jay Gorney told an interviewer: "[H]e was so fascinating and facile in his work. When finally one of us would get to the piano and play some songs, George was always

Left to right: Ann Ronell, George Gershwin, Elsie Schloss, Emily Paley, E.Y. Harburg, and Lou Paley, circa 1929, at Belmar, New Jersey (Frank Driggs Collection).

very laudatory and understanding and, in many respects, helpful. He was always glad to be of help. But it was impossible to unseat him."[35]

Ronell, who was known for helping younger musicians and composers, told an interviewer in 1950, "Much of what I try to do for beginning musicians today is inspired by what he did for me."[36] Gershwin died in 1937, but his affect on her career and life continued. Gershwin biographer Wilfrid Sheed related that fifty years after Gershwin's death, Ronell "still 'saw' Gershwin regularly in the crowds of the Upper West Side, looking as if he'd just walked out the door."[37]

There was no doubt that she was his protégé, and one he admired greatly. In 1934, when she was in Hollywood and he in New York, he was thinking of her career: "Do the muses work as well for you out there as they do in New York? In other words, have you written any swell Ronell songs?"[38] Six months later, he ended a letter: "Everybody in the East sends regards and love to you and I head the list."[39]

In her biography of George Gershwin, one which focused frequently on his romantic life, Joan Peyser wrote:

> Nowhere is there evidence to be found that Gershwin ever said "I love you" to anyone. When he gave a photograph to Ronell and inscribed it with "love," he made a point of telling her how exceptional that was, that he rarely went beyond the word "affectionately."[40]

In an interesting letter to another Gershwin biographer, Robert Kimball, Ronell was curious about his inclusions about her in his upcoming book:

> Regarding the Gershwin Book, I expect you will keep your promise to let me see what you've written about me before it goes to press finally, and am as anxious to see THAT as I am to see you again ... which is saying a lot so please save sometime soon when we can meet.[41]

But the final words on the subject, also from Peyser's biography, were from Ronell herself:

> George was a generous and helpful person. I was a 19-year-old amateur when we met and he was a 29-year-old and world-renowned....
> George was sacred to me. He was my idol. I became like a sister to the family and was his protégé.[42]

2

The First Songs and New York City: 1930–1932

"It was lucky enough to be a hit, and that's how I got started."

By the turn of the decade, Ronell was composing both words and music regularly. She claimed that for a long time, prior to her marriage, she would write "one song a day and present them to publishers."[1] But an introduction to the music publishing world by George Gershwin was not enough to get a song published. As Ronell told an interviewer, "The best way to sell a song is to be the brother-in-law of the publisher, and any other way is the long way around."[2] Modesty and lucky breaks aside, it is clear that much of Ronell's success was associated with her hard work. A few years into her career, back in her hometown of Omaha, she delineated her work ethic:

> Perseverance — stick-to-it-tive-ness— is the quality I believe ... is a good formula for anyone. First of all I think everyone should determine definitely what they want to do— and then bend all their effort to see that it is done. If you have the greatest gift in the world, it won't avail you much if you don't determine to use and develop it to the utmost.[3]

"Love and I," her first published song, was used in the *Ziegfeld Roof Show* in 1929. It was written as a concert or recital song and, though seldom used and never recorded, it was a song to add to her portfolio for presentation to publishers. As she explained in a 1963 interview: "[I]n order to break into the song-writing field at that time, an aspiring composer had to have a whole portfolio of different kinds of songs to appeal to various publishers and vocalists."[4]

When she first began composing, she knew few lyricists, and though she collaborated on songs early on, she preferred to do both words and music herself. In her eyes, this compounded the chances of being turned down. As she told an interviewer at the time, "Mind you, songwriting isn't all roses— it was a long time before I had my first number accepted and my greatest trouble was convincing people that I could write both words and music."[5]

The other problem, of course, was a gender issue. In the early thirties there were few women songwriters, composers or lyricists, as it was much harder for a woman to get a foothold in music publishing than for a man, given equal talent and effort. A convention of the American Society of Composers, Arrangers and Producers (ASCAP), circa 1934–35, had 200 attendees, and Ann Ronell was the only woman. An interviewer of Ronell in the *Women Today* section of *The Christian Science Monitor* in 1955 sympathized: "But it was not so easy to get a hearing. There were many other people with tunes at their finger tips, most of them

10

boys. Girls were few in this keenly competitive field, and most of those in it at that time dropped out later. Ann kept on — kept on writing and haunting publishers' offices."[6]

At the time, few women had made inroads into the male-dominated world, and at that, usually as lyricists. Against the wishes of her father, Lew Fields, a well-known vaudevillian and review performer and producer, Dorothy Fields began her career writing songs with Jimmy McHugh, their first hit being "I Can't Give You Anything But Love" for *Blackbirds of 1928*. She ended her songwriting over five decades later with the musical *Seesaw* with composer Cy Coleman, twenty-five years her junior. Also by 1935, Mabel Wayne had made a name for herself, penning both words and music for hits that included "In a Little Spanish Town," "It Happened in Monterey," and "Ramona."[7]

There were other female composers— Kay Swift, Dana Suesse and Anna Sosenko— but their hits were few. The women themselves did not complain, at least not publicly. To the contrary, Kay Swift told an interviewer: "We never had the feeling we weren't equal.... I don't remember ever losing any chances because I was a woman, not at all."[8]

As for getting a song published, neither Ronell's gender nor her insistence on writing both words and music was the primary roadblock. It was the state of the art itself. Just as the early classical composers needed a wealthy patron to support their next orchestral or chamber piece, so did the songwriters of Ronell's era. Rather than patrons, she and her contemporaries relied on the support of music publishers. While many were well-versed in music and aware of what was out there, and even a few, most notably Irving Berlin, were songwriters themselves, they were all businessmen. The state of the "art" was well-expressed in a humorous *New Yorker* piece over 20 years after Ronell published her first song:

> All publishers are bound together by a mutual ambition: an insatiable, gnawing, relentless, passionate desire to Have a Hit. When a publisher accepts a song it is not because he likes the music and lyrics as such. It is because he hopes someday to make money out of it; to clean up; to get rich enough to buy a golf course, an oil well, a movie company; to take over for God. The music publisher is a business man. He knows that a rival company has a smash hit called "I've Only Got One Eye, and That's on You," and he is on the alert for anything that is an undisguised copy of it.
>
> The publisher abhors unknown songwriters. They represent a probable financial loss and a possibility of making a fool of himself, so why take a chance?[9]

In more practical terms, if not as comical, Ronell had explained early in her career the plight of songwriters: "The truth is that everybody has written at least one song in his life. Everybody around Tin Pan Alley is trying to peddle a song. The office boy, elevator man or his sister-in-law, the cleaning woman's son or the newsie's mother all have songs up their sleeves. The result is that no unsolicited songs have a chance."[10]

One of her best early contacts, provided by George Gershwin, was Max Dreyfus of Chappell and Company, Inc. He and Chappell were becoming quite successful, having published much of part-owner Jerome Kern's early works. Ronell played for Dreyfus a jazz spiritual she had written, "Down By De Ribber," which Gershwin had liked much. Ronell explained what happened next: "When he discovered I had written no verse he said, 'You have to know much more about the song business before you come here!' George stepped in. He told me Dreyfus was always hard, and I should not be discouraged by him."[11]

At the time, almost all Tin Pan Alley and Broadway songs had two parts. The first part was usually a twelve to sixteen-bar verse serving as an introduction or setup to the chorus. The chorus was usually the better known part of the song, most often written in an A-A-B-A_1. Though ignoring this pattern in her jazz spiritual, Ronell, at this stage of her career and education, was undoubtedly fully aware of writing a verse. She soon learned to add verses to all her songs, at least for Dreyfus.

Ronell's first successful song, "Baby's Birthday Party," was written for a musical she had been working on for Vincent Youmans. She had an idea for a book musical that interested him, and he told her to start on some songs. "Baby's Birthday Party" was "purely a novelty," prompted by the first birthday of her nephew, Robert, her brother Sol's son. At the time, she reasoned, "Songs about dolls and doll parades had been successful. Nothing had been written about babies or baby parties."[12] She thought the idea perfect as an opening for the musical.

However, Youmans' own production of his musical, *Great Day!,* for which Ronell had been rehearsal pianist, failed, costing him dearly, and, as Ronell lamented, "my little show was out of the question."[13] She believed in the song and shopped it around to numerous publishers, seldom getting a hello, much less a hearing. Finally, an arranger at Famous Music, Jack Mason, was playing it one evening as his boss, Larry Spier, was leaving the office. When Spier asked who had written the song, Mason replied that it was "by that little girl that hangs around here every day and you won't see."[14] "Baby's Birthday Party" established Ronell as a composer-lyricist, a role she maintained throughout most of her career.

The song was written without a verse and opens with a 32-bar chorus, $A-A-B-A_1$. The melody, marked "Moderato (lightly)," is carried along with a shuffle rhythm.[15] After the first chorus, Ronell added a 32-bar interlude, meant to accelerate the festive tone of the song. Written in the major 6th of the chorus, its lyric features short phrases, aimed at attracting the listener's attention with simplified rhymes. Singer Benjamin Sears, also an archivist and historian of American Popular Song, referred to the song as "a superficially straight but surprisingly sophisticated song." He elaborated:

> "Baby's Birthday Party" begins by describing what seems to be a typical outdoor birthday party for a small child.... The middle section of the song sends a musical clue that perhaps not all is what appears, as the music suddenly switches to a Boogie-Woogie style, though the lyrics do not stray to any degree from the images of the A section. After the Boogie, the A section returns, with the lyrics continuing in the same vein, until the final statement of the musical theme.... The humor is drawn more from the contradictions between the lyrics and the music, with the Boogie section supporting traditional "Happy Birthday"–style lyrics, then the final joke in the lyrics coming during music that does not suggest "shaking a wicked shoulder."[16]

Famous Music signed on to the song and published it in 1930, and when Guy Lombardo and Rudy Vallee each recorded it, Ronell had her first hit. As she reminisced ten years later, "It was lucky enough to be a hit, and that's how I got started. Pure chance —-a shot in the dark. It's a wonderful thing to get your songs published, hear people whistling your tune — somebody else made happy by something you do under stress and strain."[17] Quite a shot it was as "Baby's Birthday Party" sold over 100,000 copies of sheet music at a time when that number meant a lot in sales.

To put that into perspective, a brief history of sound recording would be helpful. Although the phonograph and recordings had been invented by Thomas Edison in 1877, widespread availability of recordings of voice and music was not possible until the invention of the Gramophone by Emile Berliner. Though the Gramophone used shellac discs that could be mass produced, it still had to be wound up to be played. It was not until phonographs could be powered by electricity that records became popular and widespread.[18]

Even with electricity and recordings in the early thirties, families would learn the music of the day in the piano parlor of the home. One or more family members would get sheet music of the hits of the day and play the arrangements. Before there were record stores, cities and towns had sheet music stores, where a piano was available to try out songs or have them demonstrated for you. When a song reached 100,000 copies in sales, this was a benchmark of success, and the thirties equivalent of a gold record today. Jerome Kern biographer Gerald Bordman explained:

> Phonographs were the first of the technological devices to change both the nature of theatre music and, more urgently, its method of dissemination, with a concurrent change in composers' sources of income. Before phonographs replaced pianos as common household furnishings, turn-of-the-century sheet music sales reached figures that must leave modern readers incredulous— often in the hundreds of thousands for a popular song and not infrequently surpassing a million copies.[19]

This is exemplified by the fact that, despite Kern's many megahits over the years, a lesser known song, "You're Here and I'm Here," used in two different shows from 1913 to 1914, was Kern's sheet music sales champion until late into his career.[20]

Moreover, "Baby's Birthday Party" was the first time Famous Music, the music publishing arm of Paramount Pictures, had published a song unconnected to a movie, and its success prompted Famous to look more closely at Ronell's subsequent "unattached" songs.

In the years before her affiliation with Famous Music, Ronell had penned another novelty song, "The Candy Parade," published by Miller Music Corporation, but it got little attention. She renewed the copyright in 1959, and in 1965, the publishers, Miller Music, requested that she write a Christmas lyric for the song. Ronell obliged and created her one and only holiday song, lost in the shuffle of so many popular Christmas songs. The song was played and favorably reviewed at a 1997 July Fourth celebration in Boston, *American Classics— Hooray for the Ladies! Boston Globe* critic Richard Buell said about the song, "[W]hat made it special was the unstinting verve with which she took the confectionary conceit and ran with it. And ran. And ran. No she wouldn't, you kept on thinking. But she always did."[21]

Another song opportunity presented itself with the Broadway revue, *Shoot the Works!*, produced by Heywood Broun, noted newspaper columnist, raconteur and occasional performer. His plan was to use new songs by various well-known composers of the time to launch new talents he was featuring. More importantly, it was the Depression, and performers needed work. Broun's idea was for "a cooperative review — that is, nobody but the actors and chorus would reap from the box-office intake."[22]

Hearing that several songs were to be used in the revue, Ann went to the theater, hoping to get an audition for some of her songs. Aided and abetted by the conductor of the show, Bill Daly, Ann waited several days, having been told by Daly that several composers had not submitted songs as planned. Finally, Daly gave her the cue that a song was needed, specifically because the Gershwins had decided not to participate. Her song, "Let's Go Out in the Open Air," was given a hearing, accepted and was to be sung by newcomer Imogene Coca. Ronell even rehearsed Coca for the song and show, and they became lifelong friends.

Ronell's song, marked "Moderato (lightly)," is typical for the day with a 16-bar verse and a 32-bar chorus, A-A$_1$-B-A$_1$. The chorus moves along with a shuffle beat until the bridge, with a different rhythm and a key change from C major to F major. Though the lyric is mostly conventional, each section of the verse ends with an internal rhyming of three words close together which adds an attractive rhythm to the song.[23]

Shoot the Works! opened in 1931 and starred George Murphy and Broun. Other song contributors included Irving Berlin, Leo Robin, E.Y. Harburg, Jay Gorney, Dorothy Fields, Jimmy McHugh, and Vernon Duke.[24] As American popular song collector and historian, Bob Grimes, explained, "I'm always fascinated by *Shoot the Works*. They got all kinds of people to contribute to the show: songs, skits, etc., so they could just put people to work. It was like Mickey and Judy Let's Put on a Show and it seems to have worked fairly well."[25] Produced in the heart of the Depression, *Shoot the Works!* had a small budget and ran only eighty-seven performances, despite good publicity from Broun's newspaper connections.[26] "Let's Go Out in the Open Air" was later used in a movie, *The Fighting Westerner*. The sheet music was published in 1932 by Famous Music Corporation and featured singer Seger Ellis on the cover.

Months after *Shoot the Works!*, Ronell had a hit in 1932 with the publication of "Rain on the Roof," published by Famous Music Corporation. It slowly gained popularity and became a hit when it was recorded by Paul Whiteman, a progressive band leader of the time. Already popular from concerts and dance venues, his production of the *Experiment in Jazz* concert, which had premiered Gershwin's *Rhapsody in Blue* in 1924, brought Whiteman much fame in music circles. Having Whiteman and his orchestra record your song, with him pictured on the sheet music, was quite an accomplishment.

"Rain on the Roof" starts out with a typical A-A-B-A chorus, marked on original notes on the manuscript as "Moderato, Not Too Fast." The three A stanzas are musically identical. The chorus is repeated once, with different lyrics, but there is an 18-bar interlude between the choruses. The key changes from C to E-flat for the interlude, then back to C. The heart of the ballad is the interlude, where a longing tone is captured in lyric and melody.[27]

This is one of Ronell's best lyrics. In real life, she claimed to have hated the rain. On one of her songwriting days, it began to rain, and she "played the piano to drown its patter," calling the song, what else, "Rain on the Roof."[28] This song, along with the earlier "Baby's Birthday Party," conformed to Ronell's songwriting philosophy to keep things simple, an idea garnered from an English professor in a lecture on writing. Three years after penning "Rain on the Roof," Ronell expanded on the simplicity of her songs: "So far I have confined myself to the simple and the sweet little things of life. Almost everyone loves to hear rain falling on the roof. I tried to make my song just that.... My idea was to begin modestly. Songwriting is one of the professions in which modesty is the best policy."[29]

Years later, poet and critic Louis Untermeyer wrote an article on American song lyrics as a form of poetry. Among his favorite examples was Ronell's line from the song, "Silver chatter of the rain on the roof." Such a mention by the poet pleased Ronell greatly.[30]

The original copyright was 1931, and the royalty agreement between Famous Music Corporation and Ronell, dated January 24, 1931, awarded her 22 percent of net royalties.[31] Famous Music renewed the copyright in 1958–1959 and published new sheet music in 1968 as part of its *Famous Standard Publications* series. Despite the initial interest and recording by Paul Whiteman, "Rain on the Roof" garnered few royalties for Ronell over the years.

In late 1949, Ronell was approached to use her song in a commercial. In a long letter to Charles Hutaff in Cleveland, she detailed the rights and legalities of the usage, ending with: "In the meantime, I couldn't help thinking of a few lyrics for Alcoa Roofing so I wouldn't mind at all if we can start early on this project."[32] Apparently, "Rain" never fell on an Alcoa roof or at least no further mention of it was found in her records.

In the fall of 1966, a bit of notoriety was achieved for Ronell and "Rain on the Roof." John Sebastian wrote a song for his group, The Lovin' Spoonful, entitled "Rain on the Roof," the identical title as her 1931 song. Although song titles cannot be copyrighted under the Copyright Act, copyright owners may bring legal action under various states' "unfair competition" laws.[33] As explained in a later, related article in *Variety* in 1971, "The hassle is complicated by the fact that there is no copyright protection to song titles. For instance, there are dozens of different songs titled, 'I Love You, Baby,' available. In cases, however, where a particular song has achieved hit status, and the authors can establish clear economic value to a particular title, they can move to protect such titles under laws designed to curb unfair competition."[34]

To that end, attorney Stuart Kahan, for Famous Music Corporation, wrote a letter to MGM Records and Kama-Sutra Productions, Inc., the label for The Lovin' Spoonful. It included the following paragraphs:

> We are the copyright proprietor of the musical composition also entitled "Rain on the Roof" written by Ann Ronell, which is a most important standard of ours and copyrighted over thirty years ago. For many years this composition has achieved great popularity in this country and abroad and has acquired secondary meaning through sales and costly advertising and exploitation; the title has become associated in the public mind with our composition.
>
> The use of our title for your musical composition has and does mislead, confuse and deceive the public and such palpable unfairness has resulted to our detriment.
>
> Accordingly, we request that you immediately refrain from using the title "Rain on the Roof" for your musical composition.[35]

Ronell herself took legal action, retaining the services of Edmund Grainger, Jr., and the advice of Leon Kellman. In the fall of 1966 into early 1967, numerous letters were exchanged among attorneys Sidney Herman and Stuart Kahan (Paramount–Famous Music), Edmund Grainger, Jr. (Ann Ronell), John M. Gross and Miles J. Laurie (Kama-Sutra Productions).[36]

Despite attempts by the record companies to modify the song's title and presentation on the label, the efforts were insufficient. Finally, in January of 1967, Lester Cowan, Ronell's husband, wrote the following letter of exasperation to their attorney, Grainger: "Ann and I have examined the material on 'Rain on the Roof' sent to Famous by John M. Gross. Gross must think we are stupid. The title on the sheet music is still 'Rain on the Roof.' The addition in small type of "you and me and" only adds insult to injury. We must insist that "you and me and" be at least as prominent as 'Rain on the Roof' and that all sheet music copies such as the one submitted be destroyed."[37]

Finally, matters were closed February 13, 1967, with a final letter from Gross, attorney for the label, to Stuart Kahan of Famous Music, with a concession and a parting shot: "Inasmuch as you have now received the assurances requested by you from both the record manufacturer and the sheet music distributor, we are closing our file in connection with this matter. I am sure that I need not add that all changes that have been made at your request are only a courtesy to you and not a concession of the validity of any of your claims."[38]

Four years later, a similar flap occurred regarding a Stephen Sondheim song. He had written a song entitled "Rain on the Roof" for *Follies,* his ambitious musical done with Harold Prince and Michael Bennett that opened in April of 1971. This time, a letter similar to that in 1966 was sent to Harold Prince Productions by Sidney Herman of Famous Music, again utilizing the "unfair competition" aspect of the song.[39] Sondheim and his associates kindly complied, and the title in the show was changed to "Listen to the Rain on the Roof."[40]

Perhaps Ronell's best song that was passed over was her 1932 song, "Give Me Back My Heart." As much as any of her songs, it followed her dictum to "make each song paint a picture or tell a story."[41] It is another bluesy tune with a conventional twelve-bar verse, then eight bars in each A-A-B-A$_1$ section of the chorus. Much of the chorus moves along with a shuffle rhythm, but each of the A sections includes a run of eighth note triplets in the 4th measure, giving the melody a bit of a jolt.[42] This song was probably written after "Willow Weep for Me," and the feeling of the chorus is much different from those in "Willow" and "Rain on the Roof."

Ronell recognized that the song had languished and tried to revive it about the same time "Willow Weep for Me" was achieving its popularity in the early fifties. Having an acquaintance with band leader and clarinetist Artie Shaw, Ronell sent him a small collection of her songs. She explained to Shaw about "Give Me Back My Heart": "[It] got lost in the rush, as it came out the same time with 'Willow' but maybe you will like it."[43] But the song got lost again, and neither Shaw nor anyone else recorded it. Arguably, it is her best unrecorded song.

About this time, Ann made her first trip abroad. Her first passport, dated April 27, 1932, shows destination stamps in France, Italy, and Switzerland.[44] Though on vacation on this trip, the ever-busy Ms. Ronell was involved in writing music for the *Ile de France Revue* presented in 1932 at the Theatre Champs-Elysses in Paris.[45] No notable songs emerged from this project for the young composer.

Also among Ronell's early thirties songs was a waltz, "The Merry-Go-Round," an adaptable trunk tune that was used in "unauthorized performances" in two Radio City Music Hall shows, *Seaside Park* in 1934 and *Calliope* in 1935.[46] It emerged again in the 1937 Adolph Zukor film production, *Champagne Waltz*. She was in good musical company with this movie as some of the other composers with songs in it included Sam Coslow, Burton Lane, Ralph Freed, Milton Drake and Leo Robin.[47] Pictured on the cover of the sheet music are stars Gladys Swarthout and Fred MacMurray in, what else, a dancing pose.[48] Supporting actor Joaquin Garay sang the song in the film,[49] which also featured Veloz and Yolanda, an internationally known dance duo who later included "The Merry-Go-Round" in their shows. Frank Veloz wrote to Ronell at the time of the movie's production: "[We] are eager to get the record as it will take time to create a light routine to this music ... and catch the novel mood of the melody."[50]

The song is long, 94 measures, especially when considering that many of the day's songs were often only 48 measures, with 16 in the verse and 32 in the chorus. Ronell set the song with a 32-bar introduction, then with 16 bars in each section of the chorus, A-A-B-A$_1$. Ronell's bridge in the chorus is a pleasant rise to a minor key, C major to D minor, and breaks up the waltz with a few well-placed eighth note couplets.[51]

A letter that Ronell wrote to George Gershwin (June 1936) suggests that she had written the song a few years before, perhaps under his tutelage:

> I think you will be pleased to hear that "Merry-Go-Round" is to be included in this score [*Champagne Waltz*], as there really is a swell spot and meaning for this number at last. I also think you will like the other stuff (as usual) and don't give a doggone if you still treat me like a protégé.[52]

Another friend of hers in the world of music, J.C. Copeland, found distinction in "The Merry-Go-Round," complimenting and reassuring her:

> Perhaps my perspective was warped, due to the fact that I was most intent on hearing your number, "Merry-Go-Round."... Your number is the outstanding piece in the whole picture and had the best direction.
>
> We have heard your "Merry-Go-Round" on the air only a few times and cannot understand why it is not played by the larger orchestras. Fred Waring played it very well a few weeks ago.[53]

Unfortunately, *Champagne Waltz* was no hit, and the big orchestras passed over Ronell's waltz.

Most every composer went through hassles over rights and usage of songs. A recent book on the topic of American Popular Song composers asserted, "Veterans like George M. Cohan and Irving Berlin had to fight so many small fights with small people — over copyrights, royalties, credits, survival — that they remained slightly crouched and suspicious for the rest of their days."[54]

But Ronell seemed to have more than her share of fights. The difficulties surrounding "Rain on the Roof" were detailed previously. The legal maneuvering involving "The Merry-Go-Round" began in 1936, as the song was to be interpolated into Paramount's *Champagne Waltz*. Ronell had to secure the rights from the initial publisher, Leo Feist, Inc., to clear it for Paramount so she could obtain royalties from the movie.

Feist was reluctant to sign them over to her. Ronell, however, was able to prove that Feist had not published it within a year of its purchase of the rights to the song from her. To publish a song meant to offer a song for sale or provide orchestrations or arrangements for public performance. Ronell felt that Feist had made little or no effort toward publication in the first year of its ownership, and because of this, rights to the song should have reverted to her. As Lester Cowan summarized in a telegram to attorney Sol Rosenblatt in early June 1936:

RE MERRY GO ROUND ANNS PROFESSIONAL COPY STAMPED NOT FOR SALE DATED 1933 HER CONTRACT REQUIRED PUBLICATION WITHIN ONE YEAR STOP SUGGEST DEMAND FEIST PRODUCE ORIGINAL CONTRACT AND PUBLISHED COPY AS OFFERED FOR SALE AS WELL AS ORCHESTRATIONS AND ANY ROYALTY STATEMENT AS EVIDENCE OF PUBLICATION OF GOOD FAITH BEFORE KNOWLEDGE OF ANNS INTENDED USE STOP ANY FURTHER DELAY WILL GIVE THEM MORE TIME TO PLUG HOLES....[55]

Apparently, Ronell and Cowan had a good case, as Leo Feist, Inc., transferred rights to her three days later, on June 10, 1936. But this did not solve the problem. What was really needed was assignment of foreign rights, as Paramount's *Champagne Waltz* was to be distributed internationally and the foreign rights were necessary before the song could be put into the film. The latter part of 1936 was devoted to determining who held foreign rights and then reassigning them to Paramount. After a flurry of letters, clearance for the "entire world" was obtained and the song was ready for inclusion in the film.[56]

But Ronell's problems were not over. By the time *Champagne Waltz* opened in Los Angeles, Famous Publishing Company had made little effort to get "The Merry-Go-Round" out to the public. As always, she was hoping for the synergy of the release of a movie and publication of its songs. A frustrated Ronell wired her concerns to a Famous Publishing executive regarding the song's promotion:

MERRY GO ROUND GOT SPONTANEOUS APPLAUSE AT PREVIEW LAST NIGHT AND FEEL DEAD SURE THIS NUMBER REQUIRES NO MORE THAN A REASONABLE AMOUNT OF HELP FROM YOU TO COME THROUGH AS A HIT ESPECIALLY AS IT IS IDEAL FOR THE COMING HOLIDAY SEASON STOP WHILE HAVE BEEN ASSURED THAT IT HAS BEEN PUBLISHED HAVE SEEN NO COPIES ON THE LOCAL STANDS STOP WOULD YOU BE GOOD ENOUGH TO WIRE ME COLLECT PUBLICATION DATE AND SOME INDICATION OF YOUR PLANS[57]

How much promotion was done for "The Merry-Go-Round" is unclear, but her telegram was dated December 5, 1936, leaving little time for exploitation of the song for the holiday season. More perils of Ann regarding "The Merry-Go-Round" were still to come.

In June and July of 1949, the show at Radio City Music Hall at Rockefeller Center in New York was using "(On) The Merry-Go-Round" as a featured number, sung by the entire cast.[58] Ann had received no royalties for these performances and had given no permission for use of the song.

While use of a composer's song in any venue was to be acknowledged and paid for, the show at Radio City Music Hall was not just any show or venue. A *Time* magazine article of July 4, 1949, detailed the enormity of the show of the 6,200-seat Radio City Music Hall which had opened in 1933:

Grandiose spectacles, and the sumptuous grandeur of its own size and trappings, have made the $4,600,000 Music Hall a show business nonpareil and a major tourist magnet. Last year at prices from 80 cents to $2.40, it drew 16 times as many visitors as the Statue of Liberty. Of its 8 million annual customers, half are out-of-towners.[59]

As it turned out, permission for use of the song was not Ronell's to give. Rather, rights were held and granted by Paramount Pictures through their music publisher, Famous Music, Inc. Under her contract with Paramount, when they licensed one of her songs to Radio City Music Hall or anyone else, she was to receive 33⅓ percent of receipts obtained from such licensure.[60] As it turned out, Paramount, not Radio City, was guilty of noncompliance and eventually paid Ronell. The whole incident spurred Ronell to make music publishers more diligent in paying composers for royalties obtained from licensure of their songs.

Most copyright assignments were done with boiler-plate contracts, stipulating that composers assign rights to their songs to publishers, and the composers, in turn, receive from 25 to 50 percent of royalties received through sales of sheet music and recordings, radio play, movies, and other performances. Ronell and Cowan felt that payments of these royalties were often overlooked by the publishers. Years later, she and other composers sought redress through the American Guild of Authors and Composers.

But "The Merry-Go-Round" was still not finished. In 1941, it surfaced in a Paramount film, *The Parson of Panamint,* starring Ellen Drew and Charles Ruggles. Other songs in the film included "No Ring on Her Finger" with a lyric by Frank Loesser and "It's in the Cards," written by Ralph Rainger and Sam Coslow.[61] Little came of the songs or the movie.

3

"Willow Weep for Me": 1932

*"When all is said and done, it may be a lovely
song inspired by the willow trees on a New England
campus that carries Ann Ronell's name into eternity."*

Ronell's successes with "Baby's Birthday Party" and "Rain on the Roof" gave her an "in" to Irving Berlin, Inc. There, Berlin's associate, Saul Bornstein, welcomed her and listened to her newly written "Willow Weep for Me." Bornstein balked at her tempo changes and her dedication of the song. Musical historian Edward Jablonski, in a biographical essay on Ronell in *Nebraska Life* in 1997, explained: "Bornstein, as was his wont, missed the point of the song, a bluesy 'torch,' as such songs were known at the time. The measures that disturbed Bornstein musically depicted the agitated stress of the singer."[1]

Bornstein presented it to Berlin who took to it immediately. As Ronell described it in a 1932 interview, "Then Irving Berlin heard my willow song. He discovered me and used my willow weep on the radio. He's the latest person to discover me. If you want to, you can say that I've been discovered by the best people."[2]

In an interview with Ronell ten years after the publication of "Willow Weep for Me," Douglas Gilbert of the *New York World-Telegram* explained the reasons for Bornstein's hesitance:

> This was an unusual song for two reasons: One, it had a cross rhythm — the right and the left hands in different time. Now, this would require a pianist who had at least two weeks' correspondence schooling, and making songs difficult just isn't done in Tin Pan Alley.... Two, [Berlin] also let her dedicate the song to Gershwin — another Alley violation.[3]

Such a dedication was a big deal at the time, as Tin Pan Alley had its tacit rules. Gershwin was especially pleased with the inscription and had made that clear to Ronell. In July of 1937, shortly after Gershwin's death, Ronell participated in a memorial program for him. The other speakers included Harry Hershfield, producers Max Gordon and George White, composer Harold Arlen, and lyricist and Ziegfield associate Gene Buck. In Ronell's brief comments, she mentioned the inscription on "Willow Weep for Me" and added that "I am happy to this day that such little things pleased him."[4]

"Willow Weep for Me" begins conventionally with a 16-bar verse. The chorus is also a standard 32 bars, A-A-B-A, and Ronell uses eighth note triplets effectively as the chorus begins. But it is the 5th measure in each A section that distinguishes the chorus and the song, with four staccato eighth notes leading to a half note. These four eighth notes come so suddenly and unexpectedly that the listener might believe there has been a change in the time signature. Not only do the melody and rhythm catch one's attention, but so does the lyric accompanying the five notes of that 5th measure.[5] It was these staccato eighth notes that bothered Saul Bornstein and caught Irving Berlin's ear.

David Ewen, in his *American Popular Songs: From the Revolutionary War to the Present*, further explained: "This number is structurally unusual in that there is a change in rhythm notation within the refrain, a practice so unusual in Tin Pan Alley that special permission had to be obtained from the publisher (Irving Berlin) for its use in the sheet music release."[6] Even thirty years after it was published, Ronell was told by a publisher that "if I walked into an office today with 'Willow Weep for Me,' I'd never be able to sell it."[7]

"Willow" fit Ronell's belief that songs should focus on "the simple and the sweet little things of life."[8] She told an interviewer a year after it was published, "Sometimes something impresses you, the way the willows did my first year at Radcliffe. It was several years before I wrote about them. But 'Willow Weep for Me' came from that impression."[9]

Jazz writer Nels Nelson of the *Philadelphia Daily News*, in his essay about her shortly after her death, picked up on this simplicity notion: "But when all is said and done, it may be a lovely song inspired by the willow trees on a New England campus that carries Ann Ronell's name into eternity."[10]

Berlin published "Willow Weep for Me" in 1932, and it was introduced by Irene Bailey, a singer with the Paul Whiteman Orchestra. It was popularized by Ruth Etting who was pictured on the early sheet music. Despite its early associations with Berlin, Whiteman and Etting, there were no other early recordings, and "Willow" did not achieve the rapid acclaim of "Rain on the Roof" or "Who's Afraid of the Big Bad Wolf?" However, Nelson explained, "it had a longevity equal to or beyond that of the most hallowed pop standards—more than 60 years of constant growth in the esteem of the jazz musicians who recognized it from the start as a superior piece of craftsmanship."[11]

Not until the early fifties did "Willow" gain status as a standard in the American popular songbook. This was prompted by Stan Kenton's 1950 recording, popular with both jazz and big band fans of the time. Ronell was well aware of this, and when she went out on her exploitation tour for the movie and songs of *Love Happy*, she also wanted to generate publicity for her earlier songs, especially "Willow Weep for Me." The Kenton recording gave her a great opportunity to do this, for as she explained to her publisher: "The Stan Kenton record is a classic which every disc-jockey knows."[12] On the tour, radio personalities would interview her and play several of her songs, not just those from *Love Happy*. "Willow Weep for Me" was the favorite.

Frank Sinatra recorded it on his 1953 Capitol Records album, *Only the Lonely*, considered one of his all-time best.[13] Since then, the artists recording it comprise a who's who of the jazz, standard, and cabaret genres (Appendix H).[14] In 1969, jazz guitarist Wes Montgomery won a Grammy award for "Best Instrumental Jazz Performance, Small Group" with his recording of "Willow Weep for Me." The song also charted for several weeks on the Billboard Hot 100 for the English pop duo Chad & Jeremy.[15] An accounting statement from music publisher Bourne, Inc., shows royalties to Ronell in excess of $4,500 for the six-month period ending June 30, 1966.[16]

Billie Holiday was especially fond of the song, recording it at least four times, as it became one of her staple songs along with "Easy Living," "I Only Have Eyes for You," and "God Bless the Child."[17] She did a particularly moving rendition of "Willow" in the 1965 Jeanne Moreau film, *Eva*.[18]

Jazz pianist nonpareil Art Tatum recorded it five times in the fifties. As a critic wrote to Ronell about these recordings, the last one done live at the London House in Chicago in 1956,

"This was a tune that he was obviously very fond of, and it is clear that he had sort of settled into an 'arrangement' of it that he liked and repeated."[19]

In 1976, actress-singer Naura Hayden recorded an album, *And Then She Wrote*, for the Differant [*sic*] Drummer label. Hayden recorded ten American Popular Song standards, all written or co-written by women. Her album had originated as one focused on "red," the color, e.g. "Red Sails in the Sunset," as Hayden was known by her full head of red hair. However, when she discovered the musical *Redhead* and Dorothy Fields' lyrics for that 1959 show, this led her to other words and/or music written by

Billie Holiday with Ronell at the time of Holiday's recording of "Willow Weep for Me," 1954.

women, regardless of "red." She changed the focus and title of the album to *And Then She Wrote*. As she told *New York Post* columnist Earl Wilson, "I kept on looking for women composers rather than redheads and red songs. I hadn't realized there were so many women writers who, before the days of Women's Lib, were 'closet writers,' not saying much about their writing."[20] "Willow Weep for Me" was included in the album.

So enthused were the people from ASCAP (the American Society of Composers, Authors and Publishers) and their president, Stanley Adams, that a champagne reception was organized, celebrating the release of the album and honoring the distaff composers, six of whom attended.[21] Besides Ronell, the attendees and their songs recorded on *And Then She Wrote* included:

> Carolyn Leigh, lyrics, "The Best Is Yet to Come"
> Ruth Lowe, lyrics and music, "I'll Never Smile Again"
> Gladys Shelley, lyrics and music, "How Did He Look?"
> Dana Suesse, lyrics and music, "My Silent Love"
> Kay Swift, music, "Fine and Dandy"; music"Can't We Be Friends"

"Willow Weep for Me" was again celebrated in a 1982 Broadway production entitled *Blues in the Night*, a review of blues and torch songs from the thirties and before.[22] Its producers hoped to follow on the successes of similar reviews, *Ain't Misbehavin'* and *Eubie*, compilations of songs written mostly by composers Thomas "Fats" Waller and Eubie Blake, respectively. Leslie Uggams, Debbie Shapiro and Jean Du Shon starred and covered several blues by Bessie Smith and blues and torch songs from American Popular Songbook. The show had been conceived by Sheldon Epps four years previously, and directed by him, off-Broadway. Though mixed reviews greeted the show on Broadway, audiences liked it, and it enjoyed a good run.[23]

Composer-historian Alec Wilder described it as "exceptional" and a "truly fascinating song." In his oft-quoted book, *American Popular Song: The Great Innovators: 1900–1950*, he said of "Willow Weep for Me," "It's on a par with [Hoagy] Carmichael's experiments and was written, I'm sure, far from the maddening crowd of commercial songwriters. It's as if the writer didn't need any profit from it."[24]

His book was published in 1972, and some years later, after Ronell had read his comments, she wrote Wilder a note of appreciation. He, in turn, acknowledged her gratefulness, adding:

> I would have written more about other songs which I read through many years ago but couldn't remember the title or publishers of. They were extraordinarily complex for their time and very interesting music.
>
> I should have tracked you down and written more about your obviously lovely, strong talent. Were there a lot more songs, simply too complex to receive the approval of those dreadful cretinous music publishers or did you simply stop writing? I hope you didn't and that you have a great many songs tucked away. For there *is* a glimmer of sunlight on this carnival landscape.[25]

Other songwriters and artists were especially fond of "Willow." In a thank you note after a visit to Ronell and Lester Cowan's California ranch, Meredith Willson, not yet famous for *The Music Man*, wrote, "What a beautiful day I had at your gorgeous farm-ranch-hacienda-estate and such unusually nice people and elegant food and handsome dog and oh, doctor, that 'Willow Weep for Me.'"[26] Hugh Martin, who had teamed with Ralph Blane for Broadway's *Best Foot Forward* in 1941 and Hollywood's *Meet Me in St. Louis* in 1944,[27] told Ronell, "Every now and then I will hear 'Willow Weep for Me' and am astonished all over again at its beauty."[28] Jazz saxophonist Dexter Gordon had specified no eulogies at his funeral, but requested that a few songs be performed, including "Willow," sung by Lou Rawls.[29]

An apocryphal story regarding the composition of "Willow Weep for Me" evolved from singer Sylvia Syms' 1982 show at New York's Café Carlyle, residence of cabaret's grand master, Bobby Short. John S. Wilson explained in the *New York Times* (March 26, 1982):

> She has spent some time researching songs written by women and so she puts a very familiar song, "Willow Weep for Me," in fresh perspective by explaining that Ann Ronell wrote it when she, a junior counselor at a summer camp, fell in love with a senior counselor, George Gershwin — "the wail and turmoil of a very confused 17-year-old," says Miss Syms.[30]

At age seventeen, if Ann Ronell been a camp counselor, it would have been near Omaha, Nebraska, her hometown, not at an Eastern camp where Gershwin might have worked. Her first meeting with him occurred in 1926 in Boston, when she interviewed him for her college magazine. Beyond this, as mentioned above, the inspiration for her song had come from her first year at Radcliffe and its campus willows. Syms' story was a nice cabaret vignette, but doubtful.

Finally, a supreme compliment to a New Yorker like Ann Ronell, the title of her song was one of the answers to a *New York Times* crossword puzzle from Sunday, May 25, 1986. The clue: "Message from a depressed dendrologist?"[31]

4

"Who's Afraid of the Big Bad Wolf?" and Disney Studios: 1933–1935

"The song voiced the hopes of Americans
who believed that Hard Times were ending,
and the wolf at the door would be driven away...."

A good steady income was difficult to count on in the songwriting world. For every Irving Berlin, there were a hundred songwriters waiting around for their next hit. Ronell made this clear in an interview years later: "[Y]ou have to live, and let's face it, you don't make enough money from a popular song to fill in the period in between the hits."[1] To remedy this, shortly after her run of initial hits, Ronell, like many in the music business, went to Hollywood to seek work.

Walt Disney Studios in California was looking for a song to celebrate the "birthday" of Mickey Mouse. The popular rodent had come on the Hollywood scene in 1928 with the cartoon *Steamboat Willie*, Disney's first animation to synchronize sound with action.[2] Mickey Mouse had been so successful that Disney wanted to recognize the fifth anniversary of his creation. Ronell submitted her song "Mickey Mouse and Minnie's in Town," and despite the grammar of the title, Disney Studios accepted and published it.[3] In 1933, it became the official Mickey Mouse birthday song. Ronell always felt it was a "a nice little tune" but because of her "Who's Afraid of the Big Bad Wolf?" which followed closely, Mickey's birthday song "never did have a chance to put in a bid for a bit of attention...."[4]

Soon after the Mickey Mouse anniversary song, Disney Studios asked Ronell to write a theme for a new cartoon series. The synchronization of music and movement was increasingly important with Walt Disney and his staff, especially with the Mickey Mouse series. In fact, the coordination of music and cartoon movement had become known as "mickey mousing" in the industry. But music always followed animation. After the Mickey Mouse series had been flourishing for a few years, Disney told staff music director Carl Stalling:

> But we'll make another series, and they'll be musical shorts. And in them music will take precedence and we'll adjust our action the best we can to what you think is the right music.[5]

The series, with the animation following the music, became the *Silly Symphonies*, shorts that spoofed nursery rhymes and children's folk tales. They were included in movie theater programs along with newsreels and travelogues. It was for these *Silly Symphonies* that Ronell was asked to write a theme. "In a Silly Symphony" was accepted by Disney Studios in Hollywood, then published and recorded in New York.

Ronell's Disney project led to another. A Disney staff composer, Frank Churchill, had composed the background music for one of the *Silly Symphonies*, *Three Little Pigs*. Churchill had done previous recordings for Disney Studios and joined them in 1931. He had studied music at UCLA, was quite versatile and said to be "adept at developing catchy melody lines for songs."[6] It was one of these "catchy melody lines" that Churchill wrote for *Three Little Pigs*. He claimed to have written it in five minutes, loosely patterning it after "Happy Birthday."

For Churchill's melody, writer Ted Sears, who had never written song lyrics, and Pinto Colvig, a story writer and voice artist, created the words.[7] However, neither man was listed as lyricist on the sheet music.[8] Ronell took credit for the lyrics and even some of the music, though how much she did was unclear. In the New York musical world, it was said that "Tin Pan Alley consensus is that it is 'all Ronell.'"[9] She explained that she and Churchill worked from his background music to create the song. It should be noted that "Who's Afraid of the Big Bad Wolf?" is never heard intact during the cartoon, only fragments, often interrupted by the narrative. It is these fragments of melody and words with which Ronell worked, changing the lyrics to create a commercially successful song.

To be listed as a composer on a Disney song was new at the time and brought about changes at Disney Studios. Years later, she explained to friend and *Boston Herald* writer Elinor Hughes:

> Have you noticed ... how many credits are now attached to all the Disney films? Up to the time of "The Three Little Pigs" it was simply "Walt Disney Presents," but when "The Big Bad Wolf" caught on and I was announced as the author, the other people connected with the Disney pictures asked for and received recognition. Those credit lines thrown on the screen mean little to a bored audience, but believe me, they mean everything to the people they represent.[10]

Whoever wrote the song, it caught the attention of Sol Bourne, a.k.a. Saul Bornstein, the general manager of Irving Berlin Music, Inc. This was the same Sol Bourne who had balked at the syncopated rhythms and dedication to George Gershwin in Ronell's "Willow Weep for Me." Disney Studios were in the business of creating cartoons and had never considered songs as a source of revenue and sold the music publishing rights to Irving Berlin Music.[11] Bourne knew that an individual song, tied in with a movie or a cartoon, created synergy and helped sell both entities. Disney and Bourne had a successful relationship until Disney Studious formed its own music publishing division in 1950.

In a 1963 interview, Ronell recalled the initial problems with the publication of "Big Bad Wolf":

> After this song was published — and by the way, getting it published was considered a risky venture because cartoon background music wasn't taken seriously in those days and no song had even been published previously from the cartoon film industry — I was thrilled to receive copies of the lyrics translated into numerous, different languages, including Latin.[12]

The 1934 song struck a chord in several parts of the world, each with its own "Big Bad Wolf." At home, the United States was just recovering from its worst economic depression ever. In Europe and Russia, the Nazi regime in Germany was a growing threat. As musical biographer Edward Jablonski, a big fan of the song, detailed in a lengthy article in *Nebraska Life*:

> During the winter of 1933-34, the depths of what was called the Great Depression, it was impossible to avoid a perky little song entitled "Who's Afraid of the Big Bad Wolf?" It blared from radios,

was available on several recordings—from Ben Bernie to Ethel Shutta — pipingly sung by kiddies on an amateur show that proliferated at the time, not to mention the bathtub vocalists. The song's phenomenal popularity — initiating in the United States, then spreading to the rest of the world — made it an event in a year of portentous events.

The song voiced the hopes of Americans who believed that Hard Times were Ending, and the wolf at the door would be driven away; it was an optimistic answer to the previous year's despairing "Brother, Can You Spare a Dime?"[13]

Put into its historical context more specifically:

Wrung out by the Depression and bolstered by the new president [Roosevelt], the nation seemed to convert the cartoon of two carefree but short-sighted pigs and their hardworking, far-sighted brother into a parable of suffering (the world as economic adversity) and triumph (the industrious little pig as the embodiment of President Roosevelt's New Deal that promised the country relief)....[14]

Ann Ronell and wolf at Riverview Park Zoo, Omaha, Nebraska, July 1934, months after the publication of "Who's Afraid of the Big Bad Wolf?" (reprinted with permission from *The Omaha World-Herald*).

Hollywood recognized that the song resonated with the public, and it was used in several movies of the mid-thirties, including *Babes in Toyland, It Happened One Night, Los Angeles: Wonder City of the West, West Point of the Air,* and *One in a Million.*[15] Years later, when Ronell traveled to the Soviet Union to work on music for the film *Meeting at a Far Meridian,* she learned the song had had a similar effect on the Russian people:

[I]magine my complete wonderment when playing the song at the Composer's Union to have the top Soviet musicologist there point out to me that these same qualities of gaiety and laughter at fear endeared the song to his countrymen as well. According to him, the song's story and humor had provided the Russian people with a warm note of comfort at a time when it was badly needed....[16]

Though remaining in Hollywood, Ronell ended her stint with Disney Studios and moved on to others. However, the "Big Bad Wolf" would rear its head years later in a long, complicated legal action, focusing on just how much of the song Ronell had actually contributed.

She was not finished with cartoons, however, as a few years later she was asked to write a theme for Andy Panda, a cartoon character created by Walter Lantz, another animation genius with his own studio. He had attempted a various series with skunks, monkeys, and even mice, finally settling on a panda.[17] Lantz and Universal Pictures launched the character in 1939 with *Life Begins for Andy Panda.* Andy was a cuddly, mischievous creature loved by audiences, and he even had a Pluto-like dog for a pet. A song for such a character was a perfect topic for Ronell and her song, "Andy Panda," became the signature for the Andy Panda series.[18] The series did not achieve the success of Disney's Mickey Mouse, but did go on for ten years. The decision was made to have Andy age and become more adult, causing interest to wane. The last cartoon in the series was *Scrappy Birthday* in 1949, a year after Lantz had closed his studio.[19]

Among Ronell's other musical activities around this time and during much of her career was the writing of special material for numerous and varied artists (Appendix D). Special material included arrangements, medleys, and lyrics needed by singers for their solo careers, especially concerts and radio. The latter medium was at the height of its popularity, and performers were increasingly mobile and willing to tour, so special material assignments kept Ronell busy when she was not on a major project. Her clients included popular song and cabaret singers as well as numerous operatic artists.[20]

Years later, some of her best work in this area was done when she became involved with the Alberghetti family from Italy. Their daughter, Anna Maria, was a soprano who began singing professionally at age six and debuted at Carnegie Hall at age thirteen. She later won a 1962 Tony award for *Carnival!* Anna Maria's crystal-clear voice and dark eyes had captured American audiences on the weekly television variety hour *The Ed Sullivan Show*, on which she ultimately appeared a record thirty-six times.[21]

Ronell had been contacted by Alberghetti's manager, who asked her to write an English version of an Italian lullaby. Ms. Alberghetti was being promoted by Hollywood as the new Deanna Durbin, and Ronell's previous lyrics had impressed director Frank Capra. From there, Ronell began writing English lyrics to many songs from Alberghetti's operatic repertoire and adapting the arrangements into more of a "song" form. In a Bing Crosby film, Anna Maria sang Ronell's lyric "Yours the Dearest Name I Know," a translation of a well-loved Italian song, "Caro Nome." Ronell maintained a friendship with Anna Maria and her family over the years.

The end of 1934 found Ronell in her hometown of Omaha, Nebraska, composing songs and arrangements for the WAMPAS (Women of the Academy of Motion Picture Arts and Sciences) Baby Stars, touring the Midwest. This was a collection of young talent from Hollywood sponsored by the motion picture industry. Because Ronell spent little time with the troupe, she was able to do some solo performances of her own songs at Omaha's Paramount Theater, singing and playing her hits and other songs of the day.[22] While she did little of this throughout her career, performing was something she enjoyed, although down deep, she probably would have wanted to dance on stage. As she was the local girl visiting from New York, her shows were well-received:

> Miss Ronell's singing is notably good for clear enunciation and minor original effects she uses. She plays cleverly, using many keyboard tricks to get the particular interpretation she wants. Her performance was heard by large audiences at every show Wednesday.[23]

More importantly, the WAMPAS tour had brought Ronell into contact with Paramount Theater producers, Fanchon and Marco. They had commissioned her to write a show for their principal ballerina, Patricia Bowman. Ronell seldom turned down a challenge, and with her musical background, education and interests, she took on the assignment. She created a musical form — ballet-operetta — which she described thus: "Since most dancers can't sing and most singers can't dance, I evolved a form new at the time for presenting voices offstage for the dance characters. This I called Ballet-Operetta."[24]

Ronell's ballet-operetta, entitled *The Magic of Spring*, was presented as a one-hour program. The piece, also called *Like Spring* in various drafts upon which Ronell worked, called for a fifteen-piece orchestra and approximately twenty cast members. Much of the choreography was done by producer Fanchon. The libretto, written by Marcel Silver, had two protagonists — a boy, He, danced by Roy Russell, and a girl, She, the Patricia Bowman starring role.[25] The plot revolves around the boy's attempt to free her from her harsh, imposing employer, the Rag-picker, ultimately taking her to "the land of Eternal Spring."[26]

Ronell referred to the piece as a "ballet with songs," and employed just three of them — "Only Once," "The Bugle Waltz," and "Sweet Magic." The last lines of "Sweet Magic" best expressed the mood of this fantasy, comparing budding trees in spring to the magic of reciprocated love.[27]

Fanchon and Marco moved the show to the Paramount Theater in Los Angeles. A brief item in *The Hollywood Reporter* referred to the piece as "a distinctively different type of stage show."[28] The remainder of this mini-review was most favorable:

> The usual specialties are dispensed with to make way for a dance fantasy with music conceived in the fertile imagination of Ann Ronell. The setting is an old clothes shop, and the slender thread of story by Marcel Silver is a pleasing vehicle for the introduction of clever musical compositions by Miss Ronell.[29]

The review in *Variety* was tepid, describing her song as "tuneful, but having little chance of becoming popular."[30]

The Magic of Spring had a brief run in Los Angeles in March of 1934 then toured several cities in the Midwest, including the Paramount Theater in Omaha. For the Midwest shows, Ronell was the pianist in one of the numbers for the work.[31] Years later, Ronell would improve on her genre, collaborating with composer-violinist Nicolai Berezovsky on *Ship South*, calling this piece a "ballet-sing."

During all this time, Ronell continued to compose songs, both novelty ones and ballads. More than anything, she wanted to be a songwriter, hopefully an independent one, writing songs when and where she wanted to. Movie work was important, but this Tin Pan Alley girl wanted her name under the "Music and lyrics by" heading as much as possible. Larry Spier, who had published her first hit, "Baby's Birthday Party," while in charge at Famous Music, now sought Ronell out, wanting another hit on the order of "Baby's Birthday Party," and telegrammed her:

Ronell in stage dress for *Magic of Spring*, at Paramount Theatre, Los Angeles. In addition to writing words and music for the piece she called a "ballet-operetta," Ronell provided piano accompaniment for several numbers on the program (courtesy of the Academy of Motion Picture Arts and Sciences).

DEAR ANN THINK IT GOOD TIME TO PUBLISH NOVELTY SONG ON ORDER OF BBP ["BABY'S BIRTHDAY PARTY"] STOP HOW ABOUT WRITING ONE AND SENDING IT TO ME REGARDS

LARRY SPIER TB HARMS[32]

Among her next efforts was a novelty tune, "An Elephant Never Forgets." It was considered by Twentieth Century Pictures head Darryl F. Zanuck for his picture *Folies Bergere*, but was never used as it did not fit the persona of star Maurice Chevalier.[33] In such a manner did songs come and go, and so the young composer kept on plugging. Then Lester Cowan came into her life.

5

Lester Cowan and
Hollywood: 1935–1936

"Miss Ronell is wrapped up in her music.... Miss Ronell is not domestic."

Although Ann Ronell and Lester Cowan were both working in Hollywood at the time, they met at a hearing for the motion picture industry code in Washington, D.C. Cowan was there representing the Academy of Motion Picture Arts & Sciences (AMPAS), which enforced the code. Ronell was there visiting her brother Sol Rosenblatt, an attorney who was also involved in the hearings, in an opposing role to Cowan's.

Gossip maven Louella Parsons, in her column at the time of the Cowan-Ronell marriage, detailed their initial meeting: "Lester Cowan met Ann Ronell when still involved with AMPAS and butted heads with Sol Rosenblatt over the motion picture code then being instituted. When he met her, Lester Cowan did not know Ann's maiden name was Rosenblatt."[1] A New York gossip columnist gave a similar accounting of the meeting, written in "gossipese": "Lester Cowan of the Academy of Mot. Pict. Arts and Sciences, who is battling with Dep. Com. Rosenblatt of the NRA in Washington, arrived in town Fri. only to go Hollywoozy over Ann Ronell, lyricist of 'The Big Bad Wolf.'... However, he will learn here that Miss Ronell is Rosenblatt's sister."[2]

During the early months of their relationship, Cowan was attentive to getting his girlfriend entrenched in the movie music business. The projects he proposed and campaigned for her to work on included a British picture, other animated cartoons besides Disney's, and miscellaneous work at 20th Century–Fox studios.[3]

At the time, Cowan was extremely well-known in Hollywood, mostly from his position as executive director of AMPAS, known better today as the "Oscars organization." He is credited with several innovations within the movie industry including:

1. organization of the Research Council of the Motion Picture Industry which set technical standards in the industry, addressing such issues as screen size and shape, reel dimensions, and sound techniques;
2. implementation of the motion picture rating code;
3. initiation of market research of audiences, including work with Dr. George Gallup, a pioneer of market research;
4. representation of artists and technicians in their first collective bargaining which preceded the formation of the various guilds which now govern labor relations in Hollywood;

5. organization of the conciliation and arbitration framework which settled employee disputes;

6. origination of the first college course on film appreciation and film-making at the University of Southern California;

7. organization of a film training program for the U.S. Army which was used to train troops in World War II.[4]

Cowan's most prominent accomplishment while with AMPAS was the creation, in 1928, of their awards ceremonies—the Oscars. He also arranged for the first radio broadcast of the awards over NBC and CBS. For all of this, he was referred to as the "Father of the Oscars."[5] His career in Hollywood had begun after he had attended Stanford University, starting out in small studio jobs and advancing to more important positions over the years. He was production supervisor for John Ford in 1935 on *The Whole Town's Talking*, then as the thirties ended, he began producing his own films, the first two being *You Can't Cheat an Honest Man* and *My Little Chickadee*, both with W. C. Fields. As an independent producer, his films, mostly profitable, included *Ladies in Retirement* (1941), *Commandos Strike at Dawn* (1942), *Tomorrow, the World!* (1944), *The Story of G. I. Joe* (1945), *One Touch of Venus* (1948), *Love Happy* (1950), and *Main Street to Broadway* (1953).[6]

Though Ronell had had some exposure to Hollywood, marriage to Cowan was of immense help in getting her known to the profession and her finding work in the male-dominated music industry of the town. Her first Hollywood assignment outside of Disney Studios was with RKO Studios and producer Lou Brock to whom she was under contract (Appendix E). Though originally hired to write a song or two for his picture *Down to Their Last Yacht*, she also composed background music for various action and dramatic scenes, adding lyrics to the music when the script called for it.[7] Two songs from the movie emerged from Ronell's pen: "Funny Little World," a romantic tune heard during the opening credits, then sung by the crew and passengers on the yacht,[8] and "Beach Boy," a novelty song used mostly for background music.[9]

The latter song caught the ear of dance team Veloz and Yolanda, who incorporated it into their act after the movie opened. Ronell had been friends with the dance duo since their roles in *Champagne Waltz*, and they were aware of whatever she was working on. Ronell told a Universal executive: "'Beach Boy' is coming into its second childhood.... Veloz likes it so much that he arranged it as a rumba. Can you beat it? He tells me they have as many as 3–4 requests for it on each nightly broadcast."[10]

What most impressed Brock and others about her contributions to *Down to Their Last Yacht* was a "South Sea Bolero" sequence she created, including words, music, and action. It was a light, operatic piece and served as a nice diversion within the film, sung and danced by the natives of the island on which the plot unfolds.[11] Brock was to use her again later on.

Other producers were noticing her talent, including Tin Pan Alley songwriter Buddy DeSylva, who had become a Hollywood producer. In 1935, he was doing a picture with rising child star Shirley Temple, *Captain January*, and asked Ronell to do the music for it.[12] Also around this time, there was talk that Ronell would do songs for another Temple film, *Poor Little Rich Girl*.[13] Both films opened in 1936, and although Ronell probably did work on both of them, it was uncredited. The latter film had several songs written by Harry Revel and Mack Gordon, most sung by Temple or her co-star, Alice Faye.[14]

Because of her rare position as a female composer in Hollywood, reporters took notice of her, especially female ones. This appears to have been a pattern across the country, as Ronell's accomplishments would draw interviews for inclusion in the many newspaper sections devoted to women. Exemplary of this were comments written by Alma Whitaker for the *Los Angeles Times*: "So far she has exhibited a remarkable versatility, all her songs differing from each other—yet all following the same idea of presenting a definite picture in words and music and not a line censorable."[15]

Ronell and Cowan appreciated each other, personally and professionally. A family member mentioned how much they conversed with each other, and "they always had something to say to each other about what was going on."[16] They were said to have been similar in work habits—industrious and involved in a variety of projects—definite multitaskers. They both wrote endless "to-do" lists, scraps of which are still present in their records, as they seldom threw anything away. Despite all their lists, they were both disorganized, and she often had to keep Cowan from promising things to people that would come back to haunt him.

Friends and coworkers felt he was kind, especially to her, and she was much in love with him. As she wrote to ballet dancer Tamara Geva, then starring with Ray Bolger in Richard Rodgers and Lorenz Hart's *On Your Toes*, "He has the most thrilling ideas. Really, Tamara, he is the stimulating-est, the darling-est, the husband-est-est-est, and I'm sorry you didn't get to see us in New York and know him better."[17]

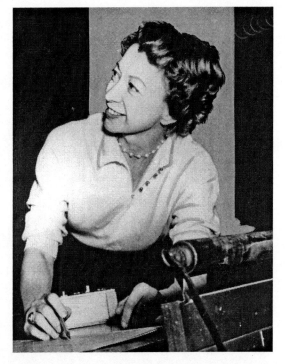

Ann Ronell at a composing table with timing device, circa 1935 (courtesy *The Omaha World-Herald* and Nebraska Jewish Historical Society).

Ann and Lester were married on November 6, 1935, on board the ocean liner *Santa Elena* en route from the West Coast to New York via the Panama Canal.[18] Their relationship appears to have been a close one over the years, governed much by their professional lives, neither one being particularly family-oriented. Two years before her marriage, a New York writer revealed this: "She can't cook and doesn't want to learn and only sews when she has to, an odd button or a torn collar or some such necessity."[19] She admitted years later that she had tried the domestic life, "but the cakes burned, the pots all boiled over, while I dashed off to write down a score bobbing around in my head."[20] And finally, from another journalist: "Miss Ronell is wrapped up in her music. Her composing is no hobby, nor is it just a profitable job.... Miss Ronell is not domestic."[21]

Soon after the wedding, Ronell and Cowan were firmly settled into California life. Always looking for a new project, she made the acquaintance of Max L. Swarthout, director of the University of Southern California School of Music, and the two of them conceived of a course for Ronell to teach. It was entitled "Music in Motion Pictures" and she was to be moderator for a series of lectures by composers, arrangers, and orchestrators within the film industry. The prospectus of the course read like a "Who's Who" of American popular song composers. Though she had the usual Ronell enthusiasm, the course was never presented due to her subsequent career commitments.[22]

Several years after they were married, Ronell and Cowan considered adoption of a child.

Ann was the impetus behind the idea and worked with Edna Gladney from the Texas Children's Home and Aid Society. At various times, Ronell and Cowan considered a four-year-old boy, but he was from a large family and aid workers wished to keep them together. Also considered were twin girls, but two children were considered too great of an initial undertaking.[23] More than anything, it appears that Ronell was pushing for the idea of adoption and that Cowan was lukewarm on the whole proposition.[24]

Ultimately, it was clear that the professional lives of Ronell and Cowan, especially at this time in the forties, were far too busy and dedicated to leave room for raising a family. As she admitted to *The Christian Science Monitor* years later: "Between my husband's career and mine, there is not much time for anything else."[25] The adoption idea slowly faded over the next several years. Ronell kidded with an interviewer years later that she had no children "but many brain children."[26] Ronell does not seem to have been affected adversely by the decision later in her life and career.

Like Ronell, Cowan had a wide range of interests, well beyond movies, and was helpful to her with her work in opera and Broadway. Like her, he had a thousand ideas and was always juggling several projects. Friends and family agree that Lester Cowan was the dominant spouse in their relationship. An interviewer surmised after a long talk with Ronell: "When there are two careers in the family, it is usually — though not always — the wife's which must accommodate home demands."[27]

While Ronell did work on several motion picture assignments separate from him, most of her film career after 1940 involved Lester Cowan productions. Cowan explained their marriage-business relationship in a 1958 letter to their attorney: "When Ann and I were married, we reached the following understanding: I would handle all the business, and she would confine her film writing to my films and would do additional writing for the theater, which she could do at home."[28] To Cowan it was both economical and possibly a control matter.

In November 1935, Ronell and Lester Cowan disembark from the ocean liner *Santa Elena* after their voyage from California and a few days after their onboard marriage (Nebraska Jewish Historical society).

Left to right: Herman Rosenblatt (Ann's brother), Ronell, Mollie Rosenblatt (mother), Cowan, and unidentified family member, on a dock in New York after Ronell and Cowan's voyage from California on the *Santa Elena* (Nebraska Jewish Historical Society).

For the most part, she seemed happy with the arrangement. In late 1946, after several years of work with Cowan, she tried to change the arrangement and get composer Louis Applebaum to replace her, at least for a year or two. As she explained to Applebaum at the time:

> My career was subjugated to his since our marriage because I felt his was so much more important and significant, his talents so much more integrated with dynamic direction, his worth as a person so much more imperative to be nourished. I still am of the same opinion, but family responsibilities & worries have diffused my value as an assistant to Lester and I am not providing the help he demands.[29]

Applebaum turned down the offer and Ronell maintained her professional position with Cowan. Fortunately, they collaborated well together, and he had numerous interesting projects over the years on which she worked.

During their best years in Hollywood, they owned a ranch in Canoga Park with over 200 acres of land, including forty acres worked to grow alfalfa. Though the couple still kept an apartment in Hollywood, the ranch served as a quiet getaway for Cowan and Ronell and frequent visitors. Among their musical friends was Leonard Bernstein, who is said to have written a good part of his 1944 musical *On the Town* while on an extended stay there. After her success with *The Story of G.I. Joe*, Ronell kept a horse on the ranch named "Linda," the title of her Academy Award–nominated song.[30]

6

Kurt Weill and
Blockade: 1937–1938

"For all the big bad wolfs ... around Hollywood, none are so fearsome as the organized group of males who long expended tremendous efforts to keep determined ladies out of the music writing departments of the film industry."

In 1937, Ann Ronell began work on a movie for Walter Wanger. By the end of the production in 1938, after changes in titles, directors, composers, screen writers and music directors, she ended up lyricist of two solid ballads, one with Kurt Weill, the other with Werner Janssen. But this convoluted Hollywood saga needs more exposition.

Walter Wanger was an independent producer, developing films as Walter Wanger Productions. He engaged director Lewis Milestone to write and direct a screenplay for a movie originally entitled *Castles in Spain*, and soon changed to *The River Is Blue*.[1] Milestone, who had a big hit with *All Quiet on the Western Front* (1930), was to co-author the screenplay with Clifford Odets.

Odets was a member of the Group Theatre, established in 1931, an assemblage of artists committed to ensemble works, method acting, and presentation of new plays and playwrights. At one point during 1935, he had four plays running on Broadway: *Waiting for Lefty*, *Awake and Sing*, *Till the Day I Die*, and *Paradise Lost*. Two years later, he had success with *Golden Boy*.[2] Odets had recently come to Hollywood from New York, a move he later considered to be a sellout, as he got used to the better income of Hollywood and worked little as a playwright. Working mostly on screenplays, then television scripts, he grew "sour and self-disgusted" toward the end of his career.[3]

Milestone and Odets adopted a plotline from a novel by Ilya Ehrenburg, *The Loves of Jeanne Ney*. They set the story in contemporary Spain, which was then going through a civil war.[4] The insurgent Nationalists, under General Franco, were getting their support from Benito Mussolini and the Fascist government in Italy and Hitler and the Nazi regime in Germany. Also sympathetic to the Nationalist cause were the clergy of the Roman Catholic Church who wanted political power in Spain to remain centralized.[5]

The existing Republic government or Loyalists were supported by communist Russia and Stalin. The Loyalists also had support from the more secular and urban members of the populace, as well as the Basques from northeast Spain who eventually wanted to separate from the country. Beginning with an uprising in Morocco in 1936, the Spanish Civil War lasted over three years, ending in 1939 with Franco firmly in control.[6]

Soon into the production of *The River Is Blue*, Wanger changed directors, hiring Fritz Lang, European-born and a friend of Kurt Weill. Lang brought Weill to the project in early 1937. Weill went to Hollywood, and in a letter dated January 28, 1937, to wife Lotte Lenya in New York, related his initial work on the film:

> I started working on the script immediately, and after one hour I had already succeeded in writing a song that will work into the story line brilliantly. It'll be a kind of revolutionary song, but at the same time a love song. Wanger, who is surprisingly nice and cultured, was enthusiastic about the idea and has great expectations for this song. What's more, I gather I'll be able to do all kinds of things in the film, because they've built entire scenes around the music.[7]

Despite Weill's productive start, troubles developed within several weeks. In a letter to Lenya on March 3, 1937, he speculated about the faltering production:

> [W]e're having big trouble with the movie, because Wanger is creating difficulties and we're trying to do the whole thing with another studio (which, however, I believe will be very hard). Wanger says he can't spend as much money on the movie as Milly [Lewis Milestone] would like him to because he thinks the film will be banned in most European countries. Well, it's all the same to me, because I'll get my money in any case, and (between us!) I'm not having such great fun working on the film anyway.[8]

Even with the pauses in production, Weill wrote almost an entire score, with various themes, to be delivered to Wanger. To complement his score, Weill asked Ronell to write lyrics for some of the themes for presentation to the producer. Ronell and Weill had been introduced by composer Ernst Toch during Weill's first visit to Hollywood two years earlier.[9] At the time, Ronell was working for Paramount Pictures and confided to friends her desire to work with Weill: "It is my pleasure to have him [Weill] wanting me as lyricist for the picture he is now doing at Paramount.... I have never heard any of his [film] music but am so fond of him personally that I am sure we'd make a swell team."[10]

Not only had Wanger delayed filming, he also brought in a new director, William Dieterle, and a new script writer, John Howard Lawson. Lawson had been an organizer of the Screen Writers Guild and years later became widely known as one of the "Hollywood Ten" during the House Un-American Activities Committee (HUAC) hearings.[11]

On top of all this, Wanger had hired a music director, Boris Morros, for his production company. Morros had recently resigned the same position at Paramount Pictures. Ronell had worked under him on two pictures at Paramount, *Champagne Waltz* and *The Big Broadcast of 1936*. Her adjectives for him, expressed in a 1979 letter to Werner Janssen, included "wily" and "tyrannical."[12] She said at the time of *The River Is Blue* that she "would not work under him."[13]

In the late 1920s, as sound was incorporated into movies, the music was created by the studios, which employed orchestras, composers, and music directors, mostly all under contract. The music directors, such as Morros, wielded much power,

Left to right: Ronell, Kurt Weill and Lotte Lenya in 1937 New York City around the time of *The River Is Blue*, later changed to *Blockade* (courtesy the Weill-Lenya Research Center, Kurt Weill Foundation for Music, New York).

assigning orchestrators and composers to films, hiring and firing personnel and, in various degrees, controlling the final product heard on screen.[14]

While Morros himself was an impediment to Ronell, it should be noted that few women were working in the music departments of Hollywood other than as secretaries. Distaff composers were few, and female arrangers, orchestrators and conductors were unheard of. Women in music did not gravitate to Hollywood. Ronell herself, during her promotional tour for *The Story of G.I. Joe* in 1945, admitted what a tough job music could be:

> I understand why women don't usually take this sort of work. I was at the studio from dawn till midnight, day after day, and before the picture was done I was down to 94 pounds.... No, unless a woman wants to spend her time doing nothing else, music director is not the job for her."[15]

Though Ronell never had children, she kiddingly compared work on a movie to pregnancy, because it takes nine months, "the same time it takes to produce a baby — plotting, charting, writing, composing, and rewriting."[16]

But there was also a true "old boys' club" atmosphere in Hollywood. Columnist Marjory M. Fisher of the *San Francisco Chronicle*, after an interview, explained, "For all the big bad wolfs (or wolves, if you must!) around Hollywood, none are so fearsome as the organized group of males who long expended tremendous efforts to keep determined ladies out of the music writing departments of the film industry."[17]

Songwriting in New York or California was still a male domain in 1938. Ronell had joined ASCAP in 1932, and between 1920 and 1949, 178 women songwriters joined ASCAP, but by mid-century, there were already hundreds of male members. Over 40 years later, writer Leslie Anderson, in a monograph entitled "Women Film and Television Composers in the United State," explained:

> Where do women fall within the spectrum of film music composition? Although women have been somewhat successful in the world of film as directors, writers and producers, as composers their impact has been minor. Unfortunately, women film and TV composers of today still fall victim to the exclusionary "all-boy" network in operation within the film business.[18]

Morros and Dieterle both wanted to get rid of Weill's score and hire a new composer and lyricist. Weill had returned to New York to work on *Knickerbocker Holiday* with Maxwell Anderson,[19] and Ronell had been overseeing musical matters for him and the stalled production. She made a plea to retain Weill's score, playing it on the piano and singing some of the songs for Wanger and the skeptical Morros, a brave act at the time. Despite her best efforts, the score was abandoned.[20]

Weill was a prominent composer with successes in Germany and recent works in America. For Ronell to be affiliated with Weill as his lyricist and musical overseer was important; Weill didn't work with just anyone. Ronell, on the periphery of songwriters at this point, felt that association with Weill, even in a futile effort, could only enhance her reputation. The elimination of Weill's music from the production was a definite setback for her.

Ronell and Weill had maintained a working relationship during this upheaval. Not only had she stayed in contact with Weill regarding the music, but her attempts to keep his score had pleased him. Despite all the production changes, copyright applications were made for two songs in March, 1938, with Weill as composer, Ronell as lyricist, and Walter Wanger Productions, Inc., as copyright owner.[21]

The first, "March — Finale," was to open and close the movie and had a forgettable set of words. The second was a love theme, copyrighted as "The River Is So Blue." It was taken from a tango Weill had written for one of the love scenes. It was published in 1938 by Ann Ronell Music and Hampshire House Publishing and is a fine expression of love, hopeful but wary.[22]

Weill's contract with Wanger had stipulated payment be made upon delivery of the music, which Weill had completed. As he gloated in a second letter of March 3, 1937, to Lenya, "The whole production has been called off. You can imagine how upsetting this was — but not for this little smarty. I get all the money as soon as I deliver the music."[23]

However, Ronell had had no agent at the time of her contract, and her agreement with Wanger, dated February 10, 1938, was that payment was to be made only after all lyric duties had been completed. Because of the economy of keeping Ronell, and also because Wanger had admired her lyrics to Weill's themes, she was retained to work with the new composer, Werner Janssen.

Weill took credit for securing Ronell's position in the rejuvenated project. As he wrote to Lenya on April 19, 1938, "Ann is very busy with the movie I got for her, on which she now works in heavenly peace with the other gentleman (they've now thrown out all my music!)."[24]

Whether Ronell's staying on with the production was completely agreeable to Weill is not known. Some displeasure is hinted at in a letter from Lenya to Weill on April 21, 1938: "I never had any doubts that that dear little Ann is quite a con artist. But one has to be fair. Naturally she doesn't want to pass up this chance, for which she has waited a really long time. But the bounds of decency can be moved by the slightest stirring of the wind."[25]

Weill was initially upset with Janssen, assuming that Janssen had engineered the switch and removed Weill's work from the production. Ronell assured Weill that it was the doing of Wanger and Morros. As she explained to Janssen in 1979, "[I] was sure that Werner had no part in manipulating Wanger into giving him Kurt's job, but with all the dog-eat-dog intrigues popular then from the sudden influx of hungry Europeans, suspicion reared its ugly head at every turn ... especially since the new citizens were so marvelously talented!"[26]

A year or so after *Blockade* was produced, Weill was in Los Angeles for a road tour of his musical *Johnny Johnson* and wanted to see Ronell. Because she liked both Weill and Janssen and still had some discomfiture over the switch on the movie, Ronell set up a "chance" meeting between the two. Despite initial misgivings, the two composers ultimately got on well.

Werner Janssen, born in New York in 1899, received his musical education in both the United States and Europe. Though he had written for the *Ziegfeld Follies* and other revues, he was mostly a classical musician. In 1934, he became the first American ever to conduct the New York Philharmonic Orchestra, went on to conduct several other major orchestras in this country, and founded the Utah Symphony. His most popular orchestral composition was "Louisiana Suite," and among his chamber music works, "Kaleidoscope" and "Obsequies of a Saxophone" were best known. However, Janssen was no stranger to film music, having completed the score for *The General Died at Dawn* a year earlier. He eventually did forty-five film scores, though only one with Ronell.[27]

As Ronell and Janssen teamed up, the production went full speed ahead. The title was now *Blockade*, and the entire action was to take place in Spain. Henry Fonda and Madeleine Carroll were the stars, with supporting roles played by John Halliday and Leo Carrillo, the latter later to star as the sidekick, Pancho, on television's *The Cisco Kid*.

Blockade opened in the summer of 1938 and was a success in England. However, mostly due to the script written by the politically active John Howard Lawson, its Loyalist-communist outlook was frowned upon by various interest groups in the United States. In support of their fellow priests in Spain, many of whom had been killed by Loyalist forces, the Catholic clergy in America denounced *Blockade*. Several Knights of Columbus posts attempted to get it banned, their national governing board demanding that the movie be labeled as propaganda.[28] The Boston city council attempted to get it banned in their city, but the mayor blocked the resolution. Because it was more anti-war and anti-bombing of civilians than anything else and not a pro–Loyalist movie, the controversy ended.[29]

Ronell and Janssen wrote a love theme, sung and played on guitar in the movie by one of her Broadway acquaintances, George Houston, in a café setting. She would later write special material for Houston's production *of The Merry Wives of Windsor* in Hollywood.[30]

"Beloved, You're Lovely" starts with a simple verse of 16 measures, marked "Moderately," with each 4 measures containing a run of quarter note triplets. The chorus, marked "Slow (*with feeling*)," is also 16 measures. The lyric is simple and, perhaps, overly romantic, but Ronell included internal rhymes into every third line which work well.[31] "Beloved, You're Lovely" was published in 1938 by Miller Music, Inc., with Henry Fonda, Madeleine Carroll, Leo Carrillo, and John Halliday pictured on the cover. Though it sounded good in *Blockade*, no recordings of it were made.

Ronell got the last laugh on Boris Morros at the end of 1938. He received criticism in his post as music director for Walter Wanger Productions. At the end of 1938, Ronell received a note from Weill: "I saw in the papers this morning that our friend Boris Morros has resigned. I always thought that his palace was built on sand (in every sense of the word), but I didn't think it would break down so fast. Well, it is good to know that there is still something like justice in the world."[32]

Ronell's positive attitude, and the way she persevered despite the vagaries of the production of *Blockade*, led to more work with producer Walter Wanger. He had purchased other artistic properties and wanted to remake a French film, *Pepe Le Moko*. Wanger had appreci-

Left to right: Dan Caste (Werner Janssen assistant), Werner Janssen, Ronell, Henry Fonda (narrator), and the program director, unidentified, during work on the NBC Radio transcontinental broadcast of score of *Blockade*, produced by Walter Wanger in 1937.

ated her work on *Blockade*, both with Weill then Janssen, and signed her to write song lyrics for the new film called *Algiers.*

Algiers was embroiled in controversy when the Acting Consul of the French Consulate in Los Angeles wanted the title changed, complaining to Joseph Breen at the Motion Picture Association of America (MPAA) that the movie gave a bad impression of the French and its North African city. He protested, "[T]he American public may be led to a misrepresentation of the character and moral standing of all French people and customs in that locality.... Such a change would be greatly appreciated and would avoid a misunderstanding which would indeed, when known in France, cause a very painful impression."[33]

Wanger would have none of it, and despite the involvement of the powerful Breen, since this was not a censorship issue, felt strongly about his film and title. He shot back to the Acting French Consul, "As remarkable as it may seem, I assure you the majority of Americans do not know where Algiers is and this picture will be of the greatest value in publicizing the name and locale. I am sure those who see it will want to go to Algiers and look for the counterparts of Hedy Lamarr and Charles Boyer."[34] The title remained.

Ronell wrote new English lyrics for the old songs as well as new ones for stars Boyer and Nina Koshetz, with music by Vincent Scotto.[35] "Algiers" was published in connection with the movie but not performed, and "C'est la Vie" featured Boyer and Hedy Lamarr on the cover and was sung by the debonair Frenchman in the movie.[36]

Also following *Blockade*, there was talk of Ronell and Weill doing a Broadway musical. He had successes in America with Paul Green as lyricist in *Johnny Johnson* (1936) and had completed *Knickerbocker Holiday* with Maxwell Anderson while Ronell was attempting to save his music in *Blockade*.[37] She was anxious to work with him, even if just as lyricist.[38] Producer Cheryl Crawford had purchased a story, *White Wings*, and wanted to pair Ronell and Weill as her creative team: "I feel that you and Kurt alone would be more imaginative about how to treat the script at this stage than a playwright. Have you talked about it yet, and have you any ideas? Please let me know. Certainly both of you have just the right quality for it."[39]

Though Crawford had backers, her composers were drawn to other projects. Weill joined forces with Ira Gershwin and created his most successful musical, *Lady in the Dark* (1940), and Ronell changed genres, turning her focus to an early interest, opera. *White Wings* was never produced.

7

Martha and Opera
in English: 1938–1939

*"We have taken the old relic down from the shelf,
dusted it off, clipped some of the bedraggled trimmings
and dabbed on a spot of fresh paint here and there."*

Ronell had begun working in a more classical vein around 1936, some of it related to her special material work with various artists. She would compose modern lyrics to classical instrumental works using, for instance, Frederic Chopin's *Nocturne in E Flat* or Robert Schumann's *Traumeri*. She also began experimenting with European operas, updating their librettos and adapting the lyrics into English (Appendix F).[1] She collaborated with Dr. Richard Lert of the Los Angeles High Schools system and Santa Barbara Music Academy and Dr. Hugo Streilitzer of the Los Angeles Junior College system. These two musician-academicians and their students were willing to work with and perform these classics in English. The operas she worked on for these ensembles included *Barber of Seville*, *Fra Diavolo*, *Tales of Hoffmann*, *The Magic Flute*, *The Marriage of Figaro*, *Merry Wives of Windsor*, and *La serva padronna*.[2]

These classical adaptations led to a collaboration with Deanna Durbin on a songbook of ten classics that Ronell had translated into English. Her intent was to push opera in English into America's consciousness with the help of an established star. Durbin was a young, pretty soprano who had done operetta and Broadway and was perfect for the big screen. Her and Ronell's 1939 project resulted in the *Deanna Durbin Album of Favorite Songs and Arias* (Appendix C).[3] Shortly after the songbook was published, Durbin performed two of these pieces in movies for Universal Pictures: "Les Filles de Cadiz" and "Je Veux Vivre." This *Album* was published in New York by G. Schirmer, Inc., and was widely distributed in music libraries of colleges and universities across America. A friend of Ronell and a well-known voice coach in the New York area, Estelle Liebling, claimed, "There never has been a student who walked into my studio without Ronell's book of 'Favorite Arias.'"[4]

With this project a success, Ronell tried further to align herself with popular singers of the day. She next worked with Judy Garland, again on a songbook of songs adapted from the classical composers, *In the Judy Garland Manner*. This project appeared to be more commercial than artistic, with Ronell and Lester Cowan attempting to interest the public in the classics under the auspices of the rising film star. With the Deanna Durbin book, Ronell and the singer appeared to have worked more closely. The financial arrangements for the Garland songbook were detailed by Lester to attorney William Hinckle:

The agreements between Ann and Judy Garland should provide that Ann give Garland a $500.00 advance against one-half of the royalties from sale of the book (but not on mechanical royalties or other revenue). In addition, she shall give Garland one-half of the royalties if the songs are published individually, utilizing Garland's pictures.... Garland agrees to use her best efforts to introduce these songs on her radio program.[5]

In the Judy Garland Manner was published in 1940 (Appendix C) but did not have the success of the Durbin work.

Also in the early forties, Ronell made overtures to screen baritone Nelson Eddy and was asked to do a song or two for a songbook featuring Lily Pons, a Metropolitan Opera soprano. Ronell reasoned, "There are as many baritones in America I am sure, as sopranos, and now with the trend singing in English becoming very popular, I am sure there would be as big a commercial success with my type of songbook with Mr. Eddy."[6] Though he liked the idea, Eddy, always the businessman, politely declined: "Many thanks for your interest — but the proposition has come up before and after some experience with it I decided not to take it up, because I sing the original music and any other presentation of these songs brings kickbacks."[7]

Not one to give up easily, she countered Eddy's comments with an explanation of her pure intentions when doing the classics. She sent him the Durbin book, published materials from *The Gypsy Baron*, an adaptation of a Chopin piece, and a letter that included the following rebuttal:

> Undoubtedly, you have the impression I was indulging in the current pastime of swinging the classics and had suggested such for your Songbook. I don't think you understand exactly what I have in mind.
>
> You will note that in every case there is no tampering with the original, the whole effect created only to serve and preserve the composer's contribution to the singer.[8]

Though Eddy was not swayed and nothing more came of the songbooks, the experience adapting and translating the classics would continue to serve her well throughout her career.

In 1938, just as the songbook projects were emerging, Ronell and Vicki Baum wrote and arranged a modern adaptation of *Martha*. It was a comic opera by Friedrich von Flotow that had opened in 1847 with a libretto by Friedrich Wilhelm Riese. Ronell and Baum had met in Hollywood, Ronell having just finished working on *Blockade* and Baum having recently moved there with her Viennese husband, Richard Lert.

Baum was born in Vienna, became an accomplished harpist in childhood, played in the Vienna State Opera and taught at the Vienna Conservatory of Music. She developed into a serious writer; her most famous work was a novel, *Grand Hotel*. It became a play by the same name, running for 13 months during the 1930-31 Broadway season, and was also a successful movie starring Greta Garbo and John and Lionel Barrymore. Though she continued to write novels and screenplays, Baum never equaled the success of *Grand Hotel*.[9] She and Ronell became close friends and corresponded sporadically for the rest of their lives. Baum, continental, cultured and multilingual, had an earthy side to her. In a friendly thank you note years after their work on *Martha*, Baum wrote to her co-librettist, "You may call me a skunk and a pig and another couple of malodorous animals for not having thanked you before."[10]

Ronell and Baum took on the task of *Martha* because both were interested in doing opera in English. Through Lert, Ronell began her collaboration with Baum. In the preface to their libretto for their translation of *Martha*, Baum made her and Ronell's case for opera in English:

> Other countries which are opera-minded — Germany, France, Italy, Russia — have every opera translated into their own language, and it is for this reason that opera is so much more popular over there.

There is a lot of entertainment, of fine sentiment or good humor buried in the books of operas, especially in the very old ones, written by the best lyric writers of their times. As a matter of fact, there are signs here and there, still isolated and infrequent, that a movement for the "naturalization" of opera art in America is under way. This new translation and adaptation of *Martha* aims to be a humble part of this movement.[11]

It was also Ronell's intention to convert their version to a screenplay, for she felt that *Martha* had "the best movie story, in my opinion, that famous operas offer."[12] More specifically, her plan was "to select the ten most tuneful and importantly familiar numbers—cut out all the recitative and pretentious parts—and do the story with a modern setting, as the music can be re-orchestrated beautifully in modern technique for the film, and also can be swung later by bands for popularization."[13]

But *Martha*, as an opera in English, was problematic. It had been written in German with a plot centered in 18th century England. However, when performed in America, it was sung in Italian, a situation which Baum referred to as "one of the flagrant riddles of opera tradition."[14] The Metropolitan Opera had last produced it in 1928, in Italian, of course.

Translation of opera had been difficult from its inception, having first been done in 1686, but the practice did not become common until translations of Mozart's works appeared in the 1780s. Most countries caught on to the idea slowly, and it was not popular until the middle of the 19th century, by which time translation of an opera was considered an "infallible mark of international success."[15]

The principles of translation were detailed by critic Sigmund Spaeth in a 1915 article in *Music Quarterly*:

Declamation, in the sense of the correct allocation of verbal stress to musical stress, is either explicitly or implicitly as the first principle to be observed by the translation. It merges into the compatibility with the musical phrase. Once these principles are satisfied, the translator must balance the various demands of suitability to the voice, fidelity to the original meaning and an appropriate sense of period and genre.[16]

Friedrich von Flotow, composer of *Martha*, carte de visite photograph by E. Desmaisons, Paris, circa 1875.

As an afterthought, the same reference on "translation" noted that after the above principles were fulfilled, there was little chance left for "good literary style."[17]

Western European audiences especially took to the idea of opera in the native tongue, and composers encouraged such treatment of their operas, as translation into the language of the listener hastened popularity of the work. One opera, Massenet's *Werther*, even premiered in German translation, rather than the composer's French.[18]

Two factors swung the pendulum back to the "opera in the original" end of the spectrum: international air travel and recording companies. Most opera stars preferred to sing in the original language rather than switch languages from city to city, and since air travel had made the world smaller, opera companies offered a production in the original language in order to attract a "big name" voice. Opera audiophiles also preferred their opera in the original, and at that time, opera recordings were popular sellers.[19]

In doing the translation, Ronell and Baum had gone back to the original libretto in German, Baum's native language. They also worked with an Italian translation and several in English, most of which had been derived from the Italian rendition. Baum referred to those available in English as "unsatisfactory ... tongue-twisting and antiquated."[20]

Ronell, Baum, and Lert aimed to streamline the opera with a compact book and to eliminate much of the "ballast" of the original libretto. They also restored passages of Flotow's music which had been lost in the Italian renditions. In doing so, they gave their audience the opportunity to hear music of Flotow never before heard in America. His music is considered graceful and charming, and though he wrote numerous operas, most of his best music is concentrated in two of them, *Martha* and *Alessandro Stradella*.[21]

Ronell and Baum realized that their Hollywood Bowl audience would not be a sophisticated opera crowd but newcomers to the art form. The two women felt it important not to discourage the interest of new listeners. Therefore, an English libretto with a compact plot, focusing on pretty melodies, would carry the evening. Baum concluded in her preface to the libretto: "We have taken the old relic down from the shelf, dusted it off, clipped some of the bedraggled trimmings and dabbed on a spot of fresh paint here and there."[22]

Martha opened August 30, 1938, to a capacity crowd at the Hollywood Bowl. Richard Lert conducted, and the four principal singers were Rosemarie Brancato, Irra Petina, Charles Kullman, and Douglas Beattie. Critics were generous in their praise of the Ronell and Baum libretto and even more for the concept of opera in English. Frank Mittauer, critic of the *Los Angeles Evening News*, opened by saying, "The reception accorded *Martha* last night by a Hollywood Bowl audience should convince the most hardened traditionalist that opera ought to be sung in the language of the country where it is presented."[23] Dr. Bruno David Ussher echoed these sentiments in the *Los Angeles Daily News*: "To me the most significant element of Tuesday's *Martha* was the greater charm conferred on this rather vapid piece by means of a fitting and bright translation. If one is willing to overlook 20th century colloquialisms from 18th century characters, the translation warrants high praise."[24]

Richard D. Saunders, writing more of an opinion piece than a review, elaborated on opera in English. He referred to the Baum-Ronell effort as "an American translation, in view of its sensible adaptations to the requirements of this country."[25] After commenting on the "unquestionably average audience," Saunders then launched into a plea for modernization of librettos:

> [F]resh eyes and ears are not reconciled to absurdities, which is the main reason why opera is not more popular in this country.
> ... If *Martha*, with its initial limitations and numerous mediocrities, could be made so enjoyable by efficient treatment, it is obvious that a similar handling of more important works is not merely desirable but actually necessary.
> ... Translation of librettos, when properly made, can achieve such modernization to the great advantage of the works themselves. But the treatment must be more than mere translation. It must include a thorough perception of poetic, musical, and dramatic values.[26]

The feelings of Ronell, Baum and the Los Angeles critics notwithstanding, the opera in English movement in the United States did not flourish, though there were scattered successes. During the 1940 opera season, for instance, the Chicago Opera Company, predecessor of today's Lyric Opera, presented 22 operas, four of them in English.[27] Those presented in the native tongue were *Martha*, *Falstaff*, *Hansel and Gretel*, and *L'Heure Espagnole* (*The Spanish Hour*).[28] The Chicago Opera Company was particularly focused on opera in English, and after a re-organization around 1940, had set its goals as follows:

> Eliminate stuffiness and stiffness as much as possible. Give American singers, both the established ones and the talented newcomers, a break. Increase the number of opera presentations in English.

VICKI BAUM . . . born in Vienna . . . played the harp as a child prodigy . . . graduated from the famous Vienna Conservatory of Music . . . returned there at 18, as a professor . . . first story published at 14 . . . married Richard Lert, the conductor . . . editor of several leading German magazines . . . wrote a number of best-sellers . . . including the world-famous "Grand Hotel" . . . now living in Hollywood . . . writing novels and screen plays.

ANN RONELL . . . born in Omaha . . . studied music and dancing . . . graduated from Radcliffe . . . went to New York . . . soon achieved fame as one of America's foremost composers and lyricists . . . noted for her distinctive popular songs . . . writes both words and music . . . and motion picture scores . . . most recent, "Blockade" and "Algiers" lyrics . . . lives in Hollywood . . . now writing new Broadway operetta.

RICHARD LERT . . . born in Vienna . . . studied music under great masters . . . began as a violinist with Vienna Phi harmonic . . . leader of operas and concerts in Germany . . . conducted in most of the capitols of Europe . . . First Conductor of the Berlin State Opera . . . married to Vicki Baum . . . they have two sons . . . living in Hollywood . . . conducting the Los Angeles Oratorio Society and the Pasadena Civic Orchestra.

Top to bottom: Vicki Baum, Ronell, and Richard Lert, from the new American libretto of *Martha* first performed at the Hollywood Bowl, August 30, 1938.

Strive for a broader base of interest by appealing to persons in industry and business. Make opera entertaining, "not an ordeal."[29]

Fortunately, the Chicago company took a liking to Ronell and Baum's *Martha* and performed it several times over its 1940–1942 seasons. *Martha* enjoyed particular success during the early forties, being also performed by the Eastman School of Music in Rochester (New York), the Peabody Institute in Baltimore, the St. Louis Opera, the Albany (New York) Light Opera

Company, and several major music schools throughout the country. At the New York City Opera, the principal roles were sung by Helen Jepson and James Melton. In 1951, there were 155 performances of *Martha* by opera companies across America.[30]

A few years later, Ronell and Baum prepared a screenplay, *The Playgirl and the Peasant*, a modern story based on the comic scenarios of *Martha*. Ronell explained, "This story is devised to show how operas can be adapted to the screen for modern entertainment."[31] Despite their best efforts, it was never produced.

In 1940, Ronell attempted to organize a national repertory opera company to present "new American librettos"[32] in major cities including Los Angeles, San Francisco, St. Louis and the East. Edwin Lester, Jr., from the Los Angeles Light Civic Opera was involved and thought that classical impresario Sol Hurok would be interested in a tour that featured lighter opera fare such as *Martha* and *The Gypsy Baron*.[33] Most importantly, Ronell had the interest of patron of the arts Albert Bender as a primary backer.[34] Unfortunately, Bender died the next year, Hurok was busy with other commitments, and the repertory plans never materialized

Ronell's final word on her initial efforts with Baum was prompted by the G. Schirmer edition of *Martha* published in 1938. Years later, she said of the publication: "This was the first new publication of a classic opera which the publishers had brought out in 39 years, so we consider their $5,000 investment terrific encouragement for the cause of Opera Adapted for the American Stage."[35] She was to revisit *Martha* twenty years later.

Ronell was serious about opera in English and wanted to demythologize grand opera. Well-versed in both classical and popular music and theater, she could see that American audiences, with movies and the spread of Broadway productions across the country, had a myriad of choices for their entertainment, and she felt that opera had to keep pace. In 1941, to foster the development of opera in English, she applied for a Guggenheim Grant. With money from the Guggenheim Foundation, she intended to take a year off and translate the lyrics of three European operas into English as well as modernize the staging and libretti.

In her "Concise Statement of Project," to the John Simon Guggenheim Memorial Foundation committee, she explained, "Because of the language barrier and outmoded theatrical techniques of opera as presently performed, the fine, cultural, and entertainment values that exist in the opera field have only reached and been enjoyed by a select few in this country."[36] To add to these thoughts in her application, she cited a speech she had given in June of that year at the National Federation Music Clubs Biennial Convention: "The opera house cannot survive if opera is treated like a hothouse flower to be enjoyed only by a chosen few. It must stand on its own."[37] To the Guggenheim committee, she added rather optimistically: "Based on my own direct experience, I am convinced it is possible for every community in America to have its own opera season performed by its own singers."[38]

Ronell was not alone in promoting opera in English, but the forces for change seldom worked in unison. She had a kindred spirit in critic Robert Lawrence of the *New York Herald Tribune*. In the same year as her Guggenheim grant application, he wrote a lengthy opinion piece regarding opera in English. Though wary of amateur productions and companies, as well as poor translations, he felt strongly that opera in America should be in English, pointing to several good translations, including *Barber of Seville* and *Pelias and Melisande*. Among his comments were the following:

> Why give opera in English? Because it would make what we see and hear more plausible; because it would bring an active sense of participation to a wider public; and because it is the only way through which we can evolve new operatic standards and create forceful new works of art.
> At present the United States and England are the only two countries where leading opera houses employ an alien tongue. Every other land uses translations, and audiences love them.

> The history of opera in almost every land has represented a gradual turning away from for-
> eign influence, a hesitant but steady growth of self-reliance.[39]

Further into her application, Ronell analyzed two impediments to the success of presenting opera to wide audiences in America: language and theatrical technique. To Ronell,
language was the bigger of the two problems. Most operas were sung in foreign languages,
usually Italian, German, or French, obviously making their comprehension difficult to those
not fluent in a particular language. As she explained in the application, "By contrast, opera
in European countries has enjoyed wide popularity. In every case, performance is in the native
language and manner of the particular country. Why America has never shown a correspond-
ing national pride as well as box-office common sense is a riddle of operatic history."[40]

Though she acknowledged that there were numerous English translations that had been
written and even performed, she dismissed most of them as "literal translations by non-pro-
fessional writers whose archaic and hackneyed wordage had only served to make matters
worse."[41] She believed that while there were numerous, talented, English-speaking writers
who could do worthwhile translations, "there is no money offered for their work and very
little to be gained after the work is done...."[42]

The second major problem with performing opera in America was the theatrical techniques. Ronell felt that American audiences, becoming accustomed to more realistic plots and
integration of the book (libretto) and music, were put off by the stilted dialogues and plots
of European opera. She felt that translations had to be less literal and more adapted to audiences of the day. She wanted operas to be more "user-friendly." Again, to the committee: "It
is on the theater side where opera hungers for improvement. When translation to the letter
is forgotten and adaptation to the spirit takes its place, we shall, instead of trying to repro-
duce the theater of yesterday, develop an opera theater of our own."[43] She believed that the
European opera stage traditions not only made it difficult for the audience but also for the
singers, who had to "observe a traditional and outmoded method of acting which most audiences find ridiculous."[44]

After detailing her philosophy of "Opera in English," Ronell proposed to the Guggenheim committee the specifics of her grant and what work she would do under its aegis and
funding. During the year of her grant, she was to translate and restage three European operas:
Rossini's *Barber of Seville*, Auber's *Fra Diavolo*. and one opera by Mozart. She assured them
that there was interest in the American opera community in performing these works as translations, as she had discussed such projects with both performers and management of several
major opera companies.

In choosing three operas, Ronell was well aware that not just any opera could be transformed, explaining, "[S]ome classic operas flex toward and benefit from adaptation more
than others." Though not choosing to do a Puccini opera among her three, she referred to
his works as "delightful stuff and story."[45] Conversely, there were operas by others that were
"so unbelievable and attuned to only the philosophy of the past as to make them museum
pieces."[46] In this category, she singled out the works of Giuseppe Verdi and Richard Wagner.

Of the three operas she had proposed, she was most excited about translating the operas
of Wolfgang Amadeus Mozart, her favorite. The thought of doing his operas made her "take
wing," as she considered Mozart "the perfect classic show writer, a composer who understood perennial theater."[47] She seemed most interested in working on *The Marriage of Figaro*.

Looking beyond the specifics of her proposal, it is clear in her application that opera in
English was almost a crusade for Ann Ronell. She closed the "Ultimate Purpose" section of
her grant proposal with the following:

It is my hope and dream that once this new and large audience for opera has been built, the efforts of our own American composers and librettists will blossom forth under the stimulation of an audience to write for.

Furthermore, I consider American adaptation of opera a National Cause, as especially in these critical times is our own opera theater necessary for the full development of our own national culture.[48]

Ronell was a true believer in opera in English.

Under the "No Ronell Project Goes Smoothly" heading is the correspondence she had with professor and composer Walter Piston, whom she knew at Radcliffe. She had listed him as a reference for the Guggenheim proposal and had sent him specifics of the proposal. In a brief reply to her, he was critical, implying she was not up to the task and stating that "the project appears to be 100 percent Hollywood."[49]

Ronell's reply was lengthy, beginning with her being "surprised and disappointed in your attitude toward the opera project."[50] She stood her ground regarding her capabilities and experience in the field. She hoped he was not opposed to "improving the theatrical phase of opera," and accused him of going "hopelessly Boston and stuffed shirt."[51] The letter was angry and indignant. Fortunately, she otherwise received encouragement and positive feedback from musicians, former teachers, and opera people. Nevertheless, her grant proposal was rejected early in 1942 though she continued her promotion of opera in English.

While working on the Guggenheim grant application, Ronell was also in contact with Earle Lewis, a manager at the Metropolitan Opera Company, a fellow believer in opera in English. She proposed to him not only operas in English, but a production combining Rossini's *Barber of Seville* and Mozart's *The Marriage of Figaro*. This proposal appears to have been closely related to those operas she proposed re-working in the Guggenheim grant. She wanted to combine music and plot elements of both in one unified musical. After outlining a story line to Lewis, she explained, "Dialog, no recitative, and highlights of both comic operas will provide a sock comedy that will trip merrily along, never repeating itself as in the originals...."[52]

She was most enthusiastic in her proposal to him, realizing that it might not play at the Met, but rather in "Central City."[53] Finally, she even suggested some titles:

I'd name this two-in-one opera, let me see — what shall it be?
THE DOUBLE FIGARO FIGARO, BARBER AND BARBERED TWO FIGAROS FOR ONE BUCK FIGARO'S AMERICAN HOLIDAY FIGARO'S FESTIVAL AND FAMILY CIRCLE FIGARO IT OUT FOR YOURSELF[54]

The production was never done. Perhaps Lewis talked some sense into her after he enjoyed a good laugh.

While never doing *The Marriage of Figaro* or *Barber of Seville* under the aegis of the Guggenheim or the Metropolitan Opera, she did work on the latter opera almost twenty years later with the Bill and Cora Baird Puppeteers. They had planned to use the voices of members of the Metropolitan Opera with Robert Merrill as the barber. The one-hour script for television, which never made it to the small screen, called for the opera to be "sung" by who else — the puppets.[55]

8

The Gypsy Baron and Light Opera: 1939–1940

"A combination of Strauss and Ronell sure to bring down the house."

Ann Ronell believed in perseverance and "stick-to-it-tive-ness," and it was never displayed better than in the spring of 1939 when, not giving up her belief in opera in English, she began work on an English version of *Die Zigeunerbaron*. This was an operetta written by Johan Strauss, Jr., of the famous musical family, successful as a conductor and composer, who often toured with his own orchestra and earned the title of "The Waltz King." His most successful opera was *Die Fledermaus* (1874), followed 11 years later by *Der Zigeunerbaron* (*The Gypsy Baron*). Though filled with the usual twists of a comic operetta, *The Gypsy Baron* also dealt with more serious topics, including war and class distinction.[1]

Ronell and her co-author, George Marion, Jr., signed a contract with the Los Angeles Civic Light Opera Association and producer Edwin Lester to do a book and lyrics in English, to be called *The Gypsy Baron*. The agreement stipulated a fee of $5,000 to each of them.[2] Marion had started in Hollywood as a writer of titles for silent pictures, and as sound came to movies, he became a screenwriter for the studios, where he met Ronell. His book for *The Gypsy Baron* was his first stage work.

As an inducement to the writers, the L.A. Civic Light Opera agreed that John Charles Thomas would star in the presentation. Thomas was an American baritone who started out in musical comedy and Gilbert and Sullivan productions. He made his debut at Covent Garden in 1928 and at the Metropolitan Opera in 1934 as Valentine in Gounod's *Faust*. He was praised for the warmth and richness of his voice as well as his enunciation and diction in several languages. One critic put it, "When Thomas sings German one declares he is Teutonic; when he sings French, one believes he must be French." Thomas preferred the concert life over opera and did a great deal of work on the West Coast. His special appearances often drew crowds in excess of 100,000 (including 165,000 at Chicago's Grant Park in 1938). He was also well-known by radio audiences for frequent broadcasts on the *Bell Telephone Hour* and the *Westinghouse Hour*.[3]

When offered the chance to work with Thomas, Ronell gladly accepted. His popularity as a concert baritone and radio entertainer was important to the success of the operetta, and she was so willing to work with Thomas that she agreed to share royalties from publisher G. Schirmer, Inc., with him. At the time of her contract with the Civic Light Opera, Ronell had entered into an agreement with G. Schirmer to publish the songs from *The Gypsy Baron* for which she had written the English lyrics and arrangements. By contract, she transferred the copyright to Schirmer for seven songs: "Love Deals the Cards Tonight," "Love Can Be Dreamed," "The World Is Wide Open to Me," "Your Eyes Shine in My Own," "When Lovers Meet," "Flirtation Intermezzo," and "Open Road, Open Sky." In return, she was to receive royalties for choral arrangements, movie and foreign rights, sheet music, and records. It was these two last royalties she was to share with Thomas, his share being one-third of the total.[4]

The presentation at the L. A. Civic Light Opera opened in June 1939. It was the world premiere for this version of *The Gypsy Baron*, and Ronell was credited in the program for "Lyrics and Musical Adaptation."[5] The scheduled run of two weeks was a success, both critically and in audience numbers. Thomas was especially popular with the audiences and "received ... enthusiastic reviews not only for his singing, but for his cartwheels and whip snapping skills."[6] Ronell was singled out in several reviews for her adaptation,[7] as she had employed over thirty sources from the orchestral and operatic works of Johann Strauss, Jr. and had "cleverly constructed them into a single offering...."[8] She had retained approximately 40 percent of the original opera *Die Zigeunerbaron*, and had adapted lyrics and other pieces of Strauss' material to complete *The Gypsy Baron*.

She had worked hard, and she and producer Lester had butted heads often, as at times Ronell could be distracted over an issue, then shortly after, be adamant on another point. A family friend was to corroborate this over fifty years later, saying that Ann was "flighty," but then was quick to add, "[W]hen she wanted something, [she] had an iron fist in a velvet glove."[9] But in the end, she and Lester became friends and were to work on other projects for the Civic Light Opera. Lester's fondness for her was revealed in a cute telegram to her in mid–June of 1939 as she left on a trip:

> BON VOYAGE LITTLE MISS LYRICIST, COMPOSER AND ADAPTOR HOPE YOU HAVE A NICE TRIP BOTH BY TRAIN AND BOAT BUT ADVISE YOU NOT TO GET DIFFICULT WITH THE CAPTAIN THANKS FOR THE BEAUTIFUL HANDKERCHIEFS MUCH TOO NICE FOR USE IN COLD BUT VERY PRETTY TO SHOW AND CLAIM THAT R ENDED UP LOVING ME AFTER ALL[10]

In a letter of early 1942 to Ronell, Edwin Lester summed up their mutual professional success: "So much for Johann Strauss. It is still the apple of my eye musically, and I still think that *Gypsy Baron*, fixed up to correct the mistakes we made the first time (which were very few, all things being considered), would get big business in New York where they still haven't had operetta done as we do it in the L.A. Civic."[11]

By 1942, John Charles Thomas had made his recordings of several of the songs that Ronell had translated and arranged for *The Gypsy Baron*. Of these recordings, "Love Can Be Dreamed" and "Open Road, Open Sky" were released on the Victor Symphony label[12] and had sold well, but not all of the songs he recorded were released. While she had little influence in the classical recording community, Thomas certainly did, and in a letter in spring of 1942 she encouraged him to approach Victor to release the remaining songs:

> If there is any chance of your speaking to Victor about releasing any of the others you recorded, please do so while you can. There is a shortage on recording materials now and there won't be as many records put on the market as before.[13]

Ronell's mention of a shortage of recording materials was a reference to the strike by the musicians union regarding recorded music. The leader of the American Federation of Musicians, James Petrillo, believed strongly that the time had come for musicians to be paid for their recording work at a rate commensurate with their live performance work. He felt that as more music was recorded, less was performed live, ultimately lessening the incomes of musicians. Petrillo said: "Nowhere else in this mechanical age does the workman create the machine which destroys him, but that's what happens to the musician when he plays for a recording."[14]

A work action of some sort had been on the horizon for months, and Ronell could see that soon there would be a dearth of recorded materials and thought she might be able to take advantage of it. Indeed, in August of 1942, the American Federation of Musicians imposed a ban on all recordings by their members. Studio recordings greatly diminished, though studio executives tried to circumvent the ban by using backup vocals instead of instruments, as singers were usually not AFM members. Despite Ronell and Thomas's best efforts, no further *Gypsy Baron* songs were released.

Always looking for new projects, Ronell, the "animated little bundle of nervous energy,"[15] took an interest in the National Music Camp of Interlochen, Michigan. She and its founder-president Dr. Joseph Maddy immediately liked each other when she visited there in 1939. She did some teaching and spent time with the students outside of the classroom. *Fiddles and Fun*, a Ronell original story based on the summer music camp, focused on a romance between two of the students as they competed for first chair in the violin section of the camp orchestra.

This story became the basis for a Paramount Pictures production, *There's Magic in Music*, starring Susanna Foster and Allan Jones. Of course, Hollywood took the story and twisted it. Foster's role became that of a young singer, out of reform school, trying to find her place at a summer music camp. She overcomes the suspicions of the faculty and students, heading the grand festival at the end of the film.[16] Ronell worked on other aspects of the movie including adapting several classical pieces into the scenes and writing words and music to a few songs. Despite Foster, a pretty young soprano who sang Ronell's "Fireflies on Parade," the movie did little at the box office. Ronell maintained a relationship with Maddy and the National Music Camp for years, providing scholarships for various students and later serving on the national advisory board.

Also about this time, Ronell had been working with Oscar Straus on a version of his operetta masterwork, *The Chocolate Soldier*. It is unclear how Straus and Ronell knew each other, but their correspondence for the operetta began in spring of 1941 with a kind note from Straus:

> It was very sweet of you to mention me to the Civic Light Opera people in Los Angeles. They wrote me a charming letter and I accepted to come there and to conduct the Festival of *The Chocolate Soldier*! I also promised them some new numbers and I would be very, very glad if you would write some of your delightful lyrics to my new tunes. I will send you a few manuscripts in the next days.[17]

The Chocolate Soldier was first presented in English in New York in 1909; this new version was produced by Edwin Lester for the 1941 summer festival of the Los Angeles and San Francisco Light Opera companies and starred Ronell's favorite baritone, John Charles Thomas.

Oscar Straus was Viennese and had worked in theatre and classical music, coming to New York late in his career. He was known for his operettas, his best works being *Ein Walzertraum* (*The Waltz Dream*) and *Der tapfere Soldat* (*The Chocolate Soldier*), both produced in Vienna in 1907 and 1908.[18] *The Chocolate Soldier* was a musical adaptation of George Bernard Shaw's *Arms and the Man*. Despite the immense success of the operetta, Shaw "loathed" it and "ruled all his work off musical limits."[19] Though he did not like Straus's operetta and did not like anyone fiddling with his words and stories, what equally bothered Shaw were financial considerations, explained by Lerner and Loewe biographer Gene Lees: "[Shaw] did not realize that because they wrote the dialogue for the operetta, the adapters of his play would by German law receive *all* the royalties. This seems to have had some bearing on his opposition to any further musical adaptations of his work."[20]

Because of the problems with *The Chocolate Soldier* and Shaw's ban on the use of his material, musical adaptations of his plays was delayed until after his death. For this reason, though a musical based on *Pygmalion* had been discussed in theatre circles for years, most seriously by Richard Rodgers and Oscar Hammerstein II, it did not come to fruition until *My Fair Lady* was written by Alan Jay Lerner and Frederick Loewe in 1956, six years after Shaw's death.

Straus's *The Waltz Dream*, along with Franz Lehar's *The Merry* Widow, ushered in an extended period of Viennese operetta on the New York stage, "initiating a rage for anything Viennese and sweeping away forever the dominance of the London musical."[21] The predominance of "American" musicals was still a decade or more in the future. But with the onset of World War I, the young artists of Europe were pulled into the war, and their talents and sources of funding were less available for the arts. As the war progressed, "German and Viennese importations were greeted with growing hostility.... The European war, as much as any other circumstance, gave America its opportunity. America grabbed it, and held on to it tenaciously and rewardingly for the next half-century."[22] But before an American musical developed, Oscar Straus had great success with his operettas, and fortunately for him and Ronell, there was still interest in them as World War II expanded in Europe.

This production of *The Chocolate Soldier* was more than a revival, as Straus had composed four new songs for which Ronell had written lyrics: "Love Comes Easy to Me," "Where Do We Go from Here," "Soldier Ballet," and "To Be in Love Is to Be." Also from Straus's themes, Ronell composed a song in a more modern vein, "April Nostalgia," used by a few classical singers in their solo acts, including multi-talented soprano Grace Moore, who Straus claimed was "crazy" about "April Nostalgia."[23] Not only did Straus compose new melodies for this new production at the Civic Opera, he also agreed to be guest conductor for its run. As producer Lester proudly stated of Straus in his "Foreword" in the program, "Ranked among the five great operetta composers of all time, the privilege of having him with us as an active participant becomes all the more notable when we realize that his achievements in this field have been world-acclaimed for over 40 years."[24]

The Chocolate Soldier was received well by critics, referred to by one as a "Grade A revival,"[25] and Irra Petina and John Charles Thomas were singled out for their singing. Ronell's lyrics were mentioned only in passing, although one studio executive assured Ronell: "I already heard about your song 'Love Comes Easy to Me,' which I understand is the 'HIT' number of the show."[26] Thomas recorded several of the *Chocolate Soldier* songs in 1941–42, but apparently none of the songs with Ronell lyrics.[27] The operetta was made into a Metro-Goldwyn-Mayer production later in 1941, starring Rise Stevens and Nelson Eddy, but it had only mild success at the box office. Straus himself continued with work in cinema with his most successful score being for *La ronde* in 1950.

In May of 1943, two years after *The Chocolate Soldier* and the initial presentation of Ronell's version of *The Gypsy Baron*, the second production of *The Gypsy Baron* was mounted on the West Coast, again by the L.A. Civic Light Opera and Edwin Lester. However, a rewrite of the book was stipulated by Lester. For this, Ronell worked with Edwin Justus Mayer. On the program, *The Gypsy Baron* was referred to as the "Ronell-Mayer-Marion" version.[28] The leads were Irra Petina and John Tyers. Tyers had done radio and occasional work at Metro-Goldwyn-Mayer, and Petina had sung secondary roles at the Metropolitan Opera and was the soprano Ronell had wanted.

Besides the original seven songs, Ronell added another solo for Petina, "Gypsy Temperament," which Ronell described as "a combination of Strauss and Ronell sure to bring down the house."[29] It was a song designed to feature Petina in the first act. She liked the song and began working on it back in New York, prior to San Francisco rehearsals. In a letter to Ronell in mid–April, Petina's agent, Dolores Hayward, explained, "Irra is keen about her 'Gypsy Temp'rament' although she had a fit about the key. Wired Edwin and he suggests changing it to C minor. She will fix it up. It is one thing to sing a song one night or even several, but not for a long-run, if the thing is too high. Anyway, she's happy about everything, particularly about getting that first act."[30]

Edwin Lester was again involved in the production, and as with most productions, there were numerous problems. Lester Cowan was involved, probably as an advisor, but also because plans continued for a New York production, possibly even Broadway, in which Cowan was a central participant. In his role, he appears to have had much to say and seems to have done some of his wife's "dirty work." In a telegram to Edwin Lester, Cowan detailed problems with the operetta's progress:

> Counting on you to do something about amateurish quality of the ensembles, especially second act opening flirtation number and third act beginning with Petina entrance. Practically all ensemble entrances and exits are slow and shabby.... At least ten minutes can be cut by injecting some discipline into cast. Petina must be told not to use whip during Arsena-Rudi scene other than as provided in the script.[31]

Despite such problems, *The Gypsy Baron* opened in San Francisco on May 10, 1943, for a two-week run, and then moved to Los Angeles for two weeks. On opening night in Los Angeles, Ronell received a warm telegram from her family:

FAMILY ROOTERS WISH TO
RECALL THEY KNEW YOU WHEN.
LOVE MOM SOL HERM AND LEEDUNK[32]

Again, the music and adaptation earned raves, but the book, having been redone by Mayer, was given mixed reviews. The operetta newcomer, John Tyers, was singled out as "young, handsome and romantic, with a first rate voice...."[33]

There was serious effort put towards a New York production for Broadway. Though the Great White Way had evolved and the Rodgers and Hammerstein era would soon take its hold, Ronell felt that an opera with an English libretto could attract an audience and sell. Her brother-in-law, Robert Cowan, himself a Hollywood executive, wished her well on the project: "It was good to learn of the reopening of *The Gypsy Baron*. I am also thrilled to learn of its renewed success. When you take it to New York it will reach its most deserving praise. You have put a lot of work on it and any great success can be blamed directly on you."[34]

Jack Kappa, an executive at Decca Records, was equally encouraging and felt he had a sense of audience tastes: "I am sure *The Gypsy Baron* will be a success, as the public is in a nostalgic mood and responds beautifully to all the melodies which they are familiar with; witness the enormous success of *Rosalinda* in New York."[35]

Lawrence Langner and his staff at The Theatre Guild were interested but wished to select the director and closely supervise the production.[36] In talks with Lester Cowan, a tentative plan for a production was made with Rouben Mamoulian to direct. Since John Charles Thomas was not available due to radio commitments, several names were batted about as the baritone lead: Frank Forrest, Jan Kiepura, John Raitt, and John Brownlee. For the female lead sopranos Irra Petina and Jarmilia Novotna were considered.[37] No doubt there were several impediments to moving *The Gypsy Baron* to New York including financing, the libretto, expenses of mounting a period piece, changing audience tastes, the war — and they all served to prohibit a Broadway version of the Johann Strauss, Jr., masterpiece.

Ronell's version of *The Gypsy Baron* evolved into an operetta, *Open Road*. Its production was to be done by the St. Louis Municipal Opera under the direction of John Kennedy.[38] The book was again reworked, this time by Milton Lazarus, building on the previous ones by George Marion, Jr., and Edwin Justus Mayer.[39] The words and music were changed to emphasize different songs. The stars were Dorothy Sarnoff and John Tyers, the latter a private in the military service at the time. They did splendid jobs, and some humor had been added to the story and songs with a group called the Why Bother quartet.

New orchestrations were done by several people, including Harold Zweifel, Darrell Calker, Sidney Fine, and Edith Gordon.[40] Her work was apparently lacking in thoroughness. In a chatty letter to Cowan, Ronell complained of her orchestrations: "I still find mistakes in places with the score she sent and am still placating the conductor over all the trouble he had on his first show of his first season."[41]

Regarding these orchestrations, there was disagreement over payments due from Ronell for them. She and Cowan butted heads over the issue with the executives of the St. Louis Opera Company (Muny). Ronell felt that her efforts and experience in the field had been responsible for a successful show and that the cost of the orchestrations should have been borne by the Muny.[42] She was disabused of that notion by the manager of the company, Paul Beisman, who informed her, "I like you and do not wish to hurt your feelings, but the full week of the *Open Road* was the only losing week this season, and its receipts were $5,000 less than the next lowest week."[43] When pressure from Cowan continued, the Muny head Laurence Schwab spelled it out to Cowan in no uncertain terms:

> I did think that *Open Road*, groomed carefully by Milton [Lazarus] and me, and worked on assiduously by Ann, would become a beautiful show for St. Louis. Otherwise I would never have suggested it. Milton delivered his book too late for any work by me and John Kennedy; Ann fluttered through her assignment. Result, an old-fashioned operetta held up by Herr Strauss' ¾ genius, that struggled through eleven nights. It did not hurt the Muny. It was satisfactory, I hope. But it certainly did not receive the professional treatment from California that the Muny had a right to expect.[44]

Running in the St. Louis 1944 summer season, *Open Road* was considered a marginal success.

Later that year, discussion was made of a movie version of *The Gypsy Baron* as well as a production to be done by Sol Hurok, the Russian-born impresario.[45] Hurok was responsible for a great deal of classical music being brought to this country, particularly that involving Russian artists and ballet companies. For the movie, mezzo-soprano Rise Stevens had signed a contract with Lester Cowan in November of 1943 to star in a "photoplay," presumably of *The Gypsy Baron*. But one year later, little had been done, and Stevens had to force the issue. Pending compensation, she agreed to be available through January of 1945 for a movie. While the agreement, signed by her and Lester Cowan, mentioned various sources as possibilities for the movie, she also agreed that *The Gypsy Baron* was acceptable to her.[46] There was also interest early on from Nelson Eddy to play the lead. However, no movie was made, nor was there ever a Sol Hurok production.

In April of 1950, Ronell contracted with G. Schirmer to create yet another *Gypsy Baron*. The main purpose was for it to become part of the Schirmer catalogue for use by whatever company might be interested in doing the operetta. She was to provide a complete libretto, score and lyrics. It was to be done within one year, and she was given a $1,000 advance against future royalties.[47]

The three previous versions, with Ronell doing the musical adaptation and lyrics, had been done with the following personnel:

Year	Book	Company	Stars
1939	George Marion, Jr.	Los Angeles Light Civic Opera	John Charles Thomas
1943	Edwin Justus Mayer	Los Angeles Light Civic Opera and San Francisco Light Opera	Irra Petina, John Tyers
1944	Milton Lazarus	Saint Louis Municipal Opera	Dorothy Sarnoff, John Tyers

From the onset, this "new" *Gypsy Baron* had problems. Ronell enlisted George Marion, Jr., again, but Edwin Justus Mayer was no longer available. Beyond this, it took several months and letters to negotiate a contract which provided royalties for the past efforts of Marion and Mayer, as well as the current writers.[48]

Of course, there were also contentions with G. Schirmer, Inc., regarding royalty percentages, television rights, and subsequent stage performances. Nonetheless, Ronell was glad to be involved with the whole project and said so to Gustave Schirmer in April of 1951: "It has been pleasurable to work with them during the periods of our active collaboration, and I am really enjoying my return engagement with Johann Strauss and George Marion more than anticipated. All thanks to you for making this possible."[49]

Ronell and Marion were anxious to complete their *Gypsy Baron* rewrite. She had planned work on a new movie or two, and he had agreed to adopt a new Oscar Straus operetta for Broadway. Beyond this, just as they were beginning, the Metropolitan Opera announced plans to do some classic presentations in English, both classic and new. The *New York Times* front page of April 4, 1951, explained that the Opera's general manager, Rudolph Bing, wanted to develop these works in English for the growing medium of television. Bing felt that it "had come to stay."[50] Equally important, these works in English were not to interfere with the regular repertory and "would enable the Met to seek out more new singers and to give increasing opportunities to the composers and librettists of our own time."[51] Quickly aware of this development at the Met, Ronell wrote to Hans Heinsheimer at Schirmer on the same day as the *Times* article, "Believing that the Met's plans for classics in English will welcome a horde of eager beavers on the same track, he [Marion] urges our *Gypsy Baron* to get in there first. A word to you may be sufficient for you know Mr. Bing personally."[52] What immediate response Heinsheimer gave Ronell is not clear, but initiation of work on *Gypsy Baron* for the Met was delayed several years.

Despite good intentions on their current *Gypsy Baron* work, Ronell and Marion had problems, mostly involving Marion's growing commitments elsewhere. It had been Ronell's plan to use the revised *Gypsy Baron* not only for G. Schirmer and amateur productions, but also to use it in its final version for a future Broadway production. As she told Marion in a letter, "...I have always felt that the right book for the professional market would be the only one which would reach the other fields. In fact I spoke about my attempts and hopes to land a Broadway or other professional prospect for production so that we could aim directly for it and publish the accepted-performed version."[53]

Marion had hoped to get the rewrite done quickly and, if necessary, to revise it for professional use. But Ronell told him:

> I have come to the opinion that it is foolhardy to force *Gypsy Baron* into a two-week job.... What little is accomplished at the end of our two weeks will only be in need of further work, and I cannot go further on revisions with you under such circumstances.
>
> After having gone through three different versions of *Gypsy Baron* and as many tryouts, I cannot afford lack of preparation on the fourth version; all the more so when this is to be final and is to be published."[54]

Matters continued to be delayed, and efforts for the revised *The Gypsy Baron* went well into 1952.

At about the time Ronell was doing the Schirmer "final" edition of *The Gypsy Baron*, movie studios began to show interest. In early 1952, she wrote letters to both Milton Pickman of RKO Pictures[55] and Olin Clark, a story editor at MGM Studios. To accommodate movie requirements, Ronell had taken the story and songs from the various *Gypsy Baron* productions and developed a movie musical entitled *The Fortune-Hunter*. Knowing the story and music as well as anyone, Ronell made cast suggestions to Clark at MGM:

> With an eye to cast, if considering this property for Mario Lanza, the numbers cued for "Rudi" can be re-adapted for tenor. The music as scored for baritone, however, would suit Howard Keel magnificently. Keel can also perform with the light touch demanded by the story. For the two star feminine leads, the vocal range is soprano: Kathryn Grayson for "Sari" and Jane Powell for "Amelia."[56]

In 1954, the optimistic Ronell was working on yet another derivative of *The Gypsy Baron*. Entitled *Music of the Night*, it was to be a stage work which would incorporate the previous versions. But this also fell short and by 1956, the *Gypsy Baron* property had been rewritten and re-titled *Josephine*.[57] It was designed for a periodic cultural show of the day, *NBC Spectacular*, which worked with an eighty-minute format. Ronell had written a three-page, three-act outline for *Josephine*. This version had thirteen songs, the bulk from her 1939 *The Gypsy Baron* score as done by John Charles Thomas.

For *Josephine*, Lester Cowan had an agreement with Walter Slezak for one of the leads.[58] He would be available at the end of his run in Harold Rome's *Fanny*, which had opened in 1954 and was still running at the time. Slezak had a good name on Broadway, having starred in Jerome Kern's *Music in the Air* in 1932 and Rodgers and Hart's *I Married an Angel* in 1938. "Ideal casting" for the television production, according to Lester Cowan, included Slezak, Gordon MacRae, Kathryn Grayson, and Shirley Jones.[59]

This same version, Cowan felt, was attractive as a movie as well, with the same cast. He wrote to Arthur L. Park of MCA Studios in April of 1956:

> I would be personally interested in producing the film in England with location in Austria.... Made abroad, with the above people, I think the picture would have an excellent chance of getting the entire $800,000 back on the Eastern Hemisphere, as I think Germany alone could earn $300,000 or $400,000.
> Slezak is going to Germany this summer to be starred in a picture about his father's life, and he is a very substantial draw in Germany.[60]

As the movie became more probable, Cowan was reluctant to have it done on television first, and that medium's production of *Josephine* was put on hold.

Ronell was anxious to do an opera on the big screen, feeling that it would have "tremendous appeal."[61] Her promotion of opera in English carried over to movies as well, as she felt strongly that the film operas must be sung in English, adding that the "mere thought of Hollywood actors singing in a foreign tongue is ridiculous."[62] As late as 1960 the project was still being discussed, still including Walter Slezak. Ronell's potential librettist at the time, Ira Wallach, had definite ideas about *The Gypsy Baron*. He told her in a letter of July 8, 1960, "I feel first of all that it must be re-written completely to make Slezak the motivating force in the show.... Slezak should arrange everything and be right about everything.... Perhaps in the future, if you have not yet settled *The Gypsy Baron*, we may work together."[63] Wallach was unavailable at the time to collaborate with Ronell, and again, nothing materialized. Despite all of Ronell's work on the *Gypsy Baron* story, the G. Schirmer edition, eventually published in 1959, had an English libretto by Maurice Valency.[64]

Ronell's last serious effort with opera in English involved the 1858 opera by Jacques Offenbach, probably his best, *Orphee aux enfers* (*Orpheus in the Underworld*).[65] It was a parody of the Orpheus myth, and Ronell felt its music and comedy well-suited to an American audience. In early 1955, she began to organize an English translation, which she hoped would be produced at New York City Opera. She had had initial discussions with City Opera's Julius Rudel, a conductor who was much interested in an English version.[66] Rudel, Viennese by birth, had been with the New York City Opera from 1943 as a conductor, his debut with them in *Der Zigeunerbaron*, though not the Ronell version. He later became City Opera's musical director from 1957 through 1979 and was known for his adventurous repertory, including some seasons devoted entirely to United States opera.[67]

At the time of Ronell's work on *Orpheus in the Underworld*, there were both French and German versions of the opera and some second-rate ones in English. Ronell wanted to entitle her translation *Orpheus* and had been in discussion with the music publishers, Boosey and Hawkes, Inc., internationally known for their publications of opera and musical theatre. However, because she was unable to get a commitment for performance of the opera, the publisher could not afford the expense of an entire libretto and orchestration.[68] Her discussions with Rudel and City Opera went no further.

9

Ship South and Nicolai Berezovsky: 1941–1942

"I just don't agree with you on the dramatic side of this opus.... I just can't stand that stuff."

Early 1941 found Ann Ronell working on the libretto for *Ship South*, a ballet-sing. This was her term for a piece devoted mostly to ballet with additional music and lyrics added for emphasis.[1] Several years before, she had worked with ballet dancer Patricia Bowman on a similar art form, which she referred to as a ballet-operetta, entitled *Magic of Spring*.[2] Ronell having been trained in classical ballet, dance was always of high interest if not a first love, and none other than George Gershwin had loved her Charleston. Moreover, in her early work days in New York, when presented job opportunities on Broadway shows she chose piano accompaniment and rehearsal over the chorus line. While piano and later composing fit her well and blossomed into a good career, there were times she seems to have doubted giving dance up.

While she did not do the *Ship South* choreography, Ronell did the outline for the story as well as additional music and lyrics supplementing the narrative. As she told one of her early interviewers, "[A] ballet, as you know, depends on color, movement and atmosphere. I worked toward this end and deliberately used symbols rather than characters, as was necessary in drawing a quick picture of the dramatic situation with the least exposition.... [T]his is my first attempt and this form, which I have called 'Ballet-Sing,' is to my knowledge quite original...."[3]

For the primary score of the piece, Ronell had enlisted Nicolai Berezovsky to compose, and they, in turn, were working with Leon Barzin of the National Orchestral Association in New York. Though she had submitted her original libretto and ideas to Barzin in March of 1941, work was stalled as she was hospitalized for a few weeks in the spring.[4] But by May, she was in steady correspondence with Berezovsky.

Born in St. Petersburg, Russia, in 1900, Berezovsky began studying violin at age eight, playing professionally in his teens. He came to the United States in 1920, studied composition and conducting, and was a violinist in the New York Philharmonic Orchestra from 1923 until 1929. His most popular compositions were a cantata, *Gilgamesh* (1947), and a children's opera, *Babar the Elephant* (1953), with a libretto by Dubose Heyward. At the time of his association with Ronell, Berezovsky was actively composing and working as an assistant conductor at CBS radio.[5] How he and Ronell became professionally linked is unclear, but their partnership appeared to be congenial, at least at the start.

Ship South, originally entitled *Pernambuco,* was set in South America and revolved around a visit there by United States citizens on a ship. Ronell's libretto focused on the meeting of the two cultures and hoped to capitalize on the then-current U.S. interest in things Pan-American.

Pan-Americanism was a political-diplomatic movement that had been growing over the previous decade, fostered by President Herbert Hoover. Up until the thirties, United States relationships with its southern neighbors had been strained, as the government frequently interfered in South American countries, often with force, to protect U.S. business interests. Hoover recognized the need for and encouraged better U.S.–South American relationships. In following his predecessor's philosophy, Franklin Roosevelt, soon after he was elected, instituted the Good Neighbor Policy, which stated that "no nation had a right to interfere in the affairs of another nation."[6] Roosevelt's policies greatly increased cooperation between the United States and South America in the years leading up to World War II.

To utilize these renewed good diplomatic feelings and to express this bicultural theme musically, Ronell had turned to Berezovsky. She was confident in her Russian partner and enthusiastic about his musical ideas, telling him in a letter of May 20, 1941, "Your idea of writing a march for Star Hope's entrance is swell. Directly cross current to the South American music announced beforehand, your march will introduce our characters with the distinctly northern flavor of vivacity, freshness, and familiarity that is the embodiment of the American spirit."[7]

Berezovsky's reputation had already been established as strongly Russian, and in a playful tone, Ronell discusses this and some of his other ideas for the ballet: "In regard to the dance of Estancero and the horses, I am amused and afraid to encourage your natural instinct to go Russian on me. I dare say the wildness of both countries are similar, but if you consciously set out to show there is no difference between South American gauchos and Russian Cossacks, the effect might be disastrous.... Knowing your flexibility of style (something I was not aware of before studying your records) I am sure that you can manage not bringing about comments from your fellow lodge members as to your being too '---' to write American music."[8]

At this point, the partners referred to the work in progress as an opera, and Berezovsky was immersed in it:

> Dear Anny,
>   Today I bought enough music paper to finish our opera. I shall start the orchestration immediately, and what an amount of work it is going to be! All my other works are put aside and please help me with your share — write the words (not all have to be lyrics) for the sequences which I pointed to you previously.[9]

Because of the war in Europe, funding for the arts was tentative, and the creative parties involved with this opera were well aware of this. However, as European tensions grew, relations between the United States and many South American countries flourished. Berezovsky and Ronell therefore felt that resources associated with Pan-American relations and business could be tapped. As Berezovsky put it in a June 18, 1941, letter to his collaborator, "Leon [Barzin] and I decided even if war breaks out we will go ahead and will utilize all the forces (Pan-American, Rockefeller [Foundation], United Fruit, etc.) to promote the work."[10]

While Berezovsky and Ronell were in agreement regarding this aspect of producing their ballet-sing, there were creative differences. Ronell had hoped to make *Ship South* a subtle work, relying on nuances of music and ballet to express emotions. This was particularly important in the scenes between the main couple of the story — the American woman, Star Hope, and Estancero, the South American. Ronell emphasized that their meeting and subsequent scenes need not be overstated:

I just don't agree with you on the dramatic side of this opus, and to me the effectiveness of Star Hope meeting Estancero in utter silence — with a moment of oomphy music to emphasize this meeting of glances and chemistry — well, such a scene is far more dramatic to me in such form than a scene you prefer with the usual breaking out into song by both parties concerned! I just can't stand that stuff.[11]

In music circles, Ronell was known to be true to elements of the music, story, etc., and this was a sticking point between her and Berezovsky. Ronell's friend and Boston journalist, Elinor Hughes, said of Ronell at the time that she "has an unusually agreeable and straightforward personality ... and an *artistic conscience* twice as big as herself."[12] Despite such differences, progress was being made, initial reactions were favorable, and Berezovsky was enthusiastic, as expressed in the following telegram to Ronell:

PLAYED FOR BARZIN OPENING AND END OUR OPERA HE IS THRILLED MISS YOU AM IN FIGHTING MOOD POOR RUSSIANS BUT THEY WILL SAVE THE WORLD LETTER FOLLOWS LOVE
  NICKY[13]

Work continued, with Ronell providing lyrics to Berezovsky's music. While she deferred to his musical strengths, her artistic integrity held fast on matters of the libretto. How Ronell was affecting her Russian collaborator is implied in a personal note from composer to librettist. A handwritten envelope is addressed: "Miss Ann Ronell, precious but sabotaging author." Berezovsky concluded the short note, dated July 28, 1941: "In reality this is a bribe, to seduce you, allure — but not to corrupt you — to write *us* more lyrics."[14]

And write she must have, for less than a week later, he telegrammed:

YOUR LYRICS ARE SUPERB FITS MUSIC AMAZINGLY HALF OUR OPERA FINISHED WILL COMPLETE BY SEPTEMBER FIRST GRATEFUL TO YOU LOVE
  NICKY[15]

But the earlier implied disagreements reached a crisis in early October as rehearsals and auditions approached. What is clear in numerous letters from Berezovsky to Ronell was that an intense romantic attachment had developed and flourished around the time of their collaboration on *Ship South*. The deterioration of their working relationship coincided with the collapse of their romance.

While dozens of Berezovsky's letters to Ronell pertaining to their affair are available, few of hers are. In a long letter of November 26, 1941, she writes to him of their waning relationship, somewhat bitter and definitely at a loss, using metaphors to the composer-violinist:

You will not destroy every beauty, despite how you wield the bow. The instrument will play to your melody as ever, but you have no more power to create harshness from me, no more art to evoke dark tones, shrill notes, unmusical vibration. That power must be lost to you — you must not hurt me more. In turn, I must not hurt you more.... If you cannot in all fairness to yourself play only that rich and wondrous sound we love and which no one else knows, then the instrument must be laid aside.[16]

From the numerous letters of Berezovsky, it is clear that they had considered divorcing their spouses and marrying.[17] For Ronell's part, however, Lester Cowan had refused to give her a divorce. Despite the discord, both Ronell and Berezovsky were committed to finishing *Ship South*.

Two different letters illustrate Ronell's frustration at Berezovsky's meddling, mostly with her libretto, as well as the dramatic focus of songs and their placement within scenes. Her letter of October 6, 1941, is addressed: "Dear Mr. Berezovsky (for you are certainly not Nicky)."[18] Though she opens with complaints regarding specific songs and scene changes, the thrust of the letter focuses on artistic control. Not only was Berezovsky interfering with her libretto, but he had an ally in Leon Barzin. As she explains to Berezovsky:

> The stage manager is the manager of the stage and not the author of the book.... I still would not relinquish my rights as author to him before my work is even rehearsed.
>
> Since my ideas no longer carry weight and you appear determined to ignore them along specific lines, I do not feel that this is a true collaborative spirit. I have asked that my revised libretto, in the order it was written, be that which you present for production. If you will not do this, I can only bow to your will, take my script, and go.[19]

What annoyed her most was Berezovsky's reliance on Barzin's opinion. She felt Barzin's artistic involvement in the work was premature and meddlesome, as he was making substantive contributions before the work was finished.

Leon Barzin, Belgian-born in 1900, played violin with the New York Philharmonic Orchestra at the same time Berezovsky was there. Most of Barzin's work, however, was as an educator and musical director of the National Orchestral Association (NOA), a semi-professional group for young musicians.[20] It was during his first tenure (1930–1959) as director of NOA that he worked with Ronell and Berezovsky in their efforts to bring *Ship South* to the stage. In a three-page letter later in October, Ronell devotes a half-page to Barzin:

> In regard to Mr. Barzin's position in this, I am of course happy that he likes the work, but am not so overwhelmed with his liking it that I forget that he is treating me rather shabbily. It is not hard to like this work....
>
> I am not ready to follow your lead, much as I should like to, in accepting his ideas as superior to mine. His record in the theater, to put it mildly, has been far from sensational. He has had his chance to try out his ideas in the theater and failed.... I found his arguments on theater dull and bourgeois ... and theatrically-minded most conventional.[21]

Ronell was also particularly angry over Berezovsky's treatment of the initial scene between the eventual lovers, Star Hope and El Estancero. She had been pleased with the dramatic device she had created for their meeting, and Berezovsky's changes to this scene completely missed the point:

> I am horrified you revert to 19th Century idealogy right before my eyes, and change my dramatic treatment of the meeting between Hope and El Estancero, which provided for the silence of chemistry, to the usual ad nauseam treatment.... My goodness, I thought you were a modernist, even if you weren't of the opinion my libretto was modern, but this is the limit. You have ruined the whole scene.... Nicky, I would sacrifice everything I had in this world for you, but not my artistic integrity.... For God's sake, get a good night's rest. If this great contribution of your dramatic sense goes thru, count me out.[22]

By some miracle, work was all but completed by early December, 1941, but when the Japanese attacked Pearl Harbor and the United States entered the war, financing became nearly impossible. (Many of Ronell's future projects were also to founder as they neared completion.) Foreseeing this, Ronell took her and Berezovsky's project beyond the National Orchestral Association. In February of 1942, she had discussions with George Balanchine,[23] Agnes de Mille,[24] and personnel from CBS Radio. Once Ronell made clear to Balanchine what was meant by a ballet-sing, his interest rose, though nothing came of it from him or the others.

Finally, in late February, 1942, Leon Barzin and the National Orchestral Association were forced to back out. With regret, he wrote to Ronell:

> From responses received to our request for financial assistance from interested parties, it was made clear that the existing emergency demanded their entire attention and that while the theme of the opera had a bearing on Pan-Americanism, the time was not propitious for such a production.

Since the National Orchestral Association is financially unable to undertake more than part of the great cost involved, and since it is impossible to raise the funds from interested parties, the entire matter must be shelved for the time being.[25]

Over the next 20 years, some attempts were made by Ronell and even Berezovsky to present the work professionally, but nothing materialized.[26] The score was reduced to a simple one for two pianos, and *Ship South* was presented by a few amateur groups.

10

Count Me In and Broadway: 1942–1943

"There is a musical score by a young lady named Ann Ronell, and that is promising."

One would think that a young woman with musical talent in New York in the thirties would have been immersed in Broadway by this point in her career. But Ann Ronell's interests were too diverse — Tin Pan Alley, opera, movies, ballet — and her experience in stage musicals had been confined mostly to piano accompaniment and voice coaching.

Her first work for Broadway was a 1938-39 Otto Preminger production, a "music-play," entitled *The King with the Umbrella*. The musical, for which Ronell supplied English lyrics, was written by European composer Ralph Benatzky; it was a hit in Europe. Benatzky, a Czechoslovakian, had worked in Germany and Eastern Europe as a conductor and composer for operettas and cabaret. His biggest successes had been in the late twenties and included *Casano*, *The Three Musketeers*, and *Im weissen Rossl* (*The White Horse Inn*).[1] He had composed several thousand songs and was said to have "catered admirably to the tastes of the time."

Ronell made her second trip to Europe in 1939 to work on *King with the Umbrella* with Benatzky, then living in the Swiss town of Thun. From there, she went to Paris to work with Oscar Straus on new songs in English for his *The Chocolate Soldier*. On that same trip, Ronell ventured to England, Holland, and Belgium, presenting concert materials to European performers for their concert and cabaret appearances.[2]

The American book for *The King with the Umbrella* was by Samuel Raphaelson, who had had successes with *Accent on Youth* and *Skylark*. *King* was to star Francis Lederer, and Preminger had started working with him and producer Ruth Selwyn in New York. Unfortunately, the story was a satire of the French government, and as World War II was breaking out and Germany invaded France, the comic premise was lost. Production ceased and was never completed.[3] But Ronell was never idle; during her work on *King with the Umbrella*, she had also been helping with music details on Lester Cowan's first movie as an independent producer, *Ladies in Retirement*, which opened in 1941. Though uncredited, she had worked closely with composer Ernst Toch on the myriad details involved with bringing a score to the screen.

Ronell got her second chance at Broadway from an unlikely group in a university setting. Walter Kerr, the future theatre critic for the *New York Herald Tribune*, and Leo Brady, a drama teacher at the Catholic University of America, had met while Kerr was earning his Master of Arts degree there. They had collaborated on biographical shows of George M.

Left to right: Cowan, Ronell, and promoter-producer Sol Hurok during a promotional tour for Cowan's production *Ladies in Retirement.*

Cohan and Joe Cook, a Broadway dancer-comedian-acrobat in the twenties and thirties, for the Theatre Department at Catholic University.

In 1942, this department, headed by the Rev. Gilbert V. Hartke, was attempting to collaborate with established Broadway and other theatre professionals. To this end, Kerr and Brady had a meeting with Ronell. They told her of the thriving theatre at Catholic University and, more importantly, of their need for someone to write the songs for a book musical, which was to be "directly connected with the war and morale efforts."[4] Ronell readily agreed to do the words and music and wrote most of them in the spring of 1942.

Six months earlier, patriotic, war-related musicals had started to emerge on Broadway. Opening in October of 1941, Cole Porter's *Let's Face It* focused on a patriotic theme. Three gigolos in the original script had been changed to three soldiers. The transfer in emphasis worked, as the show ran for 547 performances. Among other shows of 1941-1942 paying tribute to the war effort, in one way or another, included *Sons o' Fun, Of V We Sing,* and Harold Rome's *Let Freedom Sing.*[5]

Irving Berlin's *This Is the Army* opened July 4, 1942, packed the house for all of its 113 performances, and raised money for Army Emergency Relief. Berlin starred in the show which toured several American cities, Europe, and Asia.[6] His preview audiences were the stateside enlisted men and women who enjoyed his satire of the service. Though never cut out to be a foot soldier, Berlin had gone through basic training for World War I and was aware of what the troops went through. A new song, "This Is the Army," and "Oh, How I Hate to Get Up in the Morning," reprised from his World War I show *Yip! Yip! Yaphank*, were hits among the soldiers.[7] The latter song was especially relevant to the perennial Broadway night owl Berlin.

The "war effort" of Ronell, Kerr and Brady, *Count Me In*, was billed as a "Topical Musical Comedy." Kerr described it as a show "dealing with the wartime efforts of the 'average man' on the home front."[8] It opened at the University Theatre on the Catholic University campus on May 10, 1942, for a successful one-week run. Washington, D.C., reviewers were quite favorable, being caught up in the spirit and exuberance of the mostly amateur cast and show.[9] Ronell's music was described as "a vividly non-conformist score" without "a sour note in the whole production."[10]

Though a college musical, *Count Me In* attracted much professional attention. Reverend Gilbert V. Hartke, the show's original producer as the head of the C.U. Theatre Department, had numerous contacts in the theatre world. Ronell's prominence in the musical world was also a factor in garnering attention for the war-time musical. Her previous Broadway work and associations with the likes of George Gershwin and Vincent Youmans, as well as the influence of Lester Cowan, all helped to get the fledgling musical a look-see from producers who might not normally bother. She explained in a later article: "I first wrote the musical comedy last April in Washington, and it was performed there in May with success, so that we got five offers."[11]

Eventually, the Shubert Organization acquired the rights and brought the musical to Boston for tryouts at their theatre. At the New York opening, production credits were not confined to the Shuberts, but rather included "The Messrs. Shubert and Olsen & Johnson in Association with Krakeur and Schmidlapp," among these being the vaudeville team of Ole Olsen and Chic Johnson.[12]

The original cast at Catholic University had been amateur, mostly students, and had included the co-writer of the book, Leo Brady. An exception was singer Anne Blair, who had been in the Broadway and road tour productions of *Pal Joey*.[13] With the play moving to Broadway, the plan was to replace the college amateurs with stage professionals. Also to be changed were the orchestrations. At Catholic University, two pianos had accompanied the cast, but on Broadway, there would be a full pit orchestra.

In the transition to New York, there was a difference of opinion among the creators, as a few wanted to keep the collegiate freshness of the book and songs, while others wanted to make the show more topical and add Broadway sophistication. In the latter group was George Abbott, whom Lester Cowan had convinced to guide the musical to New York. Abbott was a director, producer, and librettist, best known for his work with Richard Rodgers and Lorenz Hart on several musicals including *Jumbo, On Your Toes*, and *Pal Joey*.[14] Abbott planned to start his rehearsals in July, two months after the Catholic University closing. He hoped for an opening in early September and did not wish to do any out-of-town tryouts. He had also hoped to engage composer-arrangers Hugh Martin and Ralph Blane, for whom he had just produced *Best Foot Forward*, to do the vocal arrangements for Ronell's songs.[15]

Abbott and Ronell clashed on the book and score from the beginning as he did not like many of her "corny rhymes and popular song type of writing."[16] In the same letter to Cowan, she lamented the problems with the transition:

> Everyone will have a different idea on re-writing this opus, and the original will languish in hallowed memory. Of course, Abbott is a great guy for young ideas and I suppose he'll come around to a lot of our first inspirations after we get into battle; but as it looks now, he is heavy on the topical stuff, and doesn't realize our values in the slant we've taken.[17]

Moss Hart was an ally to Ronell in all this as he had taken a look at the show at her request and made several suggestions, a development she referred to as a "victory."[18] Though not hired as a "show doctor" for *Count Me In*, his suggestions were along those lines. More importantly, they agreed on the overall philosophy of bringing the show to New York, as Ronell wrote Cowan, "Moss Hart was very admonitory about not changing the unsophistication or collegiate aspect of the writing. Gosh, how I wish he were in charge. He is the only person I have met yet without 'Big ideas' on the subject."[19]

There was also a difference of opinion between Ronell and the two original collegiate writers, Kerr and Brady. Abbott had requested that George Marion, Jr., do the rewrite, but they were opposed to it, and considered him "an inferior writer."[20] Along with this, they were holding out for a larger royalty and, in Ronell's view, had done little to help out with the transition. As she told Cowan: "They have been sheltered from all elements of turmoil in this whole enterprise, but still they demand their swelled heads get fit with the largest cap out of stock."[21] Who really did the final revisions is unclear, but Marion was never hired.

On top of this, Abbott could never reconcile himself to her score. As a courtesy, Abbott tried to blame his decision to turn down the show on contractual disagreements, but he, Ronell, and Cowan knew the true reason: Abbott just didn't think her songs were good enough to hold up on Broadway. As he stated clearly to Cowan:

> My real reason ... is that I suddenly became faced with the fact that the score was not only imma-
> ture, but that Miss Ronell did not seem able to improve it, that she had made no changes since I
> talked to her several weeks ago. I just don't think that it is smart enough and up-to-date and musi-
> cal enough to fit the kind of production I wanted to make, and so it was better for me to back out.[22]

Ultimately, Robert Ross directed the show in both Boston and New York. At the time, he had had little experience as a director. His later work as a director included a Broadway run of *Porgy and Bess* in 1943 and a Vinton Freedley production, *Memphis Bound*, in 1945.[23] The songs were staged by Robert Alton.

For the Broadway cast, Reverend Hartke recommended Mary Healy for the role of Sherry. He had performed the wedding ceremony of Ms. Healy and Peter Lind Hayes a few years before, remembered the pretty bride and thought her perfect for the ingénue role. Joining Healy in the Boston tryouts were Broadway veterans Charles Butterworth, Luella Gear, and Hal LeRoy. Newcomers included June Preisser and Melissa Mason. Dancer Gower Champion was billed with his partner as Gower and Jeanne,[24] and none of the programs or reviews gave Jeanne a last name. Her full name was Jeanne Tyler, and she had been dancing with Champion since 1931.[25]

Gower Champion began his Broadway career as a dancer in *The Streets of Paris* (1939) and had his first supporting role earlier in 1942 in Vernon Duke's short-lived *The Lady Comes Across*. Years later, he became a choreographer, but continued to dance, usually with his wife Marge. His real success did not come until the sixties, when he did several shows as both choreographer and director. His winning streak included *Bye Bye Birdie* (1960), *Carnival!* (1961), *Hello Dolly!* (1964), and *I Do! I Do!* (1966).[26]

Charles Butterworth had not starred on Broadway for years, but his successes there included Jerome Kern's *Sweet Adeline* (1929) with Helen Morgan and *Flying Colors* (1932) by Arthur Schwartz and Howard Dietz.[27] Brooks Atkinson, *New York Times* critic, called him "the limp and docile master of understatement ... an amiable comedian who is vastly amusing."[28]

Luella Gear was also a seasoned performer with starring credits including *Streets of Paris, Life Begins at 8:40, Gay Divorce,* and Jerome Kern's *Love o' Mike.*[29] Hal LeRoy, a tap dancer from his early teens, had been featured in numerous Broadway shows, among them Vernon Duke's *Thumb's Up* in 1934.[30]

Count Me In opened in Boston on September 10, 1942. Its protagonist, B.O. (Papa) Brandywine (Charles Butterworth), is a shy entrepreneur attempting to find something to do for the war effort. His wife (Luella Gear) and children (Mary Healy, Gower Champion, and Hal LeRoy) are involved, and much of the show's humor arises from Brandywine's trying their various endeavors. He fails until he takes over a complicated map project designed to confuse the Japanese.

After its Boston opening at the Shubert Theatre, next-day reviews in the *Boston Herald* and the *Boston Traveler* commended the songs, dancing and direction. Both reviews singled out the songs "On Leave for Love," "Woman of the Year," and "Ticketyboo."[31] The last title originated from an English word which had become popular in Australia and had caught Ronell's ear, fitting well into the musical's war theme. Washington, D.C., writer Bernie Harrison described the song's creation: "'Ticketyboo' is a word that won't make any sense unless you're up on your British idioms. Ann happened to pick up a New York newspaper and read an account of Churchill's flight to England, and the correspondent described the journey as 'ticketyboo' or perfect."[32] "Ticketyboo" was Ronell's most patriotic song in a most patriotic musical.[33]

"On Leave for Love" was a comedic plea for women to be aware of what they meant to their boyfriends or even more casual acquaintances.[34] It paralleled other songs of the day, most notably "You Can't Say No to a Soldier" by Mack Gordon and Harry Warren,[35] and "I'm

Finale of *Count Me In* at the Shubert Theatre in Boston, September 1942. ***Left to right:*** two unidentified cast members, Gower Champion, Jeanne Tyler, unidentified man, June Preisser, Charles Butterworth, Luella Gear, Hal LeRoy, Mary Healy, Whit Bissell, Melissa Mason, Jack Lambert (performance photograph by Richard Tucker; Billy Rose Theatre Division, the New York Public Library for the Performing Arts, the Astor, Lenox and Tilden Foundations).

Doing It for Defense" by Johnny Mercer and Harold Arlen. The latter was sung by Betty Hutton while riding in a Jeep in the 1942 movie *Star Spangled Rhythm.*[36] The chorus included "sentiments" that expressed a wish to repay a soldier's service by "Doing It for Defense."[37]

Count Me In was not a critical success in Boston, but that could not be blamed on Ronell's songs. What was criticized in Boston and even more in New York was Kerr and Brady's book. Helen Eager of the *Boston Traveler* summed up the problem: "[The book] didn't jell last evening. It only slowed down the show until the next musical number."[38] Walter Kerr wrote in the aforementioned *Theatre Arts* article:

> Toughest of the problems facing us, both in music and book, was the sustaining of a comic line, which in terms of the topical inevitably runs to satire, without giving offense or exposing any branch of the effort to foolish criticism. The line between patriotism and genuinely pungent humor is sometimes difficult to draw, and the task of keeping the situations current when the headlines were changing daily was not simple.[39]

But the failure of the book did not overshadow Ronell's song accomplishments. Elinor Hughes of the *Boston Herald* not only praised the "tuneful" and "stirring" songs, but she made a more important mention of the up-and-coming songwriter: "Ann Ronell, though a composer of great industry and varied talents, is apparently the first woman to have done the music and lyrics for a New York musical."[40] To that time, the participation of women in Broadway songs had been limited almost solely to lyrics. Listed here with their composer-collaborators and their most significant musical shows are most of the prominent women in Broadway up to the time of *Count Me In*, all lyricists with the exception of the last one[41]:

Anne Caldwell	Jerome Kern	*The Night Boat* (1920)
		Good Morning Dearie (1921)
		The Stepping Stones (1923)
Dorothy Donnelly	Sigmund Romberg	*The Student Prince* (1924)
Dorothy Fields	Jimmy McHugh	*Blackbirds of 1928* (1928)
		Hello, Daddy! (1928)
	Arthur Schwartz	*Stars in Your Eyes* (1939)
Rida Johnson Young	Rudolph Friml	*Sometime* (1918)
	Victor Herbert	*Naughty Marietta* (1910)
		The Dream Girl (1924)
Kay Swift (composer)	Paul James (lyricist)	*Fine and Dandy* (1930)

As a composer, Kay Swift (with husband-lyricist Paul James) had interpolated songs into *The Little Show* (1929) and *Nine-Fifteen Revue* (1930) and had had great success with their *Fine and Dandy* which included "Can't We Be Friends?" and the title song.[42] No woman had done words and music for an entire show. Also to be noted in the above list is Anne Caldwell, who not only wrote lyrics but usually did the book for her shows.

Sixteen song titles had been included in the original show at Catholic University, but Ronell's final version of the show, both in Boston and then New York, included ten songs which were presented as follows[43]:

"COUNT ME IN"

ACT I
Papa's Tribulation

1. All-Out Bugle Call
"All-Out Bugle Call" . . . . The Rhythmaires and Chorus

2. Life with the Brandywines
"The Way My Ancestors Went" . . . . Papa (Charles Butterworth)

3. On Duty with Alvin

"Someone in the Know" . . . . Alvin (Hal LeRoy), Tommy (June Preisser)

4. On Duty with Mama

"On Leave for Love" . . . . Mama (Luella Gear)

5. On Duty with Sherry

"You've Got It All" . . . . Sherry (Mary Healy), Dr. Heart (Milton Watson)

6. On Duty with Ted

"Why Do They Say They're the Fair Sex?" . . . . Richard (Don Richards)

7. Alvin's Post

8. Up the Block at Papa's

"We're Still on the Map" . . . . Mama, Ted (Gower Champion) and Cast

ACT II
Papa's Triumph

1. Papa's Warning

"Ticketyboo" . . . . Richard

2. Papa's Internment

"Who Is General Staff?" . . . . Mr. Moto (Joe E. Marks) and The Rhythmaires

3. Papa's Internment (continued)

4. Papa's Flight

"Why Do They Say They're the Fair Sex?" (reprise) . . . . Danced by Alvin

5. The Woman of the Year

"The Woman of the Year" . . . . Sherry and Chorus

6. Papa's Recapture

"You've Got It All" (reprise) . . . . Sherry and Dr. Heart

"On Leave for Love" (reprise) . . . . Priscilla (Melissa Mason)

7. Papa's Investigation

8. Papa's Return — Finale

Finale . . . . Entire Cast

After a ten-day run in Boston, *Count Me In* moved onto New York, where it had been booked into the Ethel Barrymore Theatre. For an original college production, albeit one with a professional songwriter, making it to Broadway was quite an accomplishment. Though Ronell's growing reputation and Reverend Hartke's theater connections were both helpful, the Shubert Organization was comprised of veteran producers, and they did not invest money solely on good names and contacts. With such an untried team, it is surprising that the production did merit a New York opening or even a Boston tryout. It may have been the desire for shows with a topical war theme or the influence of Cowan. Perhaps the veteran cast had sold the producers on the show or maybe Ronell's songs were that good. It was never clear, but to New York they went.

Count Me In opened on October 8, 1942, and was billed as "The All-American Musical Comedy." The theatre program for the show reflects the wartime atmosphere.[44] There is an advertisement featuring a serviceman receiving a letter and a carton of Camel cigarettes from home. The back page has an advertisement picturing Claudette Colbert handing out Chesterfield cigarettes as a member of the Volunteer Army Canteen Service. *Count Me In* was aimed at the same audience as Berlin's *This Is the Army*—servicemen and women and sympathetic theatergoers on the home front.

When *Count Me In* opened in New York, it was with the same cast principals as Boston.

Various contributors—cast and creators—were lauded for individual accomplishments, especially Irene Sharaff for costumes, Robert Alton for his staging of the musical and dance numbers, and Hal LeRoy and Gower and Jeanne for dancing. The singers reviewed most favorably were Mary Healy and June Preisser.[45]

But again, the book was highly criticized. Wolcott Gibbs in The *New Yorker* referred to it as "one of the silliest musical comedy books on record."[46] Atkinson was more specific: "*Count Me In* has one of the most busily useless books in years. It intends to report the frivolities of a nation at war and endeavors to find a chapter for every service. But the writing is hackneyed; the lines are flat. Never was there a book that kept pushing the show off the stage so aggressively as this one."[47]

Luella Gear and Charles Butterworth in a scene from the New York opening of *Count Me In* (October 1942). Papa Brandywine to Mama: "But Mama, I haven't had my supper yet, I'm hungry" (*New York Times* photograph; Billy Rose Theatre Division, the New York Public Library for the Performing Arts, the Astor, Lenox and Tilden Foundations).

Critics also agreed that what was probably an enjoyable and workable review in Washington, D.C., had been overworked and become too cumbersome in its transition to Broadway. Similarly criticized were "Extraneous variety acts [that] completely overwhelmed the plot."[48]

Ronell's music received mixed reviews. The consensus best ballad "You've Got It All" was sung by Mary Healy and Milton Watson. The song opens with a twenty-five-bar verse and then proceeds to an engaging chorus, featuring frequent quarter-note triplets.[49]

The comedy song singled out was "Who Is General Staff?" sung by an ensemble playing Japanese diplomats. "On Leave for Love," "Woman of the Year," and "Ticketyboo" also received frequent favorable mention among the reviews of the New York opening. Burns Mantle complimented these numbers, remarking: "There is a musical score by a young lady named Ann Ronell, and that is promising. It includes a variety of ensemble numbers of quality, a couple of good ballads...."[50]

By this time on Broadway, few women had been involved on the composing end, still a male domain. In that context, Ronell, in an interview years later, admitted what a tough project *Count Me In* had been: "It was a terrific experience writing a show at last, and I understand now why there have been so few women who ever got a hearing on Broadway."[51] Nonetheless, Ronell was proud of her "one-woman" Broadway show. As a journalist pointed out: "Miss Ronell feels that it is certainly something to be the first woman to write a major musical ... and she isn't too disappointed that she wasn't able to take all the hurdles in her path the first time out."[52]

John Beaufort of the *Christian Science Monitor* felt that Ronell had "done a job which rises above the routine."[53] Another reviewer explained that while the score "does contain some good numbers, it is none too original."[54] This sentiment was echoed by Brooks Atkinson, who also liked a few of the songs, but referred to Ronell's score as "mostly imitative work."[55]

On a positive note, the *New York Times* advertisement for *Count Me In* referred to it as "A dandy show" and "Sock entertainment." There was even a quotation from Cole Porter describing it as "The most singable score I have heard in years."[56] The ultimate critics, theatergoers, did not sustain interest, and *Count Me In* closed after sixty-one performances. Despite the cast and some of Ronell's songs, the weaknesses of the book were too overwhelming to sustain even a modest run. However, a USO (United States Organization) tour of the show was done. With Luella Gear starring, the show toured several weeks in the South Pacific.[57]

As shows move from tryout to Broadway, or (in the case of *Count Me In*) from college to professional, wholesale changes are often made. It is the rare show that needs little tinkering during its pre–Broadway run. Musical literature is rife with stories from tryout cities like Philadelphia, New Haven, and Boston of late night sessions after the performance when songs are added or removed, the book is given major revisions, new directors or choreographers are engaged, or (the ultimate cry for help) a show "doctor" takes over. Over the years, some of the more famous of these were George Kaufmann, Abe Burrows, and Bob Fosse.

When *Count Me In* moved from its campus origin, several professionals were brought in, including director, choreographer, and set and costume designers. As mentioned earlier, Ronell pared the number of songs from sixteen to ten, necessitating many script changes, and novelty acts were added, a holdover from the days of earlier Broadway. How much the book changed is uncertain, but overall, the show changed quite a bit. In 1943, Smith College had wanted to do a production of the show, and Ronell was in contact with one of the co-writers, Walter Kerr. His reply to her regarding usage of the script at Smith implies an unfavorable opinion of the show as it moved from Catholic University to Broadway: "Re the matter of Smith College doing *Count Me In,* I have just checked with Lee [Leo Brady] and we are both agreeable, so long as the script used is that of the original production. Under no circumstances would we permit the use of the Broadway version...."[58]

As it turned out, "Ticketyboo" was the only one of the show's songs to be recorded. The musical eccentric Spike Jones did it, but he "elected to the play the number straight instead of corning it up in his frenetic style."[59] No recording of it appears to be available now. That same song attracted the attention of the entertainment programmers in the War Department who liked both the spirit and content of the song; as a War Department representative wrote Ronell, "The song 'Ticketyboo' impresses us as a number that has every chance of becoming a popular hit. Further than that, it ties us in with the fact that we have allies with whom we are fighting and on whom we must depend to help us win the war."[60] Cabaret singer Hildegarde was fond of several of the songs and wanted to make an album of Ronell's songs featuring the *Count Me In* numbers. Hildegarde's manager, songwriter Anna Sosenko, wrote to Ronell of her client: "She is crazy about 'You've Got It All' and has been doing a lot of selling for it.... [E]very opportunity that Hildegarde gets, she puts a plug in for the score, and actually does the stuff on the piano for them."[61] But the problem was put succinctly by Sosenko: "I think your most unfortunate break was the recording situation because if some records had been done on your music, it would have intrigued the bands a little more and would have added a little more push for the music."[62]

At the time, there was a boycott by the recording industry of songs published under ASCAP auspices regarding sharing of profits from radio airplay of songs. From the action, Broadcast Music Incorporated (BMI) was created; it allowed composers to share in the radio profits. However, until things settled, only songs in the public domain were being played on the air, and there was no profit in recording songs. By the time the controversy ended, *Count Me In* had long closed, and there was no interest in recording the songs.

Other plans were discussed for use of the format and ideas from *Count Me In*. Circa 1950, Ronell attempted to sell the idea to television producers as a one-hour special. She had pared the show down to approximately fifty-five minutes, with much less dialogue and only seven songs.[63] As she saw the television version, the role of Papa Brandywine would be changed to a comedian unable to fit into the war effort. In that role, she felt several of the day's stars could be easily cast in that role, including Jackie Gleason, Milton Berle, Sid Caesar, Phil Silvers, or Buddy Hackett. Also of interest were Ronell's considerations for the "Boy" role: either Perry Como or Eddie Fisher.[64] Nothing came of the television project.

In 1951, with the Korean War ongoing, Ronell attempted to revive *Count Me In*, and she wrote Leo Brady, Walter Kerr, and Reverend Gerald Hartke.[65] This was soon after her success with an adaptation of Stephen Foster's music for a show entitled *Oh! Susanna*. It was written with Colin and Florence Ryerson and had been published by Tams-Witmark for regional theatres and amateur productions. Ronell's hope in her letters to her old collaborators was to rejuvenate the show for the regional and amateur companies and audiences, taking advantage of patriotic sentiments in the country during and after the Korean War.

She wrote Kerr a second time, adding to her intentions the possibility of a movie or television presentation.[66] She had also been in contact with Irving Kahn of Twentieth Century-Fox regarding a movie: "It is my hope that Walter Kerr and Leo Brady, authors of the book, will whip up a story which will make *Count Me In* saleable to films. With the war, the topical matter of the book is current again."[67]

No replies from Brady or Kerr at that time are available. From later letters of Ronell to Kerr, there had been disagreements and confusion regarding original contracts and even a matter of $740 which Kerr claimed was owed to Brady and him.[68] Ultimately, the two writers apparently did not share Ronell's enthusiasm and did not want to rework the book. With a dated story and no rights to redo it herself, she had to abandon the project and was left with hard feelings regarding the matter.

Ronell's litigious side surfaced in 1954, when a revue entitled *Count Me In* opened at the Hampton Playhouse in Westhampton, New York.[69] Although the show had nothing to do with the Broadway show, five days later, Ronell's brother and attorney, Sol Rosenblatt, sent a letter to the producers:

> Since *Count Me In* was a memorable musical comedy on Broadway ... I believe you should of your own accord not produce a new show now under the same title.
> I am sure you are not aware of your misrepresenting the property in advertising the performance of *Count Me In* at your theater this summer. The matter came to my attention when I received several calls asking me if our *Count Me In* was available for further non-professional production. Upon inquiry, I was informed that you are using our title, and am hopeful that you do not realize that this usage is misleading to the public.[70]

This disagreement occurred twelve years after the original production, and what became of it is unclear. In 1955, overtures from the Canadian Broadcasting Corporation to do a revival of the show fell short,[71] and nothing more came of *Count Me In*.

One dividend from her work on *Count Me In* was that Ronell found a niche in an unlikely musical genre for a woman — the military march. Her first march came from *Count Me In*. The score of *Count Me In* included "The Woman Behind the Man Behind the Gun." Because of its military topicality and march-like qualities, it enjoyed a short-lived popularity and was heard often on Armed Services Radio during the war.

Also in 1942, Ronell worked on film music for *Commandos Strike at Dawn* with veteran movie orchestrator and composer Louis Gruenberg. It was a Lester Cowan production for Columbia Pictures and derived from the World War II resistance movement in Norway, with

Paul Muni starring. In early correspondence with Ronell, Gruenberg, who had worked almost exclusively in Canada, was enthusiastic about his Hollywood project, telling Ronell: "I am looking forward with real pleasure to working with Lester upon so important a picture. I feel it ought to be a great success, and that wouldn't hurt any of us."[72]

The music score was done by Gruenberg and John Leipold, the latter uncredited. Though Ronell's work on the film was also uncredited, she was listed on the two songs from the movie that were published by Mills Music, Inc. She took a theme that Gruenberg and Leipold had used in their score and fashioned a light-hearted song, "Out to Pick the Berries." On the sheet music Ronell was listed as sole composer and lyricist.[73] It was not a bad song, but no recordings of it were made.

To a theme in march time from *Commandos Strike at Dawn*, Ronell added words. For the song, "The Commandos March," she was not only listed as lyricist on the sheet music but also received credit as co-composer.[74] The song was dedicated to "The Commandos of all the United Nations" and enjoyed mild success, quite apart from "Out to Pick the Berries."

Ronell's biggest success in the military march category developed from her involvement in the wartime film *The Story of G.I. Joe*. Produced by Lester Cowan for United Artists, it focused on the infantry in the trenches at the front as seen through the eyes of Ernie Pyle, the famous war correspondent. Pyle was "imbedded" with World War II troops a half a century before it became a media buzz word. Pyle's stories from the front and his ongoing efforts to communicate with the families of the ground troops made him a favorite among the soldiers.

Again, Ronell took a theme from the film's score, written by her with Canadian Louis Applebaum, and fashioned "The Ernie Pyle Infantry Match." It gained popularity quickly among the infantry and was considered the theme song of the United States Army ground troops. New York journalist and Ronell friend Alice Hughes explained the song and its purpose:

> But the infantry soldier, the doughboy, has never had a march he considered strictly his own. He has just foot slogged it to whatever the bandmaster thought up.
> Well, if the doughboy hasn't an "official" tune now, he has one as close to it as he'll probably get. Of course, he'll never learn to love to hike to *any* march![75]

"Infantry March" was "unofficially" accepted in ceremonies in Washington, D.C., and New York, at Carnegie Hall, by Chester Whiting, director of the United States Infantry Band, and was played frequently in concert by the band.

Ronell was lucky enough to hear it played in person at Carnegie Hall during the war. As Al Tamarin, publicist for United Artists, explained in a biographical article about her: "Miss Ronell says she was never as thrilled as when conductor of the band, Chester Whiting, handed her the baton, and she led the Army Ground Forces Band in rehearsal for the performance."[76]

11

"Linda" and *The Story of G.I. Joe*: 1944–1946

"I played all the music for Ernie Pyle last New Year's Eve,
and he made me play 'Linda' about twenty-five times."

With World War II coming to a close, Ronell again focused her efforts in Hollywood, where Lester Cowan was becoming more prominent, having had successes with *Ladies in Retirement* in 1941 and *Commandos Strike at Dawn* in 1942. His next film was to address problems in post-war Germany and focus on the millions of German youths raised under the Nazi regime. To create the movie, Cowan had enlisted members of the Hollywood Writers Mobilization (HWM), a 3,500-member group of movie industry talent, mostly writers, which had been organized shortly after Japan's bombing of Pearl Harbor and represented many of the writers' guilds and associations in Hollywood. During the war, this group was responsible for almost 200 documentary film scripts, 1,000 radio scripts, and 800 entertainment show scripts for bases home and abroad.[1] This wartime work was voluntary and without charge.

The film's title, *Tomorrow, the World!*, was a reference to a Nazi song sung in Germany during the war, expressing the feeling that the Nazis were in control of Germany and Europe but "tomorrow the world."[2] The featured player in the movie was just such a Nazi youth, Emil, played by Skippy Homeier. Kenneth Macgowan, a member of the Awards Committee for HWM, said of the film's protagonist: "He symbolizes the Germany and the Fascism of tomorrow, unless Fascism is smashed now within and without the German citadel. He makes us think about this problem of today and tomorrow."[3]

One of the stars, Fredric March, furthered this comment in the same program, prepared for the movie's premiere: "It scrutinized the problem of the twelve million children in post-war Germany, reducing it to such proportions that anybody may understand its complications, and at the same time, it emerges as a forceful and moving drama set in a typical American home."[4]

The picture also starred Betty Field, Agnes Moorehead, and Joan Carroll. The screenplay was written by Ring Lardner, Jr., and Leopold Atlas with a score by Louis Applebaum. Ronell was music director, but no songs emerged from the score for Ronell to lyricize, as the film's subject had no appeal for the Hit Parade. The movie derived good publicity as the winner of the First Annual HWM Award for Distinguished Motion Picture Achievement. Despite the HWM award and the probable appeal of such a topic, *Tomorrow, the World!* did poorly at the box office, most viewers feeling it was a bit contrived.

As for Ronell, another legal entanglement ensued over copyright renewal of the film's musical cues and possibly a song. From 1960 through 1965, twenty or more letters were written or received by Ronell's attorney, William Krasilovsky. The communications involved Sam Fox Publishing Company, Leeds Music Corporation, and Music Publishers Holding Corporation.[5] As usual, little came of it, including no publishable song.

In 1944, the same year as the release of *Tomorrow, the World!*, Lester Cowan began production on a film for United Artists Corporation based on the World War II writings of war correspondent Ernie Pyle. The screenwriter in the early stages of the film *The Story of G.I. Joe* was playwright Arthur Miller.[6] He collected material for the film and began to assemble a story line but was eventually replaced by the team of Leopold Atlas, Guy Endore, and Philip Stevenson. Their screenplay was taken mostly from Pyle's first collection of writings, *Here Is Your War*, published in 1943, his observations mostly of the African and Italian campaigns.

Ernie Pyle, born in Dana, Indiana, in 1900, originally wrote for a LaPlante, Indiana, newspaper, then advanced his career to the *Washington Daily News*.[7] As a correspondent with this newspaper, he filed his World War II stories, and because the *Daily News* was part of the Scripps-Howard newspaper syndicate, Pyle's dispatches were read in cities throughout the country. His view of soldiers and war was summarized by his statement: "I love the infantry because they are the underdogs. They are the mud-rain-frost-and-wind boys. They have no comforts, and they even learn to live without the necessities. And in the end they are the guys that war can't be won without."[8]

Ronell worked on the score of *The Story of G.I. Joe* with Louis Applebaum, a much-experienced Canadian, who had written over 250 film scores for the National Film Board of Canada. In addition to composition, he was active in arts education and administration, as well as workers' rights for professional musicians. He continued composing into his late sixties, including chamber and orchestral works and four ballets.[9]

The Story of G.I. Joe was Ronell's first opportunity to act as music director, though she had apprenticed on numerous films, including *Champagne Waltz* and *Blockade*. This was her biggest job up to that time and though Cowan's influence was crucial, she did express in an interview her reluctance to take it on: "I thought Lester should get a more experienced film composer because I had never attempted writing for a whole show before, but he eventually left the entire job in my hands, and now I understand why women don't usually take this sort of work."[10]

Through the years, Ronell would be criticized for seldom, if ever, working in film music outside of a Lester Cowan production. She mused in a letter to Cowan: "I guess from certain reports I am your music department by [as a result of] marriage only."[11] How much truth there was to this is difficult to tell. Though her early work in the thirties had included stints with Lou Brock at RKO Studios on *Down to Their Last Yacht*, Paramount's *Champagne Waltz* and Walter Wanger's *Blockade* and *Algiers*, from 1944 on she worked exclusively for Cowan, starting with *Tomorrow, the World!*

Ann Ronell in October 1944, during work on *The Story of G.I. Joe*, produced by Lester Cowan (Frank Driggs Collection).

Left to right: Ronell, Cowan, Xavier Cugat, Admiral Jocko Clark, unidentified woman, Aide Lt. Herman Rosenblatt (Ann's brother), in a night club on November 16, 1944.

Journalist Jerene Claire Cline, after a long interview with Ronell, addressed this topic directly:

> Much but not all of her work has been on pictures produced by her husband, Lester Cowan. Cynics may say that one could compose for pictures if her husband were a producer.
> No doubt the arrangement [marriage] has its advantage, but (1) Miss Ronell was an established composer before she married Mr. Cowan and (2) producers and their backers have a natural desire to make profitable pictures, and no favoritism will long sustain mediocre creative work.[12]

She and Applebaum worked five months on the score with Ronell doing the majority of the music. As detailed by *New York Herald Tribune* reporter Judith Klein in her interview of Ronell:

> Musically, it seemed to Miss Ronell, the Ernie Pyle film had three themes for the G.I.: battle, home and romance. For the first, she and Mr. Applebaum composed the infantry march, for the second, they arranged an American folk song, "I'm Comin' Back," and for the third, she wrote a sentimental ballad, "Linda." Reiteration of these melodies forms the complete musical background of the film.[13]

The American folk song on which "I'm Comin' Back" was based was "He's Gone Away," and mostly followed it in melody and rhythm. As Ronell told a Dallas journalist, "I find it embodies the sentiment and longing we need. I quote these four lines...: He's gone away For to stay a little while — But he's coming back If it be ten thousand miles."[14] Ronell later fashioned "I'm Comin' Back" into a concert song which was performed by singers including Burl Ives, Richard Hayes, and The Ray Shield Chorus.[15]

Though "The Ernie Pyle Infantry March" achieved some fame as it became the official march for the United States Army ground troops, it was the ballad, "Linda," that took off. The score of *G.I. Joe,* co-written by Ronell and Applebaum, received an Academy Award nomination. The individual song, "Linda," was nominated as Best Song, and Ronell was listed solely as both composer and lyricist. Moreover, the song was sung over the closing credits for the first time ever in a film drama.[16]

Ronell's Best Song nomination in 1945 occurred during the years at the Academy of Motion Picture Arts & Sciences when more than five songs could be nominated. Moreover, this was a time when the best popular songwriters were working in Hollywood, and competition was tough, as witnessed by the following list of the fourteen nominated songs, composers and lyricists. It should be noted that only Ronell did both words and music for a nominated song that year. The nominees for Best Song in 1945 included[17]:

Song	Movie	Composer/Lyricist
"Ac-cent-tu-ate the Positive"	*Here Come the Waves*	Harold Arlen/Johnny Mercer
"Anywhere"	*Tonight and Every Night*	Jule Styne/Sammy Cahn
"Aren't You Glad You're You"	*The Bells of St. Mary's*	James Van Heusen/Johnny Burke
"The Cat and the Canary"	*Why Girls Leave Home*	Jay Livingston/Ray Evans
"Endlessly"	*Earl Carroll Vanities*	Walter Kent/Kim Gannon
"I Fall in Love Too Easily"	*Anchors Aweigh*	Jule Styne/Sammy Cahn
"I'll Buy That Dream"	*Sing Your Way Home*	Allie Wrubel/Herb Magidson
"It Might as Well be Spring"	*State Fair*	Richard Rodgers/Oscar Hammerstein II
"Linda"	*The Story of G.I. Joe*	Ann Ronell
"Love Letters"	*Love Letters*	Victor Young/Edward Heyman
"More and More"	*Can't Help Singing*	Jerome Kern/E.Y. Harburg
"Sleigh Ride in July"	*Belle of the Yukon*	James Van Heusen/Johnny Burke
"So in Love"	*Wonder Man*	David Rose/Leo Robin
"Some Sunday Morning"	*San Antonio*	Ray Heindorf and M.K. Jerome/Ted Koehler

The winner was "It Might as Well be Spring." Richard Rodgers had agreed to write the music for a Hollywood musical but refused to work there, having had previous bad experiences in Tinseltown, and so all his work on *State Fair* was done from New York. In his book on American Popular Song composers, Wilfrid Sheed explained: "As Rodgers read it, in their hearts, movie people didn't really like Broadway people, beyond their publicity value, which was good for roughly one film and a half, after which the hacks with the connections resumed their sway."[18]

Ernie Pyle, Lester Cowan and Ronell formed a friendship during development and filming of the movie. Pyle liked Ann and appreciated her music, especially "Linda," as Ronell explained in her *Herald Tribune* interview: "I played all the music for Ernie Pyle last New Year's Eve, and he made me play 'Linda' about twenty-five times. He really went for sentimental ballads."[19] She, in turn, admired and recognized him as a unique, independent man from the Midwest. In a friendly letter to Pyle in the summer of 1944, after he had appeared on the cover of *Time,* she teased him about his growing fame, something he no doubt tried to eschew:

> I am writing to say that yours truly is still faithful. Am even looking forward now to getting closer to the head of the line, as many ahead of me must have dropped out after seeing that [*Daily News*] photo! They just can't take it.... You've become so glamorous, Time-ly, heroic and continental that most women think you're a cross between Boyer and Tarzan.[20]

Though "Linda" and the melodies of "The Ernie Pyle Infantry March" and "I'm Comin' Back" course through the score of *The Story of G.I. Joe,* the song is sung only once, and only

Left to right: Lester Cowan, Ernie Pyle, and Ann Ronell during work on Cowan's *The Story of G.I. Joe*, based on Pyle's correspondence during World War II. Pyle was killed by machine gun fire months later, on April 18, 1945, while riding in a Jeep on Ie Shima, an island off Okinawa (Harry Ransom Humanities Research Center, the University of Texas at Austin).

one chorus. It is sung over Berlin Radio by Axis Sally, a Teutonic version of Tokyo Rose. Preceding the song is propaganda from Axis Sally, telling the G.I.s as they are encamped in the desert before a big battle that they cannot possibly beat the German army and encouraging them to visit Germany under more "friendly" conditions.

The song in the scene was originally to be "Lili Marlene," but that song had never caught on in the United States as in Europe, so the producers turned to Ronell for something original.[21] Pyle's advice to Ronell regarding the songs for the film was "to make them sentimental. They used to listen to Axis Sally rebroadcasting nostalgic American tunes."[22]

In the film, the song is brief but effective, creating a nostalgic moment for the G.I.s but with the intent to subvert their war efforts. In the movie it is sung over the camp's speakers as the moving camera showed the faces of the lonely soldiers.

Ronell worked long on the music and lyrics with various combinations of line counts and rhyme schemes. The final version was AA-BB-CC-DD, rather simplistic for an experienced songwriter.[23] Most other versions were longer with different rhyme schemes, but what all the versions had was a longing for the girl back home. Ronell explained to the *New York Sun*: "We needed a song to set a mood, a homesick, plaintive mood, and it had to be short, just sixteen bars in the chorus."[24] An unused version by Ronell had an A-B-A-B-CCC rhyme scheme:

> Dear girl — so the letters start
> From the boy who has gone far away
> Dear girl, tho we're far apart
> We still meet the same place, the same way

I live just in mem'ries,
Sweet things we used to do
O Linda, tell me you remember too,
Oh, Linda, do you?[25]

Like many songs of the era, especially movie themes and love songs, the verse of "Linda" was little played and not heard in the film. It has a more appealing, whistleable melody than the chorus, and Ronell made good use of quarter-note triplets to move it along. The sheet music cover included pictures of both Ernie Pyle and Burgess Meredith, the actor who played Pyle, and there is much resemblance.

Opening in 1945, *The Story of G.I. Joe* was received favorably by audiences and critics. The *New York Times*' October 6 review singled out the film's reality, citing how director William A. Wellman's picture, like Ernie Pyle himself, depicted "infantry action in terms of rain-soaked, mud-caked and desperately tired men."[26] Not only general audiences, but the soldiers themselves, liked the movie. When members of the 5th Army, many of whom had participated as extras in *G.I. Joe*, saw the film, their consensus was, "This is it."[27] General Dwight D. Eisenhower, commander of the Allied Forces in Europe, called it "the greatest war picture I've ever seen."[28]

Ronell with ladies of the Boston VFW playing her songs from *The Story of G.I. Joe,* including "Linda" and "The Ernie Pyle Infantry March" (Harry Ransom Humanities Research Center, The University of Texas at Austin).

Production photograph of Burgess Meredith in the role of Ernie Pyle in *The Story of G.I. Joe* (1945) produced by Lester Cowan for United Artists. Photograph autographed by Mr. Meredith (United Artists Corporation, Ann Ronell Archive).

As for the film's portrayal of Pyle, a friend of Cowan and Ronell, Rear Admiral J.J. Clark, who had been a superior officer of Ronell's brother, Herman, in the U.S. Navy, told her: "It is a great picture. It presents an excellent likeness of Ernie Pyle as I knew him and in addition fills a much needed gap in the war records—for the unsung heroes of all wars are the 'Dough boys.' Winning war means taking the other fellow's 'real estate' and in the final analysis, it is the infantry who actually does it."[29] Although Burgess Meredith was well-known at the time, his casting as Pyle was not easy. Ronell explained to a friend: "There are so many difficulties in casting Pyle that I believe Lester will make tests of various actors before a decision can be made."[30] Apparently there was enough Midwest tough guy in the Hollywood actor to be convincing.

An ASCAP radio survey of 1947 showed that "Linda" continued to be played well into that year.[31] In the same year, another "Linda" was published, composed by Jack Lawrence; it was popularized by a Buddy Clark recording with Ray Noble and his Orchestra.[32] The opening chorus of the 1947 "Linda" was different. Nonetheless, because her "Linda" preceded that of Jack Lawrence, Ronell and Cowan felt that Lawrence's song and title infringed upon hers, and as often occurred in Ronell's professional life, legal action was considered.

The title of a song cannot be copyrighted, only the words and music. But a song may become so popular that to use its title for another song, no matter how different the words and music might be, may constitute a copyright infringement. For example, "Love" may be an oft-used title, but using it would be much safer from a legal standpoint than using, for example, "I've Got You Under My Skin." This Cole Porter evergreen is uniquely titled, extremely well-known, and one with its own legend which one might infringe upon if the exact title were to be used.

Ultimately, Ronell was given counsel by entertainment attorney Julian B. Rosenthal who advised no action. He explained that the words and music of the Lawrence "Linda" were "entirely different" and that Ronell's "Linda" at no time "achieved sufficient popularity as to have acquired a secondary meaning to the extent that anyone hearing a song entitled 'Linda' would immediately assume that it is the song from *G.I. Joe*."[33] Rosenthal's advice was heeded, and no action was taken.

In 1970, twenty-five years after its premiere, *The Story of G.I. Joe* was re-released in thirty Texas cities. This was done in commemoration of Captain Henry T. Waskow of Belton, Texas, the officer upon whom the character of Captain Walker, played by Robert Mitchum, was based. The re-release of *G.I. Joe* in Texas was successful enough to warrant a national release, timed for Veteran's Day of 1970.[34] Though the movie did well enough the second time around, there was no resurgence of the Ann Ronell songs.

12

Oh! Susanna and
Stephen Foster: 1947–1948

*"Ann Ronell has provided a score that abounds in the mingling of
spirit and sentiment that is typical of America's best-loved song maker."*

The year 1946 was a slow period in Ann Ronell's career, although she and Lester did work
on a futuristic story, *The President's Husband*. With the protagonist being the first woman
president of the United States, *The President's Husband* was to look fifteen years into the
country's future. Ronell did extensive research for the script, speaking with scientists, inventors, educators and governmental experts to see how the world might change. Little came of
the project but she kept busy with it; the project appealed to her wide range of interests.[1] During her research and initial drafts of the script, the most frequent question asked of her was,
"Will Rosalind Russell play the president?" More seriously, especially among the scientists,
what people most mentioned was concern over the future in an atomic, post–atom bomb
world.[2]

Also in 1946, Lester approached conductor-composer Leonard Bernstein with an idea to
do a film of an English novel, *The Beckoning Fair One* by Oliver Onions. Lester not only
wanted Bernstein to write the music and orchestrations, but he also wanted the handsome
musician to star and would change the protagonist of the story to a conductor-pianist. Bernstein, though a serious artist, liked the limelight and was enthusiastic for the project, telling
fellow composer Aaron Copland: "It involves score, authorship (of the screen play), acting,
and conducting. 'My' picture."[3] Cowan corroborated this in a 1985 interview: "I was to pay
Lenny twenty-five thousand dollars and build the picture around him in every respect.... I
wanted him all the way."[4]

Bernstein and his girlfriend, later wife, actress Felicia Montealegre, were invited by Ronell
and Cowan to their Canoga Park ranch in Los Angeles at the end of 1946. Ronell and the two
men were to confer about the movie and have the well-connected Cowan get Bernstein and
Montealegre better acquainted with Hollywood. The New Yorkers ended up staying a month
and announced their engagement at a party at the ranch given by their hosts.[5]

The story of the party, as told by gossip columnist Leonard Lyons, was that Ronell and
Cowan organized a hoe-down, and entertainment included Frank Sinatra and Gene Kelly.
However, hostess Ronell stole the show with a song that blended Haydn, Mendelssohn, and
Bernstein, ending with the lyrics:

Ronell and Cowan at their ranch in Canoga Park, Los Angeles, circa 1946.

> This party has been staged
> Because they got engaged.
> Len and Felicia are now officia-
> Lly two.[6]

Bernstein, though having had great success in popular music with the 1944 Broadway musical *On the Town*, was unaccustomed to Hollywood and had done no movie work. At the time of the engagement, he was devoting most of his efforts to conducting and classical composition. His mentor was Serge Koussevitzky of the Boston Symphony, with whom he often had differences, especially when Bernstein's career and energy strayed from classical work. When the movie offer came from Cowan, Bernstein was scheduled to go on a concert tour across Europe to conduct various orchestras. Because of this, Bernstein proposed that he would compose several musical themes for the film and turn them over to Ronell for expansion and orchestrations.[7] Ultimately, Bernstein, at the urging of his agent Helen Coates, Copland and, no doubt, Koussevitzky chose the conducting tour, and *The Beckoning Fair One* was never made.

Ronell remained a friend of Bernstein over the years, though she did not travel in the circles he did, especially as regards classical music. Despite the turn in his career away from Broadway, her ongoing admiration for his earlier show music brought her to write him in 1948:

> Outside of my doings, I am most anxious to shout from the rooftops that it's time for another show by Bernstein. Look at the Broadway theatre! God, is there anything more pitiful and more languishing for-want-of-a-musical-signature such as your own. If you need a book, let me know....[8]

Perhaps her plea helped somewhat, as he composed songs for Broadway's *Peter Pan* in 1950, though it was not the hit that *On the Town* was.

Top, left to right: Ronell, Leonard Bernstein, Felicia Montealegre and Lester Cowan near the Cowans's Canoga Park ranch, circa 1946. *Bottom:* Leonard Bernstein, Felicia Montealegre, Cowan and Ronell at the soda fountain in the Cowans' Canoga Park ranch, circa 1946.

In 1947, Ronell worked with playwrights Colin Clements and Florence Ryerson on a musical treatment of the early life of composer Stephen Foster. Clements and Ryerson were veteran playwrights at the time of their collaboration with Ronell. Both were born during the Gay Nineties and were involved in the theater most of their lives. Clements, like Ronell, was a native of Omaha but had not been acquainted with her there. Clements and Ryerson were married in the early forties and had some early success as a team. Their play, *Harriet*, starred Helen Hayes and was a biographical sketch of the early life and marriage of Harriet Beecher Stowe, author of *Uncle Tom's Cabin*. *Harriet* opened in 1943 on Broadway and, aided by Hayes' star power and artistry, ran for 377 performances.[9]

The other success of the Clements-Ryerson collaboration came in 1948 with *Strange Bedfellows,* a comedy derived from the suffragette movement. This was their last project as Clements died that same year. Florence Ryerson herself also had several plays to her credit, all published by Samuel French and designed for campus and amateur theater productions. Among these, *June Mad* was her most successful.[10]

In 1945, Clements and Ryerson began working on a Stephen Foster play which they had named *Oh! Susanna.* Initially, producer Michael Todd had asked them to write the play with hopes that Al Jolson would take it to Broadway.[11] When this fell through, the playwrights, especially Ryerson, decided to have music added and fashion it for high school, college, and amateur theaters. Thus in 1947, Ronell got involved. Ronell's idea was to employ the many songs of Foster, a prolific, popular songwriter in pre–Civil War America, and blend them into the Ryerson-Clements story. In addition to Foster's music, Ronell was to interpolate a song or two of her own into the work.

Playwrights Colin Clements and Florence Ryerson during work on *Oh! Susanna* 1947 (Estate of Florence Ryerson; Samuel French, Inc.).

Clements and Ryerson's story, mostly fiction, focused on the romance between Foster, a budding songwriter, and Jeannie McDowell, a young woman raised by a strict minister and his wife. Foster meets showman E.P. Christy, whose touring minstrel show comes into Foster's river town. On the same boat are Jeannie McDowell and her parents. Foster's talent, charm and good looks attract the beautiful Jeannie, but her father discourages her romance with the worldly Foster, who then becomes the resident composer in Christy's traveling show. Further plot twists include a romance between Christy and Foster's aunt, as well as Jeannie's engagement to a young stockbroker when Foster is off touring. All of this is framed within the world of the river and Christy's traveling minstrel show and ends, of course, happy and resolved.

Stephen C. Foster's actual life was less ideal. Born in 1826 near Pittsburgh, he received a strong education through high school, despite a father who was often gone and provided poorly for his large family. Foster taught himself several instruments, the flute being his first choice. His brother Morrison, in a fond biography, described his brother's talent with the flute: "[H]e learned, unaided, to play beautifully on the flute. He had the faculty of bringing those deep resonant tones from the flute which distinguish the natural flutist from the mechanical performer."[12]

Foster began composing in his teens and published "Oh! Susanna" in 1848. It became the unofficial theme song of the California Gold Rush and the pioneers in the wagon trains headed west. Never a businessman, Foster sold the rights to "Oh! Susanna" to a Cincinnati publisher for next to nothing.

Black minstrelsy songs and parlor ballads were of most interest to Foster, and it was in these two genres that he concentrated his composing and had his greatest successes.[13] Black-face and minstrelsy were popular styles of the day, and Foster is credited with raising the music and lyrics of this genre to a higher level, well above the stereotype. In a posthumous magazine article, Foster's friend, Robert P. Nevin, discussed his handling of minstrelsy songs: "If Mr. Foster's art embodied no higher idea than the vulgar notion of the Negro—as a thing of tricks and antics—then it might have proved a tolerable catch-penny affair, and commanded an admiration among boys of various growths, until its novelty wore off. But the art in his hands teemed with a nobler significance. It dealt in its simplicity with universal sympathies and taught us all to feel with the colored man the lowly joys and sorrows it celebrated."[14]

Foster's ballads included "Jeanie with the Light Brown Hair," "Beautiful Dreamer," and "Gentle Annie." His most popular minstrelsy songs were "Old Black Joe," "Massa's in de Cold Ground," "My Old Kentucky Home," and "Old Folks at Home." The latter two became the official state songs of Kentucky and Florida, respectively.

Foster's personal life unraveled, and he separated from his wife of four years, Jane Denny McDowell, in 1854. His composing slowed, though as late as 1862, he wrote "Beautiful Dreamer" and in 1864, composed the music for "If You've Got a Moustache" with lyricist George Cooper. Unfortunately, over the years, he had carelessly sold off rights to most of his songs and borrowed against future earnings. Through the Civil War years he drank heavily, and his health declined. He died in January of 1864 from complications after a fall.[15]

Ronell drew on over 300 of his songs and other works, ultimately using fifty or so, entire songs in some cases and a few measures in others. As she explained in her "Composer's Notes" for the Pasadena Playhouse program: "In wealth of discovery, I found it hard to limit the amount of material I wished to use, so I combined several lines in many instances, and enjoyably was able to handle the music as freely as if it were my own."[16]

The promotional card from Samuel French, the eventual publisher of *Oh! Susanna*, summed up the Ronell-Ryerson-Clements collaboration:

> A piece of authentic Americana is this picture of a small town on the Ohio River a hundred years ago, that lusty period when the wild frontiersmen and their womenfolk were at odds with the more settled members of the community. A series of gay scenes tells the love story of Stephen Foster and Jeanie-with-the-light-brown-hair.
>
> By adapting Foster's Ethiopian and minstrel numbers and contrasting them with his romantic love songs, Ann Ronell has contrived a superb musical background for the comedy, which includes a minstrel show, and several scenes played in front of the curtain.[17]

The three creators were hoping that this Americana, coupled with Foster's music, would make *Oh! Susanna* appeal to a wide postwar audience. To do this, they targeted their staging and musical arrangements for amateur productions—high school, college and local theater. The Samuel French promotional cards delineated the following as needed for a production of *Oh! Susanna*[18]:

7 MALES   3 FEMALES
(7 Minstrel Men, Chorus, Extras, as desired)
1 EXTERIOR SCENE   COSTUMES, 1850
LIBRETTO, $1.00   PIANO AND VOCAL SCORE, $4.00
ROYALTY, $50.00

The musical had appeal from the view of both the audience and those who might produce it. As seen above, the story, even with its subplots, called for only ten actors. Moreover, the orchestration required only two pianos for most of the songs, and the second act called for two or more minstrelsy instruments, e.g., banjo, washboard, fiddle, accordion, pots and pans, etc. Many of these instruments had the advantage that beginners could play them with some proficiency, an obvious advantage to amateur company directors, who could add minstrelsy instruments to accommodate cast additions or absences.

Further instrumentation was added in later productions, though Ronell felt that this missed the point of the musical and its antebellum setting "as I feel the use of solo instruments indicated as mouth organ, banjo, accordion (or others), is more effectively Americana flavor and in tradition than would be a full orchestra throughout."[19]

> Please note that the primitive instruments such as pots and pans, comb and paper, washboard and thimble, etc., harpsichord effects and other descriptions throughout the score were the result of much thought and sincere wish on my part to make the score a unique musical performance.[20]

The Pasadena Playhouse production of *Oh! Susanna* opened May 21, 1947; it was generally praised by the Los Angeles and Pasadena critics.[21] Though this premiere performance and run in Pasadena was not intended as a pre–Broadway trial, many of the critics gave this some consideration in their evaluations. This rankled Ronell as the initial production was never aimed at a Broadway audience. As she told Albert Taylor at the William Morris Agency: "We thought the *L.A. Herald-Express* review the most intelligent, having taken into account this was an amateur version of the play and not considering it as did the others a try-out for New York."[22]

The favorable comments about *Oh! Susanna* as a legitimate musical included:

> It's an interesting and colorful production and may develop into one of the good musicals.
> Theater-goers wise enough to have turned up at Pasadena Playhouse last night may have seen something to brag about in future years—something that might conceivably evolve into another *Oklahoma*—eventually.[23]

The Clements-Ryerson book was considered successful, especially so in the second act, where books of musicals so often fail. Ronell's music, lyrics and arrangements were well-liked. Of particular mention was her use of the Foster melodies, with her changes of the lyrics, especially for some of his lesser known songs. Most favorable were the comments in the *Pasadena Star-News*:

> Taking his tunes for a basis, using the more popular in their original version, modernizing or writing new words for other lesser known melodies, Ann Ronell has provided a score that abounds in the mingling of spirit and sentiment that is typical of America's best-loved song maker.[24]

All the critics agreed that the production needed a full orchestra and more professional voices before its creators could take it any further. Among the singers praised by the critics was a young Marni Nixon, who played Susanna and became well-known for her versatile voice, coaching skills, and Hollywood soundtracks. She would later dub singing for Deborah Kerr in *The King and I*, Audrey Hepburn in *My Fair Lady*, and Natalie Wood in *West Side Story*.[25]

Oh! Susanna continued to be well-received by California audiences, and its run was extended. Ronell and her collaborators had hoped for success for *Susanna* in amateur-academic circles. Initially, they were right on target. In the fall of that year, Ronell was happy to report the following: "I found dramatizing the Foster music and making new songs out of his lesser known melodies a rewarding job since Pasadena held over its run for five weeks and we now have lots of orders for spring performance, Princeton heading the list."[26]

Another successful professional production for *Oh! Susanna* came at the Cleveland Playhouse over two years later. Among those who had encouraged the production at the time was Arthur Loesser, brother of Broadway's Frank. Arthur, a concert pianist and head of the piano department at the Cleveland Institute of Music, was impressed with Ronell's musical efforts: "This music has real distinction. It is opera ... that is, opera as it should be. There is something for everybody; the musician and the musically-wise will appreciate its distinction, and the lay public will like the vitality and melodic quality."[27]

The Cleveland critics were more critical of *Oh! Susanna*, especially as a future Broadway work, again a presumption on their parts. One columnist liked the amateur production overall and felt that "[w]hile the show undoubtedly is too much of a conglomeration ever to succeed as a Broadway production, it nevertheless is made to order for a group of young players and singers."[28]

The *Cleveland Plain Dealer* reviewer was more harsh toward the creators:

> The play's story is pretty thin. It would have to be stronger, I imagine, to breast the winds of Broadway.
>
> The idea, apparently, is to thread the lovely sentimental melodies of Foster and the simple, lively humor of some of his songs on an idyllic and unpretentious plot which involves chiefly a love affair and consequent palpitations without much complexity of feeling or action. As it works out in the present production, it is not enough.[29]

Marni Nixon in the title role of *Oh! Susanna*, which premiered at the Pasadena Playhouse in May 1947 (Eileen Bailey photograph, Pasadena Playhouse).

Nonetheless, this Cleveland Playhouse production was quite popular and also enjoyed an extended run.

The libretto and score were published by Samuel French and Company in 1950. That first year, over one hundred performances were given by high schools, colleges and amateur theaters.[30] *Oh! Susanna* played in sixteen states, being especially popular in California, perhaps due to the influence of the original production at the Pasadena Playhouse.[31] Overall, *Oh! Susanna* enjoyed modest success over the next several years as an amateur production.

Though *Oh! Susanna* had been targeted for amateur groups, Ronell and Florence Ryerson, despite their original intentions, wanted to make the show attractive to professional companies for performance, even if never reaching Broadway. To do this, they had to secure the stock rights, which were more difficult to obtain. They felt that Samuel French, their publisher, was not adequately promoting *Oh! Susanna* and working to secure these rights. Ronell wrote to Ryerson: "It is more apparent than ever that the stock musical field is one which Samuel French has not assiduously courted."[32] As an alternative, Ronell pushed other New York publishing houses with whom she had worked to take the stock rights, especially G. Schirmer, Inc., who had published much of her opera work, and Tams-Witmark, pre-eminent in the area of musicals.[33] It was the absence of full orchestrations and the costs to do them that were impediments to obtaining stock rights which would allow the work to be performed more extensively by professional companies. A full orchestration had been overlooked by the creators because of their initial success in amateur productions with Ronell's simple, economical orchestration specifying two pianos and a few minstrelsy instruments.

But in 1947-48, when Samuel French published their work with only piano arrangements, Ronell regretted the absence of full orchestrations. As time slipped away on their project, she wrote a letter to Florence Ryerson with an almost desperate tone to it. She explained to her collaborator, who was less versed in the vagaries of the musical world:

> [T]here is absolutely no future whatsoever for *Oh Su* in stock without orchestrations, and we have none.
>
> Garrett Leverton realized the need for orchestrations and promised that French would make them at the very start of the venture. The lamentable fact of his passing has been apparent in many ways. However, the no which I didn't take for an answer seems to be permanent, and we must go elsewhere.[34]

Not only did Ronell feel a full orchestration was necessary for future considerations, but the lack of one had already impeded further productions of their work. In the same letter to Ryerson:

> Since we were already turned down because of no orchestrations by the Los Angeles City College, and by Victor Records, and by James Davidson Concert Tours who had contacted me about a concert version of *Oh Su* for 1952, and by many whom we shall never know about, I think it is only wise to face the fact that we must get orchestrations or give up any prospects of getting the full value out of our publication.[35]

Ronell, Ryerson, and Lester Cowan also felt that in addition to a full orchestra, a new book might be needed to attract a more sophisticated theater crowd and, ultimately, Broadway audiences.[36] As Ronell explained at the time to agent Martin Jurow from the William Morris Agency:

> It is my hope that you will project this property for a Broadway production, and that the book will be considered a basis for a new book.... Florence Ryerson discussed the matter with me when I was on the Coast recently, and realizes that we need a new book for Broadway and the stock field.
>
> I would be truly grateful for whatever attention you can give this matter. I feel that we have delayed too long in getting your interest since the property was published, and hope that the sixty

performances Samuel French received this last season for *Oh! Susanna* will be as encouraging an indication of its value to you as it is to the authors.[37]

Ronell was able to attract initial interest in a number of Broadway people, including independent producer Cheryl Crawford, who wrote to her in early 1951, "I'm up to my capillaries again with a new musical, opening April 8th, so all fun is eliminated for now. I'd love to have the *Oh! Susanna* score and see you after we open."[38]

More importantly, Ronell attracted the attention of Jurow. He was well-known in Broadway circles and had discussed *Oh! Susanna* with several producers, apparently to no avail. As Ronell told Ryerson, there was little interest in a revival of songs from a century before. "I saw Martin Jurow.... He was most kind and went into the matters re *Oh Susanna* in detail, but he is terribly disappointed in the vagaries of the Broadway theatre business, against which his intelligence and practical nature rebel — he thinks most producers are shoddy and ignorant of knowing what's good and what isn't."[39]

Oh! Susanna never made it to Broadway as producers felt it too old-fashioned for a Broadway influenced by the new musicals of Richard Rodgers and Oscar Hammerstein II, who had opened *Oklahoma!* and *Carousel* within the preceding five years. No full orchestration was ever done, and *Oh! Susanna* never became part of the lucrative stock field. Ronell did choral arrangements for several of the show's songs, including "De Shanghai Cockfight," "Who'll Serenade You," "The River Song," and "Aboard for Lou'siana."

As with many Ronell projects, she had several more ideas to diversify *Oh! Susanna*, including a movie, a concert version for television, and a weekly television show. The television show was conceived by Ronell as a periodical musical series, probably weekly. She envisioned the series as an extension of the *Showboat* formula with plenty of story ideas available from the relationship between Foster and Jeanie, the lives of the riverfront town citizens, and the recurring traveling minstrel show and its cast of characters. Musically, Ronell felt she could draw from Foster's myriad of songs, 300 in number, from which she had derived the music for her original *Oh! Susanna*. In her notes to pitch the idea to television executives, she referred to this music as "song hits of last century in fresh form," stressing: "You must hear it to know what it is."[40]

Though the television series never came to fruition, there were specific plans for a one-time airing of *Oh! Susanna* on the *NBC Spectacular* series. Its planning engendered much controversy because of the racial overtones of the production, especially its minstrelsy scenes. In its original form, *Oh! Susanna* included a minstrelsy show in the second act which called for that part of the cast to be in blackface. Additionally, several of the songs contained an exaggerated Negro dialect.

In the first years of productions, 1947 through 1950, such staging was apparently not a problem, as none was indicated in the correspondences of those years. In 1951, as Ronell and Ryerson were still hoping for a Broadway production, racial awareness was on the rise. Ronell wrote to Ryerson regarding their creation: "Everyone who has read our work has had a different opinion, including the people who had this month suggested contacting ANTA for their sponsorship, but added precaution [that] we should observe in deleting most of the minstrel show, as *Green Pastures* was proving [the] public did not care for Negro caricature."[41]

Ronell's reference to *Green Pastures* concerned the successful play written and directed by Marc Connelly. It was a retelling of several Biblical stories in terms of rural Southern blacks. It was well-received by the critics and won the Pulitzer Prize for Drama in 1930. It had an initial run of 640 performances and a three-year national tour.[42] *Green Pastures* was criticized by African-American artists of the time, among them poet-playwright Langston Hughes. He derided it as "white America's fantasy of the childlike simplicity of Southern blacks."[43] A revival twenty years later was not embraced by audiences and closed after a short run.

Move ahead five years to 1955–56, when planning for the television production of *Oh! Susanna* took place — the Eisenhower years — when racial tensions were increasing and integration was a pressing issue. NBC was the network planning to produce *Oh! Susanna* as part of its *NBC Spectacular* series. Several excerpts from a long letter from one NBC executive to another illustrate well the racial problems inherent in presenting *Oh! Susanna* to a national audience:

> Lester and we seem in agreement on the elimination of the more obvious Negro stereotyping words which these days all responsible broadcasters do without. I refer specifically to "darkies"...
> As to a minstrel sequence at all, I am unable to view such a job out of the context of the past five years of our RCA-NBC integration without identification policy.... Alas, we spent too many painful months persuading performers like Berle and Cantor that blackface was out of date and offensive to the customers of our sponsors and to viewers in general to take chances now.... I favor writing out blackface here and now rather than waste Lester's and our energies on even approaching the NAACP on the point.[44]

Exposure on the NBC television network on their popular *Spectacular* series would have been great for Ronell and would have given *Oh! Susanna* a rebirth. She was more than willing to revise lyrics to accommodate the NBC Continuity Acceptance Department, i.e., their censors. By the end of February, 1956, most of her reworking of the songs had been done and reviewed by NBC personnel.

A letter to her from the director of the Continuity Acceptance Department, Stockton Helffrich, makes clear what a thorough job she had done:

> I do feel the various changes in the lyrics a most positive contribution to racial amity, and I feel some of your and our other plans relating to the production will indeed both meet the brotherhood demands of our times....
> Your contrapuntal handling of these five tunes with the new lyrics you have submitted eliminates not only the ill will the titles alone used to create but also the color distinctions and condescension inherent in the words of both the titles and lyrics.[45]

Despite much planning and expense, including discussions with Gordon MacRae and Tennessee Ernie Ford about playing Stephen Foster, *Oh! Susanna* never made it to rehearsals and was never aired on television.

"Some Folks Say" was the song-choral arrangement from *Oh! Susanna* with Stephen Foster's words and music, but with Ronell's stamp firmly on it. "Some Folks Say" was presented en masse at a summer camp of the National Musical Educators' Conference in the summer of 1956. A chorus of 500 high school music camp students sang the song, accompanying it with washboards and tin pans. Ronell attended the rehearsals and performance, and the students gave her a standing ovation upon first meeting her. She said it was "the first experience of this kind I ever had."[46] NBC Television filmed the students singing her song for later presentation on one of their *NBC Spectaculars*.

Of course, what is an Ann Ronell project without litigation or the threat of it? In 1950, when *Oh! Susanna* probably reached the pinnacle of its success, such as it was, Republic Pictures was to release a film by the same title. Ronell and her representatives at the William Morris Agency felt strongly that use of this title at that time was an infringement on her work.[47] As she delineated in unpublished notes at the time which she discussed with the William Morris people:

> 1. *Oh! Susanna* is current. Other works with the same title are not. Since its debut at the Pasadena Playhouse, widely advertised and reviewed in Los Angeles papers, May, 1947, the work has been revised with constant references in the trade papers to its publication in 1949 by Samuel French....

2. This [Republic] film, *The Golden Tide*, is evidently not based on Stephen Foster songs. Republic has chosen to use for this a new title, *Oh! Susanna*, which is more valuable now in view of the public knowledge of our musical comedy work. Confusion is caused in the public's mind by Republic's use of the title.

3. We are damaged in view of being prevented from using on a future film the title which we have popularized....[48]

A month later, as things progressed, Ronell and Florence Ryerson cabled Herbert Yates, president of Republic Studios, threatening legal action:

Unless we hear from you promptly that you are not using title of our published, performed work *Oh Susanna* it will be necessary to turn the matter over to our lawyers on grounds unfair competition in view of current association by the public with our Stephen Foster property.[49]

As it turned out, Florence Ryerson was not in favor of any legal action, but Ronell had added her name to the telegram without Ryerson's permission. In a letter only three days after the telegram, Ryerson wrote to Ronell: "One thing has distressed me very much, Ann. Your sending that telegram to Republic. You must not ... you really must *not* send anything in my name without first consulting me.... Since Republic had already used the title they might be in a position to come down on us, and stirring up the lions like that might make them fierce when otherwise they would not have been so."[50]

Ronell's brother, Sol Rosenblatt, echoed her sentiment in a letter he prepared in reply to Republic Pictures:

My clients have since December, 1948, popularized a play with music entitled *Oh! Susanna*, which deals with the life of Stephen Foster, the original composer of the song, "Oh! Susanna."

In our opinion, the change by you of your title to the appropriation of my clients' title is unwarranted and unlawful and constitutes a deliberate and willful attempt by your company to appropriate good will created in the presentation of my clients' production for your benefit and is further calculated to cause confusion in the minds of the public.[51]

Legal maneuvers continued through 1951, including a "cease and desist" letter from Ronell's Beverly Hills attorney, Harold Fendler.[52] Ronell and Sol Rosenblatt continued to press the issue into 1952. Opponents of a suit against Republic, including Harold Fendler, eventually felt that Foster's story and music were in the public domain, and Ronell and her colleagues had no legal claim. As it turned out, Republic Pictures Corporation opened their picture in late 1951, a Western starring Rod Cameron, Lorna Gray, and Forrest Tucker. Its title—*Oh! Susanna*.[53]

13

One Touch of Venus and Forties Hollywood: 1947–1948

"Your battle with the mighty music department is comparable only to the fight of little David against Goliath."

In 1947, against his better judgment, Kurt Weill had allowed himself to get involved with the craziness of Hollywood for a second time. It must have been the money.

Weill's *One Touch of Venus* had opened on Broadway in 1943 and became his longest running show at that time with 567 performances. He had had success with *Lady in the Dark* with Ira Gershwin (1941) and would later compose music for *Street Scene* (1947) and *Lost in the Stars* (1949).[1] He signed a contract to have a movie made of *One Touch of Venus*, though he was reluctant, afraid his music would be mangled by Hollywood. To avoid that, he negotiated a contract ensuring that no other songs other than his could be included in the score. However, there were no assurances in the agreement that some of his songs would not be eliminated.

From a composer's standpoint, Hollywood was not like Broadway. With the latter venue, the composers and writers were involved with the show from the start — the book, choreography, casting, etc. — and stayed with it until opening night. But the movies were different. Though the composers and lyricists were generally well paid, it was understood that the songs were to be turned over to the director and film editors, and hope for the best. There was little artistic control over how the music would be used, who might sing it, and if it would even be used. Most of the "big name" composers who had started in theater, particularly Richard Rodgers, hated the system, but had to live with it or avoid it.

Work on the film began in 1945, and problems arose almost immediately. The studio felt the original show too sophisticated for the enjoyment of a general movie audience. In true Hollywood fashion, the love story and romantic elements were embellished to the detriment of the music and other plot elements.[2] This forced Weill to write additional material. As the script treatment and preproduction progressed, more and more of Broadway's *One Touch of Venus* was lost to a homogenized star vehicle for Ava Gardner and Robert Walker.

Before wholesale cuts could be made, Weill's hope had been Ann Ronell, who had been named musical director of the movie, being produced at Universal-International Pictures by Lester Cowan. Ten years previously, Ronell had been entrusted to oversee Weill's interests in a Walter Wanger movie, *The River Is Blue*. She had made a valiant attempt to retain Weill's music, but due to directorial and other creative changes, his score had been discarded in favor of one by Werner Janssen, and the film re-titled *Blockade*. Nonetheless, Weill had appreciated her efforts at the time and was now glad to have her on the new project. So in late 1947, Weill returned to New York to finish work on *Love Life*, his musical with Alan Jay Lerner to open in the fall of 1948. This left Ronell in the lion's den of a Hollywood music department, again having to fend for herself and Weill's music.

Milton Schwarzwald and his staff in the Universal music department had little appreciation for Weill's scores and orchestrations. Ronell referred to their department in an early 1948 letter as that "august stone wall."[3] A month prior to that, Ronell had warned Weill of their attitudes towards her working on the project and his music:

> Regarding adapting your orchestrations for the film score, I have found a general indisposition on the part of Hollywood men to join me in my enthusiasm — they all wish to create big jobs for themselves by saying "Leave it to me, I will do the whole score myself."
> The schwarz hearts of Schwarzwald & Co. caused such an uproar, however, when they realized my intentions were sincere to use your orchestrations for my score sketches ... that the reverberations of the loud arguments deafened the recording stage....[4]

Weill, by then no stranger to the bizarre ways of Hollywood, sympathized:

> Your battle with the mighty music department is comparable only to the fight of little David against Goliath, but, since you cannot use the sling and stone on Mr. Schwarzwald, you were bound to lose that battle. What would become of Schwarzwald and his arranger friends if they would allow the spirit of my orchestration to enter the sacred Wagnerian halls of Hollywood motion picture scoring....[5]

Ronell had suggested several names as conductor for the score, including Maurice Abravanel, Bernard Green, and Leon Leonardi. However, despite impressive classical credentials, none had done previous film conducting, and her choices were rejected out of hand by Schwarzwald. Regarding Schwarzwald's process for choosing a conductor, Ronell had written to Weill that "very few fresh and novel ideas will be looked upon by anything but a jaundiced and smug eye."[6]

Finally, all agreed upon Leo Arnaud. He had worked successfully for both MGM and Columbia Pictures as a freelance conductor and had extensive film experience. Ronell's preference for Arnaud came down to the issue of Weill's orchestrations: "Of the many men seeking the job or suggested for the job, he was the only one I was able to find who was not averse to being guided by your orchestral style and harmonic flavor."[7]

In addition to the elimination of Weill's orchestrations, most of his and Ogden Nash's songs had been discarded. The Broadway edition of *One Touch of Venus* contained thirteen songs, but a Hollywood film musical could seldom sustain that many numbers, particularly a film evolving into a light romance, with music as an afterthought. In the end, only three songs remained: "Speak Low," "(Don't Look Now But) My Heart Is Showing," and "That's Him." Weill biographer David Drew wrote that the final cut was released "amid a chorus of complaints that Hollywood had successfully obliterated a well-beloved Broadway musical."[8]

Following a 1950 interview with Ronell, columnist Tom Donnelly of the *Washington Daily News* explained the situation at the time:

> Movie audiences do not understand fantasy, anyone in Hollywood will tell you. They can't have Agnes de Mille ballets in them. And they can't have people just bursting into song. There has to be a "reason" for people singing in the movies. And Miss Ronell could only find three "reasons" for song in the celluloid *Venus*, so the other 10 numbers had to go.[9]

Ronell wrote Anya Berezovsky, wife of Nicolai, after the film opened: "It was a very difficult job to do what with the director and Universal execs being against any songs at all.... We believe

New York was disappointed not finding a big musical, because outside of New York where the show never played, the picture has enjoyed very fine business."[10] More succinctly, as Ronell replied to Donnelly's question as to why so many songs were cut: "Well, the studio didn't want a musical."[11]

The Motion Picture Association of America office had rejected the entire lyrics of "Trouble with Women" and much of "Wooden Wedding." "The Trouble with Women" was Ogden Nash at his best, a lyric filled with double entendres.[12] Both songs were eliminated early on in the production. This censorship was nothing personal toward the composers or producers, as the censors had been cutting and changing words in movies for many years. In 1938, one Jerome Kern's efforts with RKO was to be entitled *Joy of Loving*. As his biographer Gerald Boardman explained: "Filming was completed in February of 1938, but before the results were released for public inspection the title was slightly changed, apparently in response to the censors. The seemingly harmless, if vaguely suggestive 'loving' gave place to the wholesome 'living.'"[13]

Ronell was able to rewrite lines unacceptable to the censors from the Broadway song "I'm a Stranger Here Myself," but it did not survive cuts from the studio. As plot elements from the musical were eliminated, so were the songs accompanying them.

The original show's song "Foolish Heart," a waltz, also had some lines rejected by the MPAA censors. Although the dramatic situation for which it was composed had been written out of the screenplay, Ronell felt the melody too strong to be eliminated. She rewrote the lyric and saw to it that an appropriate dramatic scene was added to incorporate the song. It was re-titled "(Don't Look Now But) My Heart Is Showing." It was used in a waltz scene in Central Park sung by Dick Haymes, Olga San Juan, Robert Walker, and Eileen Wilson, dubbing for Ava Gardner.

Though Gardner was no singer, her statuesque beauty was perfect for the role of Venus. Her picture on the cover of the sheet music is stunning, as were her scenes in the film. Lester Cowan introduced his mother to Gardner on the set of *One Touch of Venus*, and upon seeing the slim star, Mrs. Cowan is said to have exclaimed: "What's the matter? You so skinny. You sick?"[14]

In a February, 1948, letter to Ronell, Weill was quite favorable about her attempts to retain his orchestrations and her work on the songs, especially the transformed "Foolish Heart":

> ... I know you are putting up a very brave fight to keep my material, as far as it is being used, intact, and I appreciate very much the fine integrity which characterizes your fight in defense of the work of a fellow artist and a friend. I realize full well what that means, and I want you to know that I realize it.
> ... The "Heart Song" scene can be effective and the new lyrics are very Ann Ronell-ish. The new ending seems alright for the different character you want to give the song, but I wrote on the music sheet a suggestion for a change of the last bars.[15]

A copyright for "My Heart Is Showing" was issued in May of 1948 with Kurt Weill as composer and Ann Ronell as lyricist, with no mention of Ogden Nash, the original lyricist.[16] Ronell had been working hard on the movie and being able to be on the same copyright with Kurt Weill was an accomplishment and a nice reward.

Work and getting on with people involved with the movie was what she was all about. This appears to be an occurrence on many of her projects, finishing a project having made several friends, later correspondents. Though Milton Schwarzwald and his crew had been tough to work with, she made many friends in other segments of the crew while working on the picture. One of them, Helen Van Dongen, wrote her: "You are the person whose letters

Ronell on the set of *One Touch of Venus* with stars Ava Gardner (left) and Olga San Juan (right) (Universal Pictures).

I love to read ... because they usually give me the feeling of a delightfully whirling hurricane ... scurrying around *Venus* like a tipsy squirrel, holding six conferences at a time."[17]

By early 1948, Ronell and Weill had exchanged several letters regarding song choices, arrangements, and singers. Even though the "musical" *One Touch of Venus* had been vastly reduced from the original, there were still a few songs to be sung. Dick Haymes, in a supporting role in the film, was to be given one or more numbers, as star Robert Walker was not a singer. Haymes had spent much of the 1930s in Hollywood as a broadcaster, bit actor, and sometime songwriter. His voice, not his songs, caught the ear of Harry James, and Haymes

Left to right: Ronell, agent Leah Salisbury, Cowan, and Kurt Weill discussing new songs for the film version of *One Touch of Venus.*

began to sing with James's band around 1940. He went on to sing with Benny Goodman and later Tommy Dorsey. By the mid-forties, his reputation rivaled that of Bing Crosby or Frank Sinatra.[18]

Though Haymes was handsome, photogenic, and had a great voice, he was somewhat difficult to work with. As Ronell warned Weill regarding a recording she sent him of one of the picture's songs: "Do not go by his melody line as you will see he does not follow the piano copy. This is evidently a habit of his 'to be different.'"[19] Because of his star status as a singer, Haymes was given much say in his pick of songs. His choice from the Weill-Nash score was "West Wind." Though a pretty song in the stage musical, those involved in the film, including Haymes's manager Bill Burton, felt it had little general appeal. Additionally, the original lyric, according to Ronell, carried "no significance"[20] to the screenplay as it had evolved.

The song choice for Haymes was important to him as he wanted to be certain that whatever song was filmed and recorded, would definitely remain in the final cut. He had just suffered a cinematic setback, along with co-star Deanna Durbin, in the 1948 movie *Up in Central Park.* Sneak preview audiences had become quickly bored with their songs and singing and had "walked out in droves."[21] So poor had the responses to those previews been that five songs were cut from *Up in Central Park* before its general release. Beyond this, the studio decided to eliminate all but the very best of slow numbers from future film musicals.[22]

To comfort Haymes and assure that his song would fit the story and make the final cut, Ronell rewrote the entire lyric and re-titled the song "My Week." As she explained to Weill, in light of the studio's slow numbers caveat, "[T]he only chance we have of getting 'My Week' into our picture is to liven it up."[23] It was published in 1948 with Weill and Ronell as composer and lyricist, respectively. But all the work and discussion were to no avail, as "My Week" was cut from the movie, the last to be so treated. Ultimately, Haymes fared well with the song lineup, singing both "Speak Low" and "(Don't Look Now But) My Heart Is Showing" in the final cut.

In addition to copyrights for "My Week" and "My Heart Is Showing," Ronell also signed Standard Uniform Popular Songwriters Contracts with Chappell and Co., Inc., for the two songs in July of 1948.[24] But to get herself and her lyrics accepted and popularized, Ronell had to plead with Max Dreyfus from Chappell to properly exploit the two songs.[25] Dreyfus and Chappell were reluctant to publish the songs with their new lyrics, not wanting to offend Ogden Nash, the original lyricist. To Ronell, it was just necessary for Chappell to publish the songs in "black and white form ... at a cost of $40."[26] With a published form, the songs could then be used by artists who had been requesting them, including Dinah Shore, Marion Hutton, Bing Crosby, and Haymes himself. Both recordings and radio usage were awaiting their publication. Moreover, producer Lester Cowan was pushing for publication of salable sheet music. He wanted it available for sale in music stores when the film opened in major cities.

Ronell's contention was that although Weill's melodies had been retained, the plot changes incorporated into the screenplay necessitated the changed lyrics. As she reasoned to Dreyfus in the letter of September 23, 1948: "Certainly Mr. Ogden Nash or those writers you are referring to cannot be so small as to object to another writer publishing completely new lyrics to fit completely new situations where in the original material was unsuitable and would not have been used at all...."[27] Ronell explained that Weill had been kept apprised of the changes in the lyrics and how the two songs were to be used, and that he was favorable toward all of it:

> He complimented me on the commercial potentialities of the new numbers and expressed delight in the plans made by the studio for their exploitation. Mr. Weill received all my music continuity notes early in the production and knew the problems I was up against in transferring material written for a stage play to a film which had new dramatic elements requiring a fresh approach to the songs.[28]

Ronell felt strongly that all contractual obligations had been met regarding use of the songs and the major changes in the lyrics she had made. In her favor were the original contracts signed by Weill, Nash et al., as well as the recently completed copyrights and the Standard Uniform Popular Songwriters Contracts signed between Ronell and Chappell, with Dreyfus himself as the signatory for Chappell. As a result, the publisher soon acquiesced and printed the songs.

The publication of these songs was part of an effort by Ronell to improve her standing in the somewhat antiquated ASCAP reimbursement system. At the time, ASCAP was the primary collection agency for songwriters, composers and lyricists. But the payment profile favored the more popular and prolific composers. The higher one's classification, D up through A, the more one was paid per song. So an Irving Berlin, who was already paid a great deal because of the number of his hits, was paid more per use of each song than a lesser composer like Ann Ronell. Truly, the rich got richer.

The problems with the ASCAP classification system in general and Ronell's issues with it specifically went back to 1933. In that year she had received a bonus payment from ASCAP because of the success at that time of "Who's Afraid of the Big Bad Wolf?," but she was still in Class D, the lowest.[29] While acknowledging hers as one of the recent "outstanding songs," ASCAP president Gene Buck made no mention of an improvement in her classification, admitting, "Classification is the most complex problem that confronts the Society. The Commit-

tee is conscious of the great changes that have taken place in our business and is doing everything possible to recognize initiative and activity."[30] Over the years, especially in the thirties,
she frequently sought to improve her status, prodding the committee over several years and
appearing before the Board of Appeals, though not always getting her desired results.[31]

To improve one's standing, a songwriter or lyricist had to demonstrate to the ASCAP
committee that his or her new popular songs, recent performances or other musical or lyrical creations were of overall significance to the ASCAP system. In the latter part of the thirties, she felt that more "credit" should be given her for the classical adaptations and translations
she had done. As she complained to Buck:

> I can't understand why writers would question the value of my work in adapting classics—cer-
> tainly they could appreciate bringing revenue to ASCAP through performance of hitherto public
> domain material ... but no, certain writers present told me my work was of little account. Thank
> goodness the majority decided that I did deserve a break.[32]

A decade later, around the time of *One Touch of Venus*, the battle continued. In a letter
to her friend, Sylvia Rosenberg, who was affiliated with ASCAP, Ronell wrote, "Re ASCAP:
Now that I have gained many new credits and performances I would like to apply for reclas-
sification. Would you kindly inform me as to when the next meeting will be held, and where,
and what procedure I should employ."[33] Besides highlighting her two new songs with Weill,
Ronell also mentioned in her mailing to Rosenberg the film score and various lyric changes
scattered around *One Touch of Venus* as well as the performance of "My Week" by Dick
Haymes on his radio show.[34]

Over a year later, her classification had been raised from C-1 to C-1A, a change she
referred to as "a slight boost ... hardly more than a nod of acknowledgement."[35] She then made
a case to be raised to the more lucrative Class B, explaining to the ASCAP committee:

> Realizing that not only am I responsible for both the words and music of numbers which have
> by themselves been raised to the classification of Standard and Classic Editions ... but that I also
> have been productive of many and varied works, with credit for the lyrics, or for the music, or for
> both, in theatre, films, concert and radio— I cannot help feeling that my ASCAP rating is not related
> to my contribution.[36]

In her request letter, she especially focused on her recent work on *The Story of G.I. Joe, Love
Happy,* and *Oh! Susanna.* Whether or not her classification was adjusted after this letter is
unclear, but her ASCAP classification represented one of her longest standing battles and
caused her to exhibit occasional ill will toward the organization. In late 1946, ASCAP was
working on publication of a biographical dictionary of its members. Perhaps Ronell was fed
up with them by this time, but for whatever reason, she requested that she not be included
in the volume. For a young songwriter, this seemed like a poor career choice. Though they
may not have shown it in their classification of her, the staff at ASCAP seems to have had a
true appreciation for Ronell. When ASCAP general manager John G. Paine heard about this,
he wrote her a most sympathetic letter:

> I am wondering what has brought you to this frame of mind. I have always regarded you as
> one of our outstanding women members, and entirely apart from my warm personal regard for you,
> I have felt that you have been a great credit to the Society. To have an ASCAP book that passed you
> over would seem fantastic....
> Won't you please write me personally, telling me what this is all about?[37]

Ronell was obviously touched by Paine's concern, answering him several weeks later,
"Your personal attention to my request of not appearing in the new ASCAP biography was
indeed appreciated. I had no idea my request was important."[38] Though her tone to Paine

was friendly and conciliatory, she did not reveal a specific reason for her reluctance to be included in the dictionary, stating only that "I don't expect you to understand the state of my humility at that time, for it is impossible for me to describe."[39] She ultimately acquiesced and was included in the dictionary.

ASCAP notwithstanding, Ronell took much pride in her involvement with Kurt Weill and the film of *One Touch of Venus*. Her view of her work on the film was expressed in a letter to producer Cheryl Crawford: "Did you like the way I got the songs into the screenplay — and did you like my score. It was a very difficult job to do what with the director and Universal execs being against using any songs at all."[40]

Despite Ava Gardner, Kurt Weill's music and Ronell's new lyrics, *One Touch of Venus* did only modest business and was one of Lester Cowan's few films to not show a profit.[41]

In the early seventies, Ronell took the basic story and songs of *One Touch of Venus* and created a show entitled *A Song Out of Heaven*.* She conceived of it as a "film story," with many of the Weill and Nash songs included.[42] Though keeping the songs, she changed the story to one with more of an entanglement of Greek and Roman gods and goddesses but still keeping the human element.

A more significant departure was her idea for an all-black cast. As always, Ronell had some strong preferences. She envisioned George Kirby in one male lead as he was multi-talented, widely experienced, and did voice imitations well. The second male lead she saw for Flip Wilson. He was immensely popular at the time because of his weekly television presence on *The Flip Wilson Show*, particularly due to a well-recognized character that Wilson played in drag, Geraldine, an outspoken black woman. So popular was the character that Ronell even hoped that it could be utilized within her story. In preliminary talks with his management, however, Wilson balked at the role. He felt his appeal crossed racial lines, and he did not like the idea of an exclusively black cast.[43]

Ronell's female choices for the cast of *Song Out of Heaven* were not as definitive. For the part of Juno, she hoped she could interest her friend Leontyne Price, a black soprano at the height of her career. Ronell wanted to find a "black Ava Gardner" for Venus and dub the singing voice in that role, as in the movie. Apparently, some Motown investors were interested in the idea, but Ronell and Cowan, for reasons unclear, were reluctant to use the singer Motown management wanted, Diana Ross. Ross had enjoyed widespread popularity on the pop charts in the late sixties with The Supremes and had also been successful as a solo act.

In addition to her two songs from the movie, Ronell also wished to use several of the original Broadway songs including "Speak Low," "That's Him," "The Trouble with Women," and "I'm a Stranger Here Myself." Beyond this, in true Ronell form, she lifted melodies from the classics and added her lyrics. The title melody, "Song Out of Heaven," was from Chopin, and a later song, "The Yearning Waltz," was a Schubert theme. As Lester Cowan explained to an interested producer-investor, in March of 1973:

> ... It was wise and clever of Ann to do this, because the melodies are classic and the music will have added distinction by a combination of Weill, Chopin, and Schubert.[44]

There was a great deal of talk and preliminary negotiations in 1973. NBC even considered financing the movie with a view toward later television rights. Nothing came of all this, and *A Song Out of Heaven* was never heard.

She originally wanted to entitle this new production The Tinted Venus. *This had been the title of the book upon which the musical had been based, written many years before by F. Anstey, a British author.*

14

Love Happy and the
Marx Brothers: 1948–1950

"Since he never talks, I let the music speak for him."

Scoring a movie is difficult enough without having the Marx Brothers complicate matters, but in the last movie the brothers made as a team, *Love Happy*, that is what faced Ann Ronell. Opening in late 1949, it was produced by Lester Cowan for United Artists in conjunction with Artists Alliance, Inc. The musical director was Paul Smith with Harry Geller doing the orchestrations and Steve Previn the musical editing. Cowan chose Ann Ronell to do the score and songs. Though he was the producer with the final say, he did have to do some talking to get Ronell okayed by writer Ben Hecht. Shortly before work on *Love Happy* began, Cowan wrote to Hecht:

> As you know, she wrote and handled the scores on both *G.I. Joe* and *Tomorrow, the World!*, and I think you will be very much impressed by the way she approaches and plans a score. Her basic advantage is being in on the picture from the very outset so that everyone is made aware of music as an integral part.[1]

During that period, there were no other women composing scores for Hollywood films. Regarding this, Ronell exclaimed, "And there aren't any others [women]. Nobody followed me."[2] A journalist at the time added: "Miss Ronell has no idea why she is the 'only' woman involved in such special work, but, one is informed, she's delighted to be standing alone."[3]

Ronell's challenge was to compose music for a fast-paced Marx Brothers comedy yet provide musical accompaniment to Harpo's "silent" scenes. She had said in an interview during her work on *The Story of G.I. Joe* that the talents of a film composer included "a dramatic ear, a split-second time sense, and a gift for improvisation."[4] But besides the usual problems of film music was that of dealing with the Marxes, who had a well-known tendency to go off-script. Ronell admitted: "It was the kind of Providence which takes care of sparrows and little children which also took care of my timing for the Marx Brothers."[5]

The intricacies of writing such a score were detailed in the March-April, 1950, issue of *Film Music Notes*. Most important was the music written for Harpo. Rather than drown the silence, Ronell sought to underscore his movements. As she explained:

> Since he never talks, I let the music speak for him. He does whistle, however, which peculiar fact gave me the idea of having him announce his own musical theme himself. Thus it is that Harpo's music in the score is his language; his gestures become rhythms, his movements mirror accent, his

Left to right: **Paul Smith (conductor), Ronell (score composer), Harry Geller (orchestrator), and Steve Previn (music editor), the music team working on the score for *Love Happy*.**

pantomimed thoughts find voice through the inflection of instruments, whose musical colors bespeak in turn Harpo's spirited style.[6]

More specifically, Ronell assigned a leitmotif to Harpo and used it in various presentations. A leitmotif is a recurrent melodic phrase associated with a specific character or recurrent situation. The term originated with the operas of Richard Wagner, but is now used more generally.[7] The recurrence of tuba notes representing the shark's presence in the *Jaws* movies might be considered a leitmotif in popular cinema. As explained in the *Film Music Notes* article by Harry Geller, the movie's orchestrator:

> For the main theme of the score, Harpo's, as central character of the story, she has written a motif which indeed contains the soul of wit in its brevity. Heard first in the score as Harpo's whistle, the theme is continued throughout the picture as such. First stated instrumentally by piccolo in the noise of the street where Harpo is discovered eyeing groceries, this theme is repeated in variation by the actor in live whistle when he spies a cop watching him, and is thereupon taken up by the orchestra when the music cue begins.[8]

This theme Ronell used repeatedly and with great versatility throughout the movie, underscoring the speechless Harpo. As musical conductor Paul Smith concluded, "The first time I heard Harpo's theme sung over the phone to me, I was impressed with its providing a fine basis for comedy character."[9] Ronell featured Harpo's theme throughout the film, but also wrote individual themes for Chico, Groucho, Rita (Ilona Massey), and a character called The Whammy.

Besides the melodic coordination with characters and action, Ronell also took pains to time the rhythms with the action. Because few movies had the fast-paced action of *Love Happy*, a simple stopwatch could be used for the timing of their scores. Ronell explained, "The stopwatch method which I'd employed before for timing music and action of other pictures now failed to capture the split seconds of zany mania in which I spun."[10] To better synchronize the activity and music, conductor Smith utilized the clicktrack method of scoring, a more precise technique. As he explained it:

> Defining the clicktrack, almost all normal actions, mechanical or physical, are for music-comedy purposes reducible to a rhythm which is translatable in terms of music. This in itself is not the prime purpose of music for a comedy picture, but if the music can assert itself within the set pulse as music and still point action, it is successful. The flow of the music is of prime importance.
> Technically discussing the clicktrack, themes call for their own tempo within a margin of any one out of ten and clicks must first be selected to fit. A metronomic beat of 129 could be handled at 105 to 135 but beyond this margin the theme is distorted unduly, due to lack of proper tempo, so taste and judgment alone are involved as to choice of beat.[11]

While employed to facilitate the composing process, the clicktrack method could be restrictive to both melody and rhythm. Ronell told an interviewer in her hometown of Omaha, "You write by the second or by the foot or, in many cases by the frame. That's called the

"Mickey Mouse technique," a reference to a cartoon music technique employed by Disney Studios.[12] But it eventually worked out for her, and conductor Smith felt she adapted well: "In spite of the limitations of the strict clicktrack, Miss Ronell achieved great musical variety by seeking points of repose, these accomplished by means of sustained chords, diminution and augmentation."[13]

Several reviews of the movie commented on the music. Harry MacArthur, in the *Evening Star* in Washington, D.C., declared, "The comedy of all three [Marx Brothers], incidentally, is heightened by a fanciful musical score contrived by Ann Ronell, one of the most imaginative decorations of a comedy sound track in some time."[14] Ronell corroborated this view of her work to a 1950 interviewer, when asked to sum up writing for the

Ronell at piano with Chico Marx during the scoring of *Love Happy* (United Artists).

Dance rehearsal on the set of *Love Happy. Left to right:* Billy Daniels (choreographer), unidentified assistant, Marie Bryant (cast member), Vera-Ellen (star), Ronell (score composer), unidentified male (United Artists).

movies: "Music is really a subconscious narrator. It should not detract from the drama but appeal to the subconscious, heighten suspense, and accentuate a break in mood."[15]

Ronell had begun work on the songs in the fall of 1948. She sent "first draft lyrics" for the title song to the promotional firm for the movie's advertising campaign. Anticipating many changes, she asked it not be labeled as a lyric to be performed in the movie or printed on sheet music copies.[16] This first draft lyric bears little resemblance to the final set. Within ten days of the above letter and lyric, Ronell had written another set which she much preferred, expressing this to Lester Cowan in October of 1948:

> After you called last night I thought I would write some different lines for *Love Happy*, in case you preferred them, as I do, to the first draft.... I have written a verse preceding this refrain and have sung the song to several strangers to see how they liked the lyrics. On all accounts the reaction has been most gratifying as they say the lyrics are not the usual stuff now being heard. I realize the latter half of the song took a nose dive and hope to revise it with you when you return.[17]

Lyricists go through extensive changes of their words and often abandon songs altogether. *Love Happy* needed a title song, and while it could not be dropped entirely from the film, Ronell changed the lyric drastically. A comparison of the initial and final lyrics shows just how much:

First draft	*Final lyric*
Tonight the sky is star happy	Love Happy, I'm Love Happy,
The moon is shining like new	It's wonderful to know
I'm so in love I guess that	The meaning of "happy"
I'm Love Happy	And if I do
And all because of you.	'Tsall because of you.
The trees and breeze are song happy	Heart happy, I'm kiss happy,
With melodies that thrill thru	Who ever would believe
And every dove is cooing	That I'd be this happy,
She's love happy	Why are skies blue?
Because you love me too.	'Tsall because of you.
My heart's in a haze	Oh my darling, my daisy
Lost in a daze	I may be crazy but haven't you found
But keeps repeating that phrase	That we're doing what we like
I love you like crazy.	And gee whiz we feel like
	Kids on a merry-go-round!
When you smile I'm dream happy	Tonight happy and day happy,
With a Seventh-heavenly view	I see a future where
Just name the day and darling,	I'm gonna stay happy
I'll stay happy	And I know why
Love, Love happy with you.[18]	All my dreams come true,
	'Cause you're Love Happy too.[19]

Orchestrator Harry Geller had high praise for Ronell's title song, feeling it an important contribution to the picture:

> What kind of a song fits into this kind of a score is a consideration too often underestimated. Vitality of detail stimulated arrangements of this theme from dance settings ... to statement for merry-go-round in the park scene, and the vocal renditions by Marion Hutton and The Mello-Larks, which marks the start and finish of the movie.[20]

"Love Happy" as sung by Hutton and The Mello-Larks was up tempo. Beyond the movie, the song was recorded in 1949 by Doris Day and Buddy Clark for Columbia Records. With this Columbia recording by Day and Clark, Lester Cowan, his promotional executive Barney Rossen from Artists Alliance, Inc., Lester Sacks of Jewel Music Corporation, and Mannie Sachs of Columbia Records began a campaign for the song and its tie-in with the movie. As Cowan expressed to Mannie Sachs of Columbia Records, "The Columbia recording by Doris Day and Buddy Clark of our title song *Love Happy* assures us of a top rendition by top stars. To further the sale of this record, we are prepared to put back of it an intensive and well-integrated campaign in ... 31 key cities...."[21] Typical of music and movie promotional campaigns of the day, the synergistic components of the two media would include disc jockeys, juke boxes, radio play, interviews, and promotional tie-ins. With openings scheduled for the next year in several cities, hopes were high for both *Love Happy* and its title song.

As for promotional tie-ins, product placement was well-practiced in Hollywood even then. Bulova watch, Wheaties, and Mobilgas each had prominent placement in the film, and the three companies were involved in advertising costs in the film totaling $300,000. Ronell was writing some of the commercial lyrics for Wheaties through their advertising shop, Knox-Reeves Advertising Company. Her proposed lyrics for the cereal ads, sticking closely to the meter of "Love Happy," included:

> Love Happy, I'm Love Happy
> It's Wonderful to Know the Meaning of Happy
> Eat Wheaties— Eat Wheaties

> Love Happy, I'm Love Happy
> It's Eating Wheaties Daily Makes Me Love Happy
> or
> It's Wheaties, Wheaties, Wheaties Keeps Me Love Happy[22]

It is unclear whether any of these words were ever used in Wheaties commercials.

Despite her foray into the world of advertising, Ronell was focused on developing "Love Happy" into a popular song. Ronell liked the Day and Clark version and encouraged the duet concept done by them. In a letter of July 15, 1949, to Lester Sacks of Jewel Music Co., the song's publisher, she gave instructions to that end:

> If word DUET is marked alongside 2nd chorus lyrics, on sheet copy, use the designations (He) (She) (Both) as marked — for novelty....
> Please work with the Modernaires to get a happy, gay rendition, using the 2nd chorus lyrics as well — especially if another singer records with them (as Doris Day did before). You can get an unusual rendition, somewhat like a duet by give and take between boys and girls with special lyrics.[23]

In a letter ten days later to singer Hal Dickinson of the Modernaires, Ronell was even more specific:

> Special lyrics have been written for the second chorus in duet fashion, and it was my intention to your using them between the boys and Miss Kelly somewhere in your arrangement....
> The recording from the sound track of the film is being sent to you today from this office so that you can hear how Marion Hutton and The Mello-Larks present the vocal in the picture.[24]

The Modernaires recording is still available on the Sony Music compact disc "The Complete Modernaires with Paula Kelly on Columbia, Volume 4 (1949–1950)."[25] The arrangement is brisk, and both choruses are used, with a duet arrangement featuring Paula Kelly. Ronell was pleased with the Modernaires' rendition and as usual, was optimistic about the song's success. She sent orchestrations to several of the day's well-known bands and song copies to singers including Martha Tilton, Eileen Wilson, Frank Sinatra, Dinah Shore, Margaret Whiting, Dick Haymes, and David Street. The Modernaires version was well-liked, and Lester Sacks thought it would be a great boost to the exploitation campaign. However, in early fall of 1949 the campaign began to falter. In a detailed letter to Ronell in mid–September, he explained what had been done so far but more importantly, what had not been done:

> Cooperation between the producer's office, record company and publisher lack coordination as there is no one that has the authority to carry out any of the contemplated plans or suggestions you made at the time that you were in New York. Many meetings were held on what was to be done by the producer but nothing has been done.[26]

Specifically, Sacks felt that availability of records to disc jockeys and the attendant promotion with them was out of synch with the upcoming opening of the movie. To Sacks, the record executive, the radio promotions had to precede the movie, and he felt "we have missed the boat." He then summarized, "So far I have put forth a great deal of effort in the promotion of the song and my staff is hard at work, working on the song but I am very much disappointed in what has been done by the producer."[27]

Love Happy opened October 10, 1949, in San Francisco, then across the nation to good reviews. Besides the title song, Ronell also wrote a light number done by Marion Hutton, "Who Stole the Jam?," on which Harold Spina and Walter Bullock were also credited. Her classic, "Willow Weep for Me," was incorporated into a dance sequence entitled "Sadie Thompson Number," danced by Vera-Ellen and the chorus.[28]

Though Ronell's music was favorably mentioned in reviews,[29] the promotional campaign for "Love Happy," the song, continued to be a struggle. Again Lester Sacks sent a letter to

Ronell detailing the gaps in the promotion and the failure of the producer and his staff. In a letter to Ronell in late October, Sacks's criticism of Cowan intensifies: "All these things were done with the hope of making the song a profitable hit and I fully feel, had Lester Cowan kept even one of his promises a better showing might have been made, as we had created a desire by the disc jockeys to play the song."[30] So harsh is the letter that one wonders if Sacks knew Ronell and Cowan were married.

As the campaign progressed, Ronell put more emphasis on Marion Hutton's MGM recording and urged that it be made available to disc jockeys. But often, when Ronell would make a guest visit to a radio show, no recording had been made available to the station. For this reason, she always carried her own copy of the song which the disc jockey would play. As she expressed to Jesse Kaye of MGM Records as late as December 21, 1949:

> Since there was no MGM recording available in town I played my own copy whenever possible. Many of the disc jockeys asked me to send them Marion Hutton's recording which they promised faithfully to play.
>
> Incidentally, one of the largest music stores in New York, G. Schirmer, 3 East 43rd St., had requests for the MGM recording of "Love Happy" during October and November but these orders have remained unfulfilled as of this time.[31]

Delays and missed deadlines plagued Ronell's solo promotional tour for the song well into 1950. From the several letters of Ronell and others, there appears to have been almost a group effort against her and her song. In May, she sought to acquire full rights to "Love Happy" from Jewel Music, Inc. She wrote to her attorney, Peter Pryor, "I believe you will have no real difficulty in obtaining the material for me since Sam Wigler of Jewel very definitely indicated to me about two months ago that his firm would be willing to return the song, since they have been unable to fulfill their obligations under the contract."[32]

By June, though initial interest in the movie had passed and she had not as yet acquired full rights to the song, Ronell's promotional tour picked up and was successful in Chicago and Minneapolis. She met with disk jockeys and radio personalities, getting numerous radio plays of "Love Happy" and several other of her songs. Her multi-city tour extended from the fall of 1949 into the summer of 1950, and from all accounts, she was an excellent and pleasant interview. As one follow-up letter exclaimed: "Has anyone ever told you that you should be in radio??!"[33]

15

Main Street to Broadway and *Tin Pan Alley Girl*: 1951–1953

"A very strong case could be made that Tin Pan Alley
is far too rough a place for a girl. Very few have succeeded."

Taking on problematic jobs was something Ann Ronell never avoided. Over the years, she agreed to tasks others rejected or *would* have had there been an offer: voice coaching stars who might have a talent for acting or dancing but not necessarily singing; writing songs for an ill-fated Vincent Youmans musical; adding lyrics to Disney's "Who's Afraid of the Big Bad Wolf?" to make it marketable; writing songs for a musical by a group of college students that actually made it to Broadway; trying to convince the music community in America that opera in English was a viable form of art; "saving" Kurt Weill's music, first in *Blockade* and later in *One Touch of Venus*. After all these, writing a score and songs for a group of Hollywood stars while Rodgers and Hammerstein looked over her shoulder was just another day at the office.

In 1951, Lester Cowan began production on a movie titled *Main Street to Broadway*. It was done in collaboration with the Council of the Living Theatre (CLT) and Cinema Productions, Inc. (CPI). The CLT was based in New York, and its membership included major Broadway producers and theatre managements. Cinema Productions was an association of motion picture exhibitors.

At the time, though Broadway was doing well, there was much concern by New York management that touring shows had not been successful. In turn, theatergoers across the country felt that not enough Broadway productions were touring. To remedy these problems, the CLT was formed, as playwright Robert E. Sherwood, its first president, explained, to "bring more people to the theatre and more theatre to the people."[1] More specifically, CLT intended "to stimulate interest in the theatre on a national subscription basis." According to composer Arthur Schwartz, president of the CLT at the time of *Main Street to Broadway*, "The cities are deeply desirous of flesh-and-blood shows, and they embraced our proposal that 'you supply the audiences and we'll supply the plays.' Committees were organized, with civic and social leaders as chairmen, and in some of the cities as many as five hundred local men and women did the actual recruitment of subscribers."[2]

To raise both awareness of and money for the CLT and its mission, Lester Cowan had the idea of a movie love story within the world of the theatre.[3] The exhibitor members of CPI would promote the film, and CLT would provide some of its best talents, both acting and production. In return, CLT would net a percentage of the profits.

A collaboration of theatre producers and movie exhibitors seemed incongruous at the time, as they were competing for the same audience. However, both groups hoped to benefit. Arthur Schwartz explained, "It is curious how alike are the woes of the people of the theatre and motion pictures. Once nominal rivals, we now face similar perils to our prosperity alike, harassed by the new forms of competition that have invaded the night hours once sacred to us."[4] These sentiments were better detailed by John Beaufort of the *Christian Science Monitor*:

> ... *Main Street to Broadway* reflects Mr. Cowan's conviction that motion pictures and the theater are much closer than the leaders of either industry realize. Both depend upon paid admissions, as compared to television, whose entertainments are free. Both must concentrate increasingly on quality, leaving to television the "B-picture" type of mediocrity which once was part of stage fare but which in turn was taken over by the movies.[5]

Cowan enlisted Ronell to compose and direct the movie's music. Leo Arnaud was to do orchestrations and conduct and assemble the orchestra, and Steve Previn, who had worked with Cowan and Ronell on *Love Happy*, was to oversee the scoring sessions and act as music editor. Ronell was also to compose a song for the love story and to coordinate the music scenes with the various stars within the picture.

Financing of the production began in 1951. Much of the financing was based on the potential value of the numerous Hollywood and Broadway stars who were to be in the film, mostly in cameo roles. More bankable was the participation of Richard Rodgers and Oscar Hammerstein II, at the height of their popularity. As he explained to an executive at Bankers Trust in June of 1952, "...Hammerstein-Rodgers' participation alone is worth $100,000, and the 8–10 stars another $250,000, so that the $275,000 value is considerably below market value. (Irving Berlin, for example, just made a deal with Fox for the title song of *No Business Like Show Business*, a feature picture, and got $250,000 for it.)"[6]

To secure his loans, Cowan had to convince Bankers Trust of his ability to produce profitable films. In another letter to Bankers Trust a month later, he wrote:

> Of these nine productions, seven were profitable. Only one, *One Touch of Venus*, will show a loss. All of these films, with the exception of *Love Happy*, were produced within or substantially under budget. *Love Happy* exceeded the budget by $85,000, and represents the single instance when I had to draw upon completion monies to finish a film.[7]

Although financing had not been secured, filming had started in late May of 1952 and continued through August. The story was written by Robert E. Sherwood, the first of many contributions from the Council of the Living Theatre members. Samuel Raphaelson, with whom Ronell had worked on *The King with the Umbrella* in 1938, wrote the screenplay, and Tay Garnett directed.

The screenplay had a boy-girl plot but also had a story within a story, allowing the actors, dancers, and other creative talents within the CLT to participate. New York theatre critics were also to become involved. Some of the celebrities were to be used within this story, while others were to be filmed coming to its "premiere." The male lead was taken by Herb Shriner, and the ingénue role by Mary Murphy.

The star of the inner story was Mary Martin, who came in from London to shoot her scenes and had a ten-day window in her schedule to complete the film and song recordings. Ronell had done specialty material for her over the years, and though the two were friends, the demands of the shooting schedule allowed little time to renew acquaintances. Ronell lamented in an article in *Film Music*:

> Glamour, be gone. I had to locate and work with her accompanist and arranger on the vocal, choral and orchestral settings of the routine, to get the music copied and written in her keys, check with

Mr. Rodgers for last minute changes, obtain personnel for the recording session, and prepare all other cues possible to get recorded at the same session.[8]

Later that year, Martin wrote a note to Ronell and Cowan, postmarked London, grateful for their time with them:

> We both adored being there with you, even for so brief a time — and send the warmest best wishes for the success of your picture — and for your happiness —
>
> Love, Mary[9]

The film was well into production by the middle of 1952, and Ronell was in the thick of things. As she wrote to close friend Eleanor Lattimore in early 1953, "The picture is so complicated, with so many stars, so many scenes, so many prima donnas, so many moods, lines, changes of costume, set, lights, ad infinitum.... But maybe it will turn out. We've had not a moment of rest in between."[10]

During her exploitation tour for the movie, a Toronto interviewer expanded on the complexities of Ronell's role:

> It was a difficult picture to make because these busy people are difficult to get together when you want them.... She worked from a script of the movie, but often had to write themes for parts of the film not yet completed. Then, after the scenes had been shot, she had to go back to her music and edit it to fit it perfectly to the film.[11]

Richard Rodgers and Oscar Hammerstein II wrote a song, "There's Music in You," to be done by Mary Martin. The script also called for brief appearances by the two songwriters; despite their lack of acting experience, Cowan felt the scenes with them were important to the film's success, especially the one involving their song, having pitched them as bankable in his financing efforts. Ronell wrote to Cowan's Hollywood secretary Natalie Boardman on August of 1952:

> I'm working with Rodgers & Hammerstein (when I can get them) on the song for the film and on their appearance in screen action, so needed the notes for a conference yesterday. The song is lovely and will be recorded on tape t'mw with a singer who will interpret the song according to Rodgers' coaching.[12]

Although the song scene with Rodgers, Hammerstein and Martin, done mostly ad lib due to technical problems,[13] was included in the final cut, the song itself never caught on, even with a Mary Martin performance.[14]

Ronell's main song in the film, "Just a Girl," was done by Herb Shriner in a casual scene with accompaniment by Perry Botkin, who had played ukulele for Bing Crosby. The song, true to movie songs of the day, had a verse and a chorus, each 16 bars long. The first line of the verse set the scene. Then as a nice change of pace, as the chorus ends, Ronell adds a refrain, notating it as a "Chanty." The lyric is forgettable, but the opening bars of the verse are hummable.[15] Ronell also wrote a "Theme from *Main Street to Broadway*," subtitled "Blue New York," written in a "Slow blues tempo."[16] Though as quickly forgotten as "Just a Girl," it deserved more attention.

Ronell undertook an extensive publicity tour, referred to in those days as exploitation, when the movie opened. It began in Canada in May of 1953, including Toronto, Stratford, Ottawa, and London, Ontario, and ended in August in Detroit. The radio interviews and shows allowed her to play not only the *Main Street to Broadway* music, but also highlighted her individual songs, which she often sang and played. Newspaper articles featured her and her music in addition to the movie publicity.[17]

At that time, piano sheet music still sold well and was important in disseminating the

Top: Filming of the "Just a Girl" sequence from the 1953 MGM movie *Main Street to Broadway. Left to right:* Perry Botkin, Mary Murphy and Herb Shriner (stars), Ronell (composer), Dolores Rubin (script girl), Elaine Shriner (wife of Herb), Tay Garnett (director) (MGM Studios). *Bottom:* Ronell on the set of *Main Street to Broadway* with director Tay Garnett, left, and Richard Rodgers, who appeared in the movie and wrote a song for it, "There's Music in You."

On the set of *Main Street to Broadway*, left to right: Ronell (composer), Ethel Barrymore, who appeared in the movie as herself, Mrs. Tay Garnett (wife of director), Lester Cowan (producer).

music of a production, whether a movie or a Broadway show. As she asked one of her promoters regarding this matter, in a letter of July 21, 1953:

> I do hope you will ask the leading music stores to display copies of the songs in their windows the week our picture opens so that we get advertising through this medium.... We have had wonderful tie-ups in the past with records and music displays where the covers are effective advertising for a picture....[18]

Ronell worked hard for the movie in Canada and continued the same in the States. At the end of her Canadian tour, Arthur Manson of MGM of Canada wrote her in thanks and referred to her as a "good trouper."[19] Despite all the star cameos, the movie did poorly at the box office. Reviews were tepid.[20] The *New York Times* critic, while acknowledging the "very best of intentions" of all involved, used adjectives that included "dull," "awful," and "faintly vulgar."[21]

Despite the demands of *Main Street to Broadway* or for that matter whatever project she was focused on at any given time, Ronell always had others on the back burner. She may not have been the master of any genre, but her diverse interests and education in music and literature made her a jack-of-all-trades, always willing to take on something new. Her myriad friends and professional contacts and the correspondence that accompanied them show a woman who, if not engaged in a specific work, was interested in starting another or in helping out on those of others. Her ideas-to-be-pursued files were large and included the following: radio shows, screenplays, musicals, a line of simple, minstrelsy-like instruments, oral

Ronell at MGM during the scoring and editing of *Main Street to Broadway* (1953) with her best friend.

histories of Tin Pan Alley songwriters, contributions to the Save-the-Cable-Car movement in San Francisco including a song, and more operas in English.

As further evidence of her eclectic interests, she wrote a song, "The River," based on the folk themes from an Indian movie of the same name. How she became involved is unclear. The movie was released in 1951 by United Artists, produced by Kenneth McEldowney and directed by Jean Renoir with the original title in French, *La Fleuve.* It told the story of a teenage English girl growing up in colonial India against the backdrop of the sacred Hooghly River.[22] Although Ronell did not write the score of *The River*, she made a study of Indian music and wrote a feature article in *Film Music* about the film's score. In the article, co-written with music scholar Alva Coil Denison, she discussed the quarter-tone scale used by Indian and other Eastern musicians, as well as their adherence to ragas, the fixed melodic patterns of Hindu music.[23] With this background knowledge of Indian music, she approached the song.

"The River" was written in Western fashion with the usual twelve tone scale and notation. Both the verse and chorus have sixteen measures with the verse marked "Freely." The chorus, though marked "Slowly," was also notated by Ronell with "Raga-jala rhythm bass throughout." This rhythm was modified somewhat from a Hindu rhythm and featured a run of sixteenth notes as the fourth beat of each measure.[24]

The lyric of the verse is directed to a quizzical child and is then followed by a philosophical refrain, focusing on the relentlessness of life and the river. The second refrain then ends with a twenty-four-bar tag which continues the philosophical tone.[25]

Soon after the song was published, Ronell wrote a letter, dated March 6, 1952, to the Consul General of India in New York, Arthur S. Lall. She expressed her gratitude to him and expressed her feelings regarding the entire project:

> I cannot quite explain what this whole experience of writing and publishing the song has meant to me. It was more than just meeting a challenge in musical techniques and composing a song blended of eastern and western characteristics well enough liked to be published as an American popular song.[26]

In corroboration of Ronell's feelings regarding "The River" and Indian life and music, Lall responded shortly after, adding to his words of thanks:

> May I add that I thought you had really experienced something of the impact of Indian life which you have put down so beautifully in the music and words for the song. I do hope it becomes a great success.[27]

Also of note in her March 6 letter to Lall was a paragraph mentioning her "Who's Afraid of the Big Bad Wolf?": "Perhaps this song of India will cross national boundaries in the same way as another one of my songs 'Who's Afraid of the Big Bad Wolf?' which was written during equally strenuous times."[28] "The Big Bad Wolf" had been written in 1934, and years later, the song became a metaphor for the Axis enemies. In 1952, the publication year of "The River," the United States was still fully engaged in the Korean War, her current reference to "strenuous times."

As with so many of Ronell's songs and projects, she had to go to great lengths to get "The River" more widely published and recorded. Letters to publishers and record companies reveal that she had tried to get Frankie Laine to record it, as he apparently had a penchant for off-beat songs. In a letter to Milton Krasne at General Artists Corporation in May of 1952, she explained:

> The song is very unusual, based as it is on Hindu folk music, and will present a novelty to a singer who is constantly looking for "different" numbers. Since Frankie is the song-writer's dream, you are besieged with songs for him, I know, and I would not send anything but an unusual song to him.[29]

Mitch Miller, executive at Columbia Records, took an initial interest in the song, but nothing came of it. At the time, Miller was working with several big names in the jazz and pop fields, and his endorsement of a song could mean nearly instant success. As Ronell put it in a letter to Walter Lowenthal of Transfilm Incorporated: "I believe Mitch Miller was sent the material and that it all might still be resting on his desk — which, I understand, has been practically static since his trip to California. Don't ask who told me, but she has a slightly German accent — very glamorous."[30]

Surprisingly, there were even problems getting "The River" published in India. Apparently, there was reluctance on the part of the producer, Kenneth McEldowney. Beyond this, translation of the lyric into Hindustani and transcription of the music into Indian music script were problematic.[31]

Eventually "The River" was recorded by Carl Ravazza, for United Artists Corporation, being done as a non-commercial demonstration. There was limited air play of the recording in several East Coast cities as well as some sheet music sales of the song. In Springfield, Massachusetts, "The River" was used as the "Mystery Tune" on a local radio show.[32]

On the flip side of the Ravazza recording, Ronell wrote a dance tempo format, the "Raga-Jala," to further exploit the song's "pop possibilities."[33] As she noted in a letter at that time, Goddard Lieberson of Columbia Records strongly believed "The River" to be a "pop song."[34] At the time, Lieberson, known for his "amazing ear," had begun his successful string of original cast recordings of Broadway shows and would become head of Columbia Records in 1955.[35]

Ronell wanted her article in *Film Music* to be used more to promote the song. She was particularly annoyed with Gustave Schirmer at G. Schirmer for his lack of interest, detailing to him, in a letter of April 3, 1952, what she and her associates had been doing to promote the song and chastising him for his firm's lack of effort:

> Let me say at this point that you have not taken advantage of the magazine tie-up and it looks as if all my work on this as far as Schirmer is concerned meant little. I am deeply disappointed. We could have made all the music magazines all over the world with proper promotion under your supervision.[36]

Despite Schirmer's tepid interest, other artists or their record companies were impressed with "The River." Artie Shaw had wanted to record it but never did. Martin Gabler and Morton Palitz at Decca Records were to show it to both arranger Gordon Jenkins and the folk group The Weavers, but again, to no avail.[37] Ronell also worked hard with folk singers Hillel and Aviva, on both the presentation and arrangement. They were to audition for Mitch Miller in hopes of doing a commercial recording, but nothing came of it.[38] Although the song was published in America, England, France, and Italy, no commercial recording of it was made. Opera singers Jan Peerce and Brenda Lewis included the song in their solo concerts and recitals, but beyond that, "The River" flowed no further for Ronell.

During her work on "The River" and *Main Street to Broadway*, she was also tinkering with an autobiographical story entitled *Tin Pan Alley Girl*. At the beginning of her career, Ann Ronell was, if anything, a Tin Pan Alley Girl. She had tried to write a song a day and had hawked these songs in dozens of music publishing offices, finally breaking into that world with her first hit, "Baby's Birthday Party." To support herself during these efforts in Manhattan, she had been a rehearsal pianist, voice coach, model for adolescent clothing and other jobs necessary to pay her rent. She had friends and associates throughout the songwriting world in New York, Tin Pan Alley artists themselves, with varied levels of success. It was these early struggles of a single girl in Manhattan that Ronell and Lester Cowan wanted to capture.

Their original idea, beginning in 1952, was to produce a television series, then a feature film, both biographical. Cowan discussed these two possibilities with both MCA, Ronell's agents regarding television, and the William Morris Agency, a multi-versed entertainment firm Cowan had consulted on several matters over the years. Serious discussions were also had with Louis de Rochemont Associates, a company which had done biographical movies. All parties agreed that the television series could be sold. Cowan enlisted the services of veteran writer Sam Dann and later a director, Bill Colleran, who was then directing *Your Hit Parade.*[39]

Early outlines show that the television series was to feature Ann's travails not only in New York as a single girl but also in the mostly male world of song publishing. The series was set mostly in Greenwich Village, where the heroine rented an apartment, and in Tin Pan Alley and the theatre, where she worked. Notes on the production at the time explained the conflicts of the plot: "Tin Pan Alley is a rough world, moral scruples are perhaps lower than in any other form of show business.... A very strong case could be made that Tin Pan Alley is far too rough a place for a girl. Very few have succeeded. Ann is the only one who has succeeded as both composer and lyricist."[40]

Each week, the story was also to focus on one or more of her songs going from composing to selling to publication. Early episodes were to feature her songs "Baby's Birthday Party," "Candy Parade," "Rain on the Roof," and "Willow Weep for Me." With each of these songs, there was a story to be told of its writing and eventual acceptance. These stories dovetailed well with the rest of her life as a *Tin Pan Alley Girl,* the title of the series. Numerous characters from the theater and music world were to be part of the story lines. In typical Ronell fashion, she drew up a list of over 150 celebrities-artists who might fit into one story or another.[41]

To highlight these song publication efforts, writer Sam Dann created a publisher with whom Ronell worked and did battle. This publisher was a composite of the characters she had encountered in Tin Pan Alley getting her songs accepted. Proposed scenes included vignettes such as Ronell getting into Saul Bornstein's office to sell "Willow Weep for Me" and her riding in a car with Florenz Ziegfeld and star Marilyn Miller, for whom Ronell was serving as voice coach. In her notes for the series, she detailed an experience with Miller and Ziegfeld:

> He always took great care that the fur robe was placed over Miss Miller's beautiful gams and that an orchid was blooming in the bud vase attached to the side window.[42]

Ronell's character, named Mary Powell in outlines, was discussed with Polly Bergen, Jeannie Carson, and Giséle MacKenzie.[43] All three were interested in playing the Ronell character, but nothing came of the series. Perhaps Lester Cowan's unfamiliarity with the new medium of television was a hindrance, or perhaps the stories were too old-fashioned. This was early television and while dramas were aired, audiences clamored for comedy. There was plenty of it, some of it classic, including *I Love Lucy, The Milton Berle Show* and *Your Show of Shows* with Sid Caesar and Imogene Coca. For whatever the reason, early audiences of the small screen never heard the stories of the *Tin Pan Alley Girl.*

16

The Eisenhower Years
and Political Songs: 1953–1960

*"I think it is you who have paid too big a price.... [T]here is a
sad waste of talent in the helter-skelter of our national campaign."*

In 1953, playwright Arthur Miller and producer Jed Harris hired Ann Ronell to write incidental music for Miller's play, *The Crucible*. Set in seventeenth-century Salem, Massachusetts, a community of Puritans, *The Crucible* dealt with a hysteria that enveloped the small town, focusing on choices available to the townspeople and one man's reliance on the truth, ultimately leading to his death. Miller's play not only focused on the historical and moral issues of this incident, but it was also felt to be an attack on the fear-mongering and anti–Communist environment that surrounded the McCarthy and House Un-American Activities committees of the era.[1]

Among the music Ronell wrote was a short lullaby to which she added lyrics, entitling it "Sleep, My Babe, My Darling." Publishing company Samuel French included Ronell's music in its publication of the play for amateur production. Her original manuscript still exists, with all its changes and erasures, mostly in the lyric.[2] The music is marked "Gently" and is written in thirty-two bars for three voices, not in chorus, but consecutively.

There was also a Ronell arrangement for two sopranos with a counter melody to be sung against the lead voice for the latter part of the song.[3] She felt the added depth and color of additional voices would be effective, telling the producer Kermit Bloomgarden:

> Having worked in theater and film material, I know that additional color is often required in performance which at first seems adequate enough solo; so in case additional voices are needed for your atmospheric mood at the time of the play wherein the lullaby is cued, you will have the music ready.[4]

"Sleep, My Babe, My Darling" was eventually sung solo and *a cappella* by Beatrice Straight as Elizabeth Proctor. Straight, a dramatic actress, had been coached and rehearsed by Ronell for the production.[5] Though only a short, incidental song within the drama, the music was effective. Jean Dalrymple, a friend of both Ronell and producer Jed Harris, wrote to her, "Jed is back in town after a couple of weeks on his boat in Florida. He did a magnificent job on *The Crucible* and you should come just to hear how touchingly your music is used."[6]

No audio or video recordings of the original production of *The Crucible* are extant. Snippets of "Lullaby" can be heard on the 1967 television version of the play which starred George C. Scott and Colleen Dewhurst.[7] As Elizabeth Proctor, Dewhurst sings quietly to her baby in the cradle, just prior to a scene with Scott as John Proctor. No mention was made of Ronell or the music in the end credits.

As her work on *The Crucible* was ending, Ronell was involved with a John Wayne western, *Hondo*. The composer and musical arranger was Hugo Friedhofer, and Ronell assisted on several aspects of the music. Friedhofer, born in San Francisco in 1902, started working in films in 1929, first as an arranger, including collaborations with Max Steiner and Erich Wolfgang Korngold. He eventually became a composer-arranger, doing his best work in *The Best Years of Our Lives* (1946), *The Bishop's Wife* (1947), and *The Young Lions* (1958).[8] He continued to work through 1971.

The main theme from *Hondo* was arranged into 30-bar song, "Hondo! Hondo!," with Ronell writing the lyric.[9] The production company, Warner Brothers, and their producers, were indifferent to the song and did little to encourage its publication or to promote it.[10] Ronell wanted a photo of John Wayne for the cover of the sheet music, which she had hoped to get published by the time *Hondo* was released at Thanksgiving time of 1953. Foot-dragging by the producers made this impossible, and even though Ronell relied on simple art work for the cover, the sheet music did not come out until nearly 1954, missing the tie-in with the opening of *Hondo*.[11]

Continuing into 1955 with more movie songs, Ronell wrote the theme for a Swedish nature documentary, *The Great Adventure*. The film's score was written by a Swedish composer, but the production company, Louis de Rochemont Associates, asked her to write a theme attractive to American audiences. Her song, by the same title, was inspired by a baby fox, one of the "stars" of the movie. The opening lyric for the chorus is a call for a new day, to anyone young, especially the fox.[12]

Peter Lind Hayes and Mary Healy used the song in their act in Las Vegas and Los Angeles.[13] Healy had had a supporting role in Ronell's musical, *Count Me In*, in 1942. Hayes was a frequent guest on Arthur Godfrey's CBS radio show and sang "The Great Adventure" on that nationally broadcast program. Hayes, who had started in vaudeville, had some success in television with *The Peter Lind Hayes Show* in 1950–51 and later on with *Peter Loves Mary* in 1960–61. The song was recorded by Joe Leahy and His Orchestra in 1955 and cabaret singer Hildegarde in 1956.

Ronell's version was released by Seeco Records, and credit for the composition went to a "G. Branscomb." This eventually came to Ronell's attention in 1959, as no royalties had been received. She, in turn, employed her attorney, Edmund C. Grainger, to investigate and stir the legal pot.

What he discovered was that the recording company, Seeco, had requested mechanical (recording) rights from one of the performing rights organizations, SESAC, the Society of European Stage Authors and Composers. The request from Seeco was for rights to "The Great Adventure," but one by a different composer with a different publisher. The mechanical rights and royalties, usually a few cents per song, paid by Seeco Records to SESAC, amounted to a miniscule $26.58 from September, 1956, to March, 1959.

Nonetheless, attorney Grainger involved the publisher and licensor of the "wrong" song, as well as ASCAP and Harry Fox, a mechanical licensing agency. A small flurry of letters cleared up what appeared to be a legitimate error.[14] SESAC refunded the $26.58 to the recording company. Ronell received legal satisfaction and a few dollars in royalties.

In the mid-fifties, never able to sit still, Ronell continued with various projects. During 1955–56, she attempted to revive a work she had written — plot and songs — in 1937 entitled *The Customer Is Always Right*. She called it a "modern musical comedy" and was hoping to have it produced for television.[15] Ronell's story focused on the competition between two large department stores, Ezli's Emporium and Dooper's Department Store, and its plot complications included a romance between rival personnel, a wealthy kleptomaniac, corporate spies, and a store detective.

Ronell used two alternate titles in her notes on the work, *Love on Time* and *Very-Very Too-Too*. Her retail-oriented songs included "Song of the Skirt," "Be Very Saks–Fifth Avenue," and the title number. She made numerous calls and contacts, including old friend Peter Lind Hayes, to whom she wrote, "We have a good title, a fresh, modern background and a potentially unique idea for the finish."[16] Ultimately, she and Cowan could not sell it.

Because of no significant movie work and the failure of *The Customer Is Always Right*, Ronell had a lull in her career and projects. Always interested in politics and a lifelong liberal, she turned her efforts to a political campaign. In 1956, the Democratic Party faced an uphill battle in the presidential campaign. Their candidate for the Oval Office, Adlai E. Stevenson, was running on their ticket with Senator Estes Kefauver from Tennessee as vice-president. But Stevenson had already lost to President Dwight Eisenhower in 1952 and was finding him difficult to unseat in a prosperous postwar economy.[17]

One hope of the Democratic Party was to attack the vice-president, Richard M. Nixon. Eisenhower had suffered a heart attack in 1955 and had other health issues. He was considered to be a part-time president, more often seen on the golf course than in the Oval Office. Because of Eisenhower's health, Nixon becoming president was considered a real possibility.

Prior to becoming vice-president, Nixon had been U.S. Senator from California. In his campaign for the United States House of Representatives in 1946 and the Senate in 1950, Nixon had portrayed his opponents as communist and socialist. During the latter run, his Democratic opponent labeled him "Tricky Dick," a name that would haunt him during the Watergate scandal in 1973–74 which forced him out of the White House.[18]

Beyond these earlier campaign practices, there had been an incident during the 1952 presidential campaign when Nixon was accused of maintaining a political slush fund for personal use. To clear his name, he gave his famous "Checkers" speech explaining the matter, saying that he would rather resign his post than be forced to return the family cocker spaniel, Checkers, that his daughters loved and that he had received as a gift. With all this "baggage," Nixon was considered to be a liability by many Republicans. Moreover, Harold Stassen, an advisor to Eisenhower on armaments, was appealing to the more liberal Republicans to replace Nixon with Governor Christian Herter of Massachusetts.[19] Despite all this, Eisenhower believed in Nixon and retained him as a running mate.

Ronell had written a campaign song in 1942 for Massachusetts Governor Leverett Saltonstall and, still a staunch Democrat, she turned her talents to a song for the Democratic party entitled "Too Big a Price." Written in a calypso rhythm, it focused not on Eisenhower but rather on Nixon.[20] Finishing it in early summer of 1956, Ronell promoted it to the Stevenson for President Committee, the Democratic National Committee, and the advertising agency involved with the campaign, Norman, Craig and Kummel. Ronell had pitched them the idea of using the song prominently at the opening of the convention, then changing the lyric daily during the Chicago convention as issues and personalities developed through the week.

She conceived the idea of herself as a "song reporter," explaining this to advertising agency executive Walter Craig in a letter of August 3, 1956:

> Ann Ronell goes to Convention in role of special commentator in song, daily new lyrics would be written which could be performed as part of interviews with noted commentators like Ed Murrow, John Daly.... The climactic performance [of the song] would be the 17th, the night of the big show, and [the lyrics] would consist of the platform and campaign issues as developed by the Convention.[21]

A week later, she was selling the idea to the Stevenson for President Committee: "The number is perfect for use in the campaign as a jingle, and I am hopeful that the theme can be used during the Convention as there are many times when a little jingle with a repetitive refrain comes in handy to emphasize the name of your candidate."[22]

In further promotion of the song, Ronell had the Mello-Larks record it with four different sets of lyrics including a special set for the farmers. But by late August of 1956, Ronell was still trying to get through the party bureaucracy and obtain an okay for use of the song at the convention, then only a few weeks away. As she explained to Paul Ziffren of the Stevenson for President Committee, "Everyone is most enthusiastic on hearing my jingle but there seems to be a lack of coordination between committees, and I'm beginning to take the title of my song personally."[23] By this time, with the convention finished, she was hoping to have "Too Big a Price" used anywhere in the campaign, locally or nationally. It was heard at rallies and cities on the East Coast. "Too Big a Price" was sung several times by jazz singer Thelma Carpenter, accompanied by Ronell. Carpenter had sung with the Count Basie and Teddy Wilson bands and later became famous for appearances in *The Wiz* and as Dolly Levi in the all-black cast of *Hello, Dolly!*, replacing Pearl Bailey.[24]

It was clear that Ronell was pushing her song a bit too hard to a Democratic party with bigger worries than what to do with a little campaign ditty. Lyricist Alan Jay Lerner was a member of the Rockland County Stevenson for President Committee and had organized several Democratic rallies,[25] and in a note to him in mid–October, she conveyed her urgency to get the song more widely used in a campaign running out of gas:

> My number [is] being performed tonight by Thelma Carpenter at Woodmere, Long Island, in conjunction with talks by Kefauver, Lehmann, Cahagan. Don't you think it worthwhile someone from your committee cover and report audience reaction, particularly effect of participation by colored singer.[26]

The song was never played much and received no air play, and as in 1952, Stevenson was roundly defeated by Eisenhower. Though acknowledging its scattered distribution, Ronell summarized the "Too Big a Price" project in a letter to a friend in 1960: "I am sorry to say the idea was neglected by those of the political regime I was able to contact."[27]

In that same year, she sent the candidate a copy of the song as a memento for him, as he was nearing retirement from political life. Always better with the written word than as a public speaker, Stevenson dropped Ronell a kind note: "I think it is you who have paid too big a price.... I am afraid there is a sad waste of talent in the helter-skelter of our national campaign."[28]

17

Walt Disney and Who's the Real Big Bad Wolf? 1954–1958

*"She created a song which had a form, a beginning, an end,
she told a story; not the parts spoken by the pigs, but wove the
whole story into a composition which was new and original."*

The trouble began with *The Toast of the Town* show on CBS television in January of 1954. Hosted by Ed Sullivan, a syndicated gossip columnist with the *New York Daily News*,[1] *The Toast of the Town* was a one-hour variety show featuring singers, dancers, circus acts, and Broadway excerpts. It first aired in June of 1948, conceived as a "vaudeville hour," and Sullivan was perfect as the emcee as during his varied career in show business he had been "most successful as a master of ceremonies in vaudeville."[2]

The show was renamed *The Ed Sullivan Show* in 1955 and was a top-rated program through the mid-sixties. As an example, the new musical *Camelot* had opened in December of 1960 and was having problems at the box office. Sullivan had occasionally devoted a part of a show to a composer or lyricist, and as a boost to the musical, he decided to present the music of composers Alan Jay Lerner and Frederick Loewe featuring their new songs from *Camelot*. What follows gives an idea of the show's influence:

> Burton, Andrews, and Goulet did twenty minutes of *Camelot*'s high points on Sullivan's show which was immensely influential at that period....
> The next morning Lerner got a call from the manager of the Majestic, telling him he'd better get down there and take a look. When Lerner arrived, he viewed a line stretching halfway down the block.... The show was a hit.[3]

Though top acts were usually scheduled, and there was always something to interest children, the Sunday show's success was due in large part to its emcee, Sullivan himself:

> His deadpan face, monotone voice, and stiff mannerisms made him an easy subject for comedians, many of whom mimicked him on his own program. His clumsiness and low-key demeanor baffled critics who tried to analyze his popularity, some saying that the audience must have felt sorry for him and others saying his sincerity made people like him. Whatever the reason for his popularity, millions of viewers tuned in every Sunday night.[4]

It was to a large Sunday night audience that Sullivan paid tribute to America's most-respected and best-loved producer and cartoonist, Walt Disney. By 1954, Disney was a household name. He had been making animated films since 1922 and had early commercial success with his Disney Brothers Studio in the late twenties with their *Oswald the Lucky Rabbit* series which included the merchandising of chocolate bars of the same name. Always a technical innovator, Disney won his first Academy Award in 1932 with *Flowers and Trees*, a cartoon done in the then new three-color Technicolor process.[5] His studio achieved phenomenal success with the long-running Mickey Mouse series which began in 1928 with *Steamboat Willie*, flourished during the thirties, and did not end until 1995 with *Runaway Brain*, the 120th cartoon in the series.[6] His annual income in the mid-thirties was estimated at $400,000.[7]

Disney Studios began doing feature-length cartoons with *Snow White and the Seven Dwarfs* in 1937, followed by *Pinocchio* and *Fantasia* (1940), *Dumbo* (1941), and *Bambi* (1942).[8] Leading up to his appearance on *The Toast of the Town* in 1954, Disney had continued to capture young audiences with adventure films like *Treasure Island* in 1950 and *Robin Hood* in 1952, and a nature film a year later, *The Living Desert*.[9] Disney was closely identified with his films, was well-liked by the public and worked hard on a relaxed, avuncular image. Paying tribute to Walt Disney was a sure-fire draw for Sullivan's show.

At the start of the program, Sullivan began to discuss with Disney how he had decided to make *Three Little Pigs* and the song that eventually was associated with it, "Who's Afraid of the Big Bad Wolf?"[10] Disney's response to his host was a humble "disclaimer":

> Well, Ed, when you say me, I think it's as good a time as any to explain something. When you see Walt Disney over a picture, it doesn't only mean me, but it means a lot of other guys too — teamwork. Yes sir. So, with the help of some of those boys that were there with me at the time, I would like to reenact that first story meeting on *Three Little Pigs*.[11]

This cued the start of a taped sketch of Disney and four of his writers creating *Three Little Pigs* and some of its music and lyrics. The only musician at the original session in 1934 was composer and pianist Frank Churchill, who had died by 1954, and whose role in the kinescope was played by writer Frank Thomas. Script excerpts of that kinescope tell the story of the cartoon's song[12]:

> ED PENNER: That's right, we need a change of pace. Ya know, something simple, just three or four characters.
>
> WALT DISNEY: Well, how about the one we've always wanted to do, and never got around to, The Three Little Pigs?
>
> TED SEARS: Well, offhand, I don't get much out of those pigs.
>
> DISNEY: Well, ya got somethin' simple, four characters, three pigs and a wolf.... And it's a good story. It's timely, and not only that it's timeless.... They won't be ordinary pigs, we'll do something; give them personality....
>
> PENNER: Hey, how about getting a tune in this one too. Ya know, something to express the theme....
> (Group moves to piano)
>
> DISNEY: Let's see, ya want a pig with a fiddle, maybe the other one with a flute.
>
> FRANK THOMAS: Yeah, that's good.
>
> SEARS: We'd better get a lyric writer in on this.
>
> DISNEY: Oh, no, let's keep it simple.
>
> THOMAS: Okay, what's your first line?
>
> DISNEY: Well, ya know, the brother's always worrying about the wolf, so it would be, "Who's afraid of the wolf," or somethin.'
>
> WARD KIMBALL: How about, "Who's afraid of the big old wolf?"
>
> THOMAS: No, it would be "big bad wolf." Now, what comes next?
>
> KIMBALL: What rhymes with wolf?
>
> PENNER: Well, what's wrong with wolf?
>
> KIMBALL: Yeah, let's repeat it.
>
> DISNEY: Big, bad wolf.

THOMAS: Hey, this is going to work. Let's try it.

DISNEY: Okay, you start.

PENNER: Who's afraid of the big bad wolf?

SEARS: Big bad wolf.

DISNEY: Big bad wolf.

KIMBALL: Who's afraid of the big bad wolf?

DISNEY: Hit it.

   ...Dissolve to closeup of pictures being put on [story] board ... and cartoon sequence, Three Little Pigs.

At this point in the show, Sullivan talked about Walt Disney's "integrity":

   [H]e was the one who suggested that he reassemble those original members of his staff who wrote that song just the way it's described there. Just the way it was acted out.... The only one that was missing was the original piano player and composer, you heard them refer to him as Frank, and actually that represented Frank Churchill.... He wrote "Who's Afraid of the Big Bad Wolf?" He wrote "Heigh Ho." He wrote "Some Day My Prince Will Come."[13]

This kinescope was shown again on February 16, 1955, on American Broadcasting Company's *Disneyland*, a Disney television production with a wide audience. Though Ronell saw neither of these showings, she was apprised of them by friends and colleagues. The first showing had angered her, especially because of the large audience that watched *The Toast of the Town*, but the second showing on a similarly popular program put her over the edge, and she and Lester Cowan decided to bring suit.

The original suit was filed April 11, 1955 — *Ann Ronell vs. Walt Disney Productions and Walt Disney* — in a United States District Court in New York by the law firm of Butler, Jablow & Weisman. The Original Complaint stated that the defendants had shown their kinescope of the making of the song, "willfully and purposely attributing the composition of said song to other than the plaintiff and neglected and refused to give credit for the composition of this song to the plaintiff...," adding that they had "intended to and did convey the following meaning: that someone other than the plaintiff had written the musical composition 'Who's Afraid of the Big Bad Wolf?'"[14] In less formal language, the complaint claimed defendants did "palm off the work of the plaintiff as that of their own."[15] Though initially $350,000 was sought, the eventual total of damages asked for was $90,000. This was comprised of the following claims:

- $25,000 loss of composition work and income from sale of rights to story of her life;
- $15,000 from loss of reputation and credibility;
- $25,000 damages for failure to give credit on song and subsequent loss of work;
- $15,000 due to pain and mental anguish;
- $10,000 due to damage to reputation for any future employment opportunities.

Ronell's deposition was taken five months later, and she gave a much different interpretation of the creation of the song than Disney and his men had. As she described it to defendants' attorney George Leisure, she had seen the ten-minute cartoon short *Three Little Pigs* at the RKO Theatre on Broadway, found it charming, and felt that its music and themes would conform well to a popular song. She contacted George Joy, the general manager at Irving Berlin Music, Inc., which had published many of her songs, including "Baby's Birthday Party" and "Willow Weep for Me." Joy's response to her suggestion was given in several of Ronell's answers early in the deposition:

   He didn't believe that a song could be popular from a cartoon. Most songs of that period were from [Broadway] musical comedies, and there had been no songs which had issued as popular material from the cartoon industry ... he laughed. He said that no songs came out of cartoons. They weren't taken very seriously, as far as music goes, and that he doubted it.[16]

Being Ronell, she convinced Joy to get the musical manuscript from Disney Studios so that she could fashion a popular song out of all the music. A few weeks later, Ronell received a two-inch thick score from the music of the cartoon.

As with so much in litigation, even this part of the story was disputed, though not by Disney, but rather by George Joy himself. A 1934 letter from Joy to Sol Bourne, one of the owners of Irving Berlin Music, contained Joy's recollections of the song's creation:

> I do definitely remember that we all decided it [*Three Little Pigs* music] would have to be altered and lengthened because it was no good as a popular song in its original form. I thought of Ann Ronell to do the job because we had a pretty big hit of hers right about then in "Willow Weep for Me," which I had taken from her about a year back.... She was a bit puzzled as to how it could be done and Johnny Burke, who was under contract to the firm at the time, offered, as a friendly gesture, to help her with it, though he did not want payment or credit for anything he contributed to it. He worked with Ann on it, though what part was his and what part was hers, I do not know.[17]

Johnny Burke was a little-known lyricist at the time under contract to Irving Berlin Music and the same age as Ronell, with his biggest hit up to that time being "Annie Doesn't Live Here Anymore." He would later pen numerous hits for the movies including "Polka Dots and Moonbeams," "Swinging on a Star," and "Like Someone in Love," working most successfully with composer Jimmy Van Heusen.[18] Burke was an amiable guy and probably would have given Ronell help, though with her experience and education, it is difficult to believe that she "was a bit puzzled as to how it could be done," as Joy had suggested. Moreover, at the time, Ronell and Burke were working on a theme song for the movie *Palooka*,[19] and it seems far more likely that whatever contact the two had with Joy and Irving Berlin Music was more related to their song "Palooka (It's a Grand Old American Name)." Whatever the situation was, Burke received no credit on any part of the song and probably worked little if any on it, especially since the problems with it were more musical than lyrical.

What became the central issue in the *Ann Ronell v. Disney* case was "the song," and who wrote it — Disney and his men or Ann Ronell. In the kinescope, what Disney portrayed was the inception of the cartoon *Three Little Pigs* and the seed of its song and music. When the cartoon premiered, the song "Who's Afraid of the Big Bad Wolf?" did not exist as a commercial, published song, but the lyric line "Who's afraid of the big bad wolf?" did, and it had been created by the Disney staff.

What Ronell and Joy planned was a popular song, drawn from the musical themes and lyrics of the cartoon. Up through 1934, though Disney Studios' personnel were greatly successful in cartoons, they paid little attention to the development of their music into commercial songs and up to that time had no songs, much less hits, associated with their cartoons. To cartoonists, music was something incidental used to accompany action of their characters. It took Ronell with "Mickey Mouse and Minnie's in Town" and "In a Silly Symphony" to educate them on the importance of a salable song related to the cartoons. Even with some awakening, Disney was still willing to turn over sheet music rights for Mickey Mouse and the *Silly Symphonies* to Irving Berlin Music, Inc.,[20] a deal fashioned by Berlin's partner Sol Bourne, which was extended to most of Disney Studios' music until the early fifties.

Unlike Disney's musicians, Ronell was accustomed to popular songs — recognizing, creating, and polishing them. There was a diamond in the rough in the words and music of *Three Little Pigs*, especially their lyric, "Who's afraid of the big bad wolf?," and she was confident she could fashion a hit song out of all of it. In the cartoon, four characters — three pigs and the wolf — sang bits and pieces to portray their feelings, but there was never one cohesive song that could be sung by one person. It was this problem that faced Ronell. When the defendants' attorney suggested that she had merely done a "rearrangement," she answered decisively, "A song form is a creation, and it is not a rearrangement of themes. I first of all felt that a song that would be popular would have to be pretty strong physically; that is, have a very strong form in which a singer could present a musical composition to the public, and it wasn't a question of rearranging themes. I first had to decide what my format was going to be."[21]

After she had been deposed by the defense, her own attorney, Richard Jablow, posed a few questions to clarify this matter of song development:

> JABLOW: In your opinion as a composer, would it be possible or plausible for the soundtrack to be sung by any one individual?
>
> RONELL: No
>
> JABLOW: Why?
>
> RONELL: Because the soundtrack was related to the characters and their involvement in the dramatic action of the cartoon, in which each spoke or sang according to the dictates of the action.
>
> JABLOW: In other words, it would require more than one person to sing the soundtrack?
>
> RONELL: Yes.[22]

Her contention throughout all phases of the legal action was that she had created a commercial song out of the musical fragments of the cartoon. Lester Cowan felt similarly, and in a letter early in the case to her attorney, John Schulman, put Ann's efforts into perspective vis-à-vis Disney's musical personnel: "If Disney or any member of his staff had the talent or imagination to see a popular song in the cartoon, they would have said so or done something about it. As the deposition indicates, it was all Ann's idea and her accomplishment.... In the very next film, *The Grasshopper and the Ant*, the form which Ann had created for "The Big Bad Wolf" was copied for the song "The Grasshopper and the Ant," but the writers being amateurs, they were unable to match Ann's talent and ingenuity."[23]

In a pre-trial letter three years later, Cowan was more specific regarding Disney and his musicians: "Disney could have asked Churchill to write the song instead of Ronell, but Churchill had never written a published song."[24] In an ironic twist, it was Ronell who sponsored Churchill's membership into ASCAP on the strength of one song, "Who's Afraid of the Big Bad Wolf?." Only a few years earlier, Ronell had needed more songs and more time to be accepted into the same society, a fact which stuck in her craw through the years of the dispute with Disney.

During her deposition, Ronell faced several questions regarding whether she had truly added to the compositions from *Three Little Pigs* to create "Who's Afraid of the Big Bad Wolf?" or had she merely latched on to a nearly finished piece and taken credit for it. John Schulman stated Ronell's claim as composer in his Opening Statement in the trial, which commenced on December 1, 1958:

> Now, the background music in the cartoon is not a song; it can neither be sung as a song, nor can it be published as a song; it isn't a song in the accepted sense which can be popular either from the viewpoint of performance or the viewpoint of sales of copies of records....
>
> She created a song which had a form, a beginning, an end, she told a story; not the parts spoken by the pigs, but wove the whole story into a composition which was new and original.[25]

Disney's attorney, George Leisure, in his Opening Statement countered:

> There was music in this cartoon, and it was much more than background music; it had lyrics. You could come out of the theatre whistling it, you could come out of the theatre singing the lyrics. The repeating refrain, "Who's afraid of the big bad wolf?" was repeated fourteen times in an eight-minute cartoon.[26]

In her deposition three years earlier in response to several questions from Mr. Leisure, she had held fast to her position that while she had used themes from the cartoon, the song was her creation:

> The whole format is mine. I composed the form of the song, which entails X amount of bars from a reel and a half of film music. Naturally in the doing of such I composed the relation of the themes used in my song according to my selection of these themes from that music, which is quite considerable....[27]
>
> There are various bars that have been created solely by myself. However, the whole composition in its entirety — in form — constitutes one hundred bars, which I put together, shall we say — and I mean "put together" in the musical sense, which is to juxtapose the various selections that are used for the score, harmonically and continuously, to create an entity — no less — a song.... I put together the whole form out of a possible ten minutes of music from the ... *Three Little Pigs*.... I don't think there is one phrase in it that appears in the same juxtaposition as it appears in the cartoon.[28]

To corroborate the opinions of Ronell and Schulman, well-known musicologist-historian Dr. Sigmund Spaeth was called as an expert witness. Spaeth had accomplished much in music as an author, lyricist, and radio broadcaster as the "Tune Detective." He had worked with Rudolph Friml and several other composers but was best known for his book, *A History of Popular Music in America*.[29] Prompted by several questions from her attorney, Richard Jablow, Spaeth was definitive about Ronell's accomplishments in creating the song:

> In the song, however, the larger part of the music, by far the greatest part, is a completely new lyric which tells the story of the picture, and which has actually two verses which can be preceded and followed by the little refrain, and those sections which represent nine-tenths, certainly at least three-quarters of the song as a whole are entirely Ann Ronell's work as far as words are concerned, and also represent her work in the creation of a — well, of a song in standard form, the sort of song that could be published.... [M]y frank opinion and my honest and sincere opinion is that this is definitely an original creation by Ann Ronell.[30]

When George Leisure, in a question to Spaeth, contended that the core of the song — the lyric "Who's afraid of the big bad wolf?" — was of the essence and that the published version added little to the song and its popularity, Spaeth countered, "I know of no case in which a song of a motion picture became popular without the help of a published version. In fact, it has always been the published version that has popularized a song, even when it stood out in a picture, even when it has been sung as a complete theme song, a title song. Even in those cases I would deny the song could become really popular without a published version."[31]

Years later, in a related case involving copyright renewal of "Big Bad Wolf," expert witness musicologist Harold Barlow made a similar contention regarding creative contribution to the song: "[O]f the four hundred and some-odd measures of *Three Little Pigs,* four melodies were taken and made use of to formulate 'Who's Afraid of the Big Bad Wolf?' In so doing, these melodies were now placed in a different order, with one of the melodies now being transposed to another key for a better relationship to create a format so that it could then be presented in the form of a popular song."[32]

The contention of the defense on this point was that Ronell's work on the song did not take place until several months after the release of *Three Little Pigs*. During those months, because of the popularity of *Three Little Pigs*, the song became popular without published sheet music and without her contributions. In a Post-trial Memorandum, the defense held, "It is apparent that during the intervening four months from the time the cartoon was released in May, 1933, the music in the cartoon became widely known as 'Who's Afraid of the Big Bad Wolf?' and was extremely popular before plaintiff had anything to do with it. In view of the repeating refrain in the cartoon, the song in the cartoon could not be known by any other title."[33]

Disney biographer Neil Gabler stressed that in the early months of release, the effect on the public of the cartoon and its song went far beyond that of mere popular music: "The film had been open only a short time when the song began sweeping the nation — not just a musical phenomenon but a cultural one that played incessantly.... A few observers even credited it not just with reflecting the Depression but with helping vanquish it.... Whatever the cartoon's impact on sagging morale, 'Who's Afraid of the Big Bad Wolf?' indisputably became the nation's new anthem, its cheerful whoop hurled in the face of hard times."[34]

During Ronell's testimony, Leisure continued to press the point that the song became popular well before Ronell's contributions, citing comments from reviews that had been printed in national papers during the summer of 1933, months before Ronell's involvement with it:

> The heading is "Popular Tunes: 'Who's Afraid of the Big Bad Wolf?,' the theme song of the production, already has assumed a familiarity of a national anthem. Citizens sing it to traffic cops and tax collectors. Its buoyant melody lilts through political proclamations."
> Now let me read to you a clipping from the *Detroit News* dated June 15, 1933: "The handling of the idea, the execution of the cartoon work and the tinkling of the theme song 'Who's Afraid of the Big Bad Wolf?' combined to make this a number that will delight all."[35]

Plaintiff's attorneys disagreed with Leisure, of course, believing that "Big Bad Wolf" was not a song until their client got ahold of it. They used a closely related argument regarding the practice of using themes from film music to create a popular song. To make their point, they focused on several commercial hits which had evolved from the themes of popular movies. Testimony from Dr. Spaeth and comments from producer Cowan supported this. In his comments under questioning, historian Spaeth discussed three well-known hits which had evolved from the musical themes of their movies — "Laura," "Song from *Moulin Rouge*," and "Around the World in Eighty Days."[36] In these cases, popular song composers — David Raksin, Georges Auric, and Victor Young, respectively — used movie themes to create popular songs.

Cowan had explained to Schulman that the proper reference on sheet music for the composers of the popular songs was to reference on the title sheet that the song was "based on themes from the score of," citing that done on "Around the World in Eighty Days." Cowan stressed, "In other words, instead of crediting Churchill as co-author, Ann could very well have credited the song to herself, as based on themes from Walt Disney's *Three Little Pigs*."[37]

When the original sheet music was published, the "based on themes from the score of" phrase was not used, but the song was credited to co-composers: "Words and music by Frank E. Churchill and Ann Ronell." This was the decision of Irving Berlin Music, Inc., the publishers, and Disney Studios' people had little to do with it, as they had turned the sheet music matters over to Sol Bourne at Irving Berlin Music. The initial publication of the music went smoothly until Churchill read the sheet music credits and was quite angry about the wording. Prior to this, none of Disney's musical personnel had ever been credited with any of the music and lyrics in the cartoons, such as they were. Churchill thought the time had come.

Walt Disney then became displeased with Ronell as he had a small uprising among his staff of musicians who, until *Three Little Pigs*, had been conforming to the ways of Disney. In his 1955 deposition which was read into the trial record, Disney emphasized what a problem the misplaced credits had caused:

> Well, it wasn't a conversation [with Churchill]; it was damn near a calamity.... I can't remember the incident in any detail, but it was a very unpleasant thing. Churchill was terrifically disturbed, and we were never consulted by Berlin or Bourne when the music was put out. In fact, I never — I didn't know about it until after it was out. I just can't recall the thing but Churchill was very disturbed.[38]

The rest of the Disney staff supported Frank Churchill and resented that an outsider, no less a woman, got equal credit for something they felt they had created.

For her part, Ronell was proud of the fact that she had been instrumental in getting acknowledgment for her work in the form of credits on the song, and as later evolved from this "Big Bad Wolf" controversy, she had played a role in Disney's acknowledging credit to his employees for various work on the cartoon and music. In an interview years later, she explained, "[W]hen 'The Big Bad Wolf' caught on and I was announced as the author, the other people connected with the Disney pictures asked for and received recognition."[39]

The whole issue went deeper than Ronell's obtaining credit on the song. Disney had always been reluctant to credit his people individually, thinking that writing, cartooning, music composition, etc., were all part of a collaborative, creative process at the studio. But with the credit assignment on the sheet music of "Who's Afraid of the Big Bad Wolf?," the lid was off. Lester Cowan knew well the inside workings of Hollywood and was especially aware of credits and compensation for the creative personnel behind the scenes, having represented various artists and technicians in their early collective bargaining agreements and having organized the arbitration framework for studio employees while working at the Academy of Motion Picture Arts and Sciences.[40]

As an insider, Cowan was also aware of Walt Disney's reluctance in the whole area of credits, as they meant royalties—more expenses. In a letter to attorney Schulman two days prior to Disney's deposition, Cowan stressed:

> I am sure you will question Disney about his personal contact with Ann and about his preoccupation and the trouble caused him at the studio. Apparently there was a strike and thereafter Disney had to give credit on the screen to his writers and technicians.
> ... [I]t is important that Disney be asked to express himself on the question of the importance of credit to writers. Certainly one of the fundamental purposes of the Writers Guild and code is to see that the writer receives fair credit. Hollywood credits are perhaps the most important factor in building a writer's earning power.[41]

Cowan's reference to "personal contact" between Ronell and Disney was directed at her visit to Disney Studios soon after "Big Bad Wolf" was published. Ronell, during the second day of her testimony, remembered that in their meeting at the studios in California, she had asked Disney why he had not used her song "In a Silly Symphony," which was to be the overall theme song for his *Silly Symphonies* cartoon series. He told her that her credit as co-composer on "Big Bad Wolf" "caused me a lot of trouble here."[42] She remembered that she then asked Disney "Why?," to which he answered:

> It is a credit situation. All the writers here now want credit; up to this time no one had had their name on the screen as having written or drawn or had any part of Walt Disney cartoons. By your having a success as an outsider of the studio with a song that came from the studio, the writers now all want their names on the material which they are writing, and I am having a terrible time.[43]

The meeting became so hostile that when Ronell asked to meet Frank Churchill, Disney refused and said "he didn't want anyone to meet me."[44]

After Disney protested the wording of the credits, Sol Bourne published a new edition of the sheet music which specified the composer as Frank E. Churchill with "additional lyrics by Ann Ronell." Bourne, after all, wanted to keep Disney happy as he was now going to be publishing music from the Disney cartoons and anticipated a long, mutually profitable contract with the Disney Studios. Bourne explained to Ronell's attorney, Loyd Wright, in a 1934 letter: "The original credit line, however, was objected to by Mr. Disney, and as we had acquired the song from him and all of our rights ... we had no choice other than to change the credit line ... as directed by Mr. Disney."[45] Beyond this, Bourne was planning for Ronell to continue writing material for Disney as he recognized her talent and felt a continued association would be good for all involved.

Roy Disney, Walt's brother and partner, appears to have been the voice of reason during the years of litigation, having both Ronell and Cowan's trust and respect. In testimony he made years later in a litigation involving copyright renewal rights for "Big Bad Wolf," Roy's testimony summed up the view of the organization in the first years of the controversy:

> Ann Ronell's additions were just that, some additional lyrics to adjust it so it was in sheet music form suitable for sale, as was the custom of the day.... [T]he boys fight pretty hard for their credits. Churchill and Walt Disney were not intending to give anybody a part of the copyright just for a few additional lyrics, and that was the controversy. This is how it was settled, by the phrase "additional lyrics by Ann Ronell."[46]

Sol Bourne's letter to Loyd Wright had been prompted by the problems Ronell was causing because of the changes in the credit line and because of the royalties which she was to be paid. In representing Ronell, Loyd Wright had accused Bourne and his company of compromising Ronell's royalties and credit on the song to improve his position with the Disney company:

> It is our information that you sacrificed the usual production royalty in order to accomplish the successful contractual relations with Disney covering other items in which and with which Miss Ronell is not interested.
> Obviously this works to the disadvantage of Miss Ronell, and she is entitled to compensation on the usual basis.[47]

She had dug in her heels and did not want the wording of the credits changed. Even though they were changed, Bourne had managed to maintain Ronell's percentage of the royalties — 25 percent — though she had originally understood them to be 33⅓ percent. She apparently gave the management at Irving Berlin Music a hard time, as a month after Bourne's letter, general manager George Joy complained to Ronell's older brother, attorney Sol Rosenblatt, "I have gone out of my way to help Ann — and her name on the song has helped her in so many ways, including the American Society [ASCAP] and her prestige in general — and she received 25 percent of the royalties after the song was written and released in the picture. It seems that instead of appreciation, I am receiving very unfair treatment. It was an effort to get Disney to agree to the 25 percent for Ann."[48]

As the months of 1934 passed, Ronell relented and at the encouragement of the Berlin management, began cashing her royalty checks, thereby assenting to the royalty agreement and the credit lines, though she wrote no further songs for the Disney organization. However, the ultimate arrangement preserved her status as one of the composers of a song which had truly swept a nation recovering from a long Depression. Authorship of such a song was a feather in the cap of a young composer. As the years went by, everyone in the business thought of her as the creator of "Who's Afraid of the Big Bad Wolf?" That is, until the *Talk of the Town* broadcast in 1954 with Ed Sullivan and Walt Disney.

As detailed above, Disney and his staff played out a skit describing the creation of the cartoon *Three Little Pigs* and some of its music, including the phrase, "Who's Afraid of the Big Bad Wolf?," prompting Ronell to file suit for damages. As stated in the Plaintiff's Trial Memorandum-Preliminary Statement of December 1, 1958, just as the trial was beginning, "If the first telecast [*Toast of the Town*] produced suspicions ... as to the plaintiff's representation of ownership, the second telecast [*Disneyland*] certainly confirmed these suspicions and created a grave cloud on the plaintiff's credibility, as well as her professional reputation. Thereafter, this suit was commenced."[49]

This same Trial Memorandum, in the opening paragraphs, stated what the offense to the plaintiff had been:

> They [defendants] depicted the circumstances under which the said musical composition was composed, and were calculated to convey, and did convey, in the listening and viewing audiences that said song was composed by Walt Disney himself, or in conjunction with some of his employees, none of whom was the plaintiff herein. As a result, Miss Ronell's undisputed authorship of said song has been seriously questioned and her professional reputation and earning capacity seriously impaired.[50]

The same memorandum went on to suggest that more than just an oversight, in depicting Ann Ronell as a co-author of "Big Bad Wolf," "The defendants' activities in denying credit ... are the culmination of their long-running intentional campaign to remove Miss Ronell from credits on her song."[51]

One oddity of the case was that Ronell had never seen the kinescope as it was shown, either originally on *Toast of the Town* or any of the showings on the *Disneyland* series. Thus, when friends and associates called her about the airings, she was all the more shocked. As she explained in her deposition under questioning from George Leisure: "People in the profession who told me about it [*Toast of the Town*], knowing that I was co-author on the song and was not mentioned when the song was talked about, called it to my attention."[52] But it wasn't just the mention of it that was offensive to Ronell, it was the repeated questions from people she would meet: "Did you write it? Didn't you write it? What did you do? How did it happen?"[53]

Ronell's most embarrassing moment regarding the authorship of the song came at a party she attended with The Mello-Larks, a group interested in one of her songs at the time. The incident, related during her deposition, seems apocryphal but was told under oath:

> [A]t a party to which they took me, they introduced me as the writer of "Big Bad Wolf," where there were many people congregated, among them was a six-year-old girl, and in front of everyone she turned to me and said, "No, you are not the writer." Everyone turned to listen to this conversation, since it aroused attention, and I said, "What do you mean, I am not?" She said, "I saw *Disneyland*, and Mr. Disney wrote the song. You didn't."[54]

More importantly, there were also financial aspects to the matter of denial of credit on her song. In the nine-page Original Complaint, Ronell's attorneys detailed that their client had been:

(1) "negotiating a number of contracts for the writing of musical compositions on the basis of the fact that she was the composer of the musical composition "Who's Afraid of the Big Bad Wolf?";

(2) "since the beginning of 1954, negotiating for the rights to produce the story of her life in motion pictures and on television";

(3) "unable to consummate the aforementioned transactions and has been damaged in the sum of $100,000"[55]

Of course, because it was a legal dispute involving many aspects of the entertainment world, *Variety* told its own version of the controversy:

Says Disney Cold Shoulder Has Hurt Her

"Life has been harder," says Ann Ronell, ever since she demanded credit from Walt Disney for writing the song "Who's Afraid of the Big Bad Wolf?".... John Schulman, songwriter's attorney, called it a "cause célèbre in the struggle for an author's credit rights.... By not crediting her with the song's authorship, Disney in effect discredited her and such projects as her film biography and television life series have suffered as a result."[56]

Cowan's version of the impact of the kinescope was even broader in scope:

> After *Main Street to Broadway*, we moved to New York in 1953.... Ann's purpose was to acti-
> vate her music publishing firm and give up movie scoring and embark on a new career as writer for
> television and as a recording artist. This new career depends on using her many contacts in the enter-
> tainment world to enable her to develop as a personality. The Disney broadcast ruined her entire
> plans....[57]

As to the first matter in the Original Complaint — the "writing of musical compositions" — Ronell was a go-getter, always on the lookout for a song to write and the possibility
of creating a hit. In late 1953, she had been working on the song "Hondo, Hondo," with movie
composer Hugo Friedhofer; she believed it was a song that a certain type of singer might be
able to forge into a modest hit. To that end, she had been in contact with several singers including Burl Ives, The Mello-Larks, Frankie Laine, and Art Lund. The reception Ronell most often
encountered while hawking the song was best addressed in two answers given during her deposition:

> [A]ttitudes tell what they are thinking of, and I found I was on the defensive during this period,
> sort of like having a black eye, and I didn't realize to what extent that could hurt me until much
> later....
> In the course of several meetings, Mrs. Ives [wife and manager of singer Burl Ives] called atten-
> tion to the fact that it was too bad I was not mentioned or alluded to in any respect in connection
> with "Who's Afraid of the Big Bad Wolf?," because credit is so important to a writer in promoting
> a new venture such as "Hondo" was for me at the time.[58]

Artists, while sympathizing with Ronell, did not want a new project to be tainted by anyone, including a composer who might be misrepresenting her authorship of a song. The Preliminary Statement concluded: "It has become almost a matter of fact that writers live by their
past reputations and their future earnings depend upon it."[59] More succinctly, when discussing
the matter of her not being mentioned in the kinescope, the consensus of the profession was
that "It was too bad."[60]

Lester Cowan, in his pre-trial letter to John Schulman, assured him that "Disney knew
that he was discrediting Ann before millions of people and as a professional he knows the
degree of damage."[61] In so far as "Hondo, Hondo" was concerned, Cowan was right. Ronell
could never get an artist to commit himself, and it was never recorded or heard outside of
the film's music track.

In the Original Complaint, "the story of her life in motion pictures and on television"
referred to the work Ronell and Cowan had been doing to sell *Tin Pan Alley Girl*. Efforts had
begun in 1952 with Cowan involving talent agents-consultants MCA and William Morris
Agency to sell the idea to movie studios or the fledgling television industry. Plot outlines and
scripts had been prepared. There was even talk that Doris Day might star.[62]

Louis de Rochemont Associates, a production company that had done biographical films,
was interested in Ronell's life as a songwriter, thinking that the "depiction of the creation of
my works ... would make excellent dramatic entertainment."[63] Despite the gradual encroach-
ment of rock 'n' roll on the music industry, the Tin Pan Alley–Hollywood songwriters were
still a commodity, and it was thought that the career of a young woman succeeding in such
a male-dominated profession would make a good story line. In the preceding ten years, there
had been several film biographies of composers[64]:

Rhapsody in Blue	George Gershwin	1945
Night and Day	Cole Porter	1946
Words and Music	Richard Rodgers and Lorenz Hart	1948

Cowan asked Schulman to press Disney about these matters:

> I think it would be in order to question Disney about the vogue in making life stories of com-
> posers.... Ann may not have written as many hits as some of these composers, but being the only
> girl who has ever written words and music for such hits ... the story is far more dramatic and inter-
> esting and can be made into an exciting musical.... By discrediting her publicly, he may have ruined
> the project....[65]

As production was nearing, the producers balked at the project with the first airing of
the Disney kinescope, then cancelled it altogether with the second broadcast on *Disneyland*.
As Ronell explained on her third day of testimony:

> Well, Mr. Mace [of deRochemont] spoke to me about the damaging effect the omission of my
> name had, on the broadcast, and then when Disney's broadcast [on *Disneyland*] went on following
> that, that was sort of the coup de grace, so far as my position being questioned was concerned, my
> veracity, my credibility, the whole works.[66]

As for the television project, the aura of Walt Disney and Disney Studios hung over that
project. Disney held much influence on producers and advertisers alike, and no one wanted
to get involved in a controversy with him, no matter how distanced it was. On her third day
of testimony, Ronell singled out Disney's effect on people in the industry: "I have found that
in explaining to everyone it is not the case of what my story is, it is a case of the weight of
power which Mr. Disney has, which effects [*sic*] the impression or the reaction people have."[67]

Cowan explained in his brief testimony in the case: "In television, it practically destroyed
the marketability of the property because of the sensitiveness of sponsors who either are
potential advertisers with Disney or who, in any event, want to avoid anything controversial."[68] To Schulman, Cowan specified the amount of loss: "For the TV series, Ann would
receive $1,500 for each of the first 39 episodes, plus 20 percent of the stock in the producing
company. For the feature film property our object was to get $100,000, payable over a ten-
year period, plus ownership of all of the musical rights, including albums."[69]

A television show and movie were the main commercial interests that were lost, according to the suit, but there was also the matter of lost revenue on jingle writing for the advertising firm of Young & Rubicam. Ronell had spoken at length with Lucy Sokole, a Young &
Rubicam representative who was familiar with Ronell's music, having written several songs
with her in the early thirties, and Sokole thought that the style of her songs, especially "Big
Bad Wolf" and "Candy Parade," showed promise for the advertising field.

There was also talk by the advertising firm of putting Ronell to work composing and
arranging for some of the shows sponsored by their clients, including a musical variety hour,
The Max Liebman Show. But then the kinescope happened, and everything fell through, or
so the suit claimed. As Ronell testified on her first day of deposition, she had discussed work
with one of the music supervisors of these Young & Rubicam shows: "He said that it was just
too bad that my credit had been neglected in the entire credits stated on the broadcast.... He
agreed that it was wise on my part not to try to contact people further, and to wait. He said
that it is the most unfortunate circumstance."[70]

Other important work Ronell felt she had missed out on was involvement in a new musical of *Peter Pan*. It started out as a production of the Los Angeles Civic Light Opera done by
Edwin Lester, with whom Ronell had had a great relationship during their work on *Gypsy
Baron* and with whom she definitely had an in. But *Peter Pan* opened in late October of 1954
with several songs by Moose Charlap and Carolyn Leigh and later ones by Jule Styne, Betty
Comden, and Adolph Green.[71] As Ronell lamented on her last day of deposition, "I referred
earlier to *Peter Pan*, and I know that the job of writing the music for that show could have
been mine if I were not in that particular state of grace which was caused by *Disneyland*....

Being considered for work depends on how 'hot' one is at the moment. If there is any blight upon one, they are not 'hot.'"[72]

Beyond listing specific missed opportunities, there was Ronell's overall reputation in the entertainment community which at any given time might provide her with employment or the chance to work on a new song. As her attorney Richard Jablow contended, "In addition to those specific names given, there would be every motion picture house, every network, every recording company, every song-publishing company, and anyone else in the entertainment field who might be interested in Miss Ronell's work who would be a potential employer."[73]

Battle lines were drawn. Ronell and her attorneys felt that she had contributed considerably to the final edition of "Who's Afraid of the Big Bad Wolf?" and in doing so, deserved proper credit for it whenever the song was discussed. Because Disney and his associates had failed to do this in the kinescope, her reputation suffered, which in turn caused her a loss of significant income on various projects. For loss of reputation and money, Ronell wanted recompense.

In their defense, Walt Disney Productions and Disney countered that the kinescope only went as far as the creation of *Three Little Pigs*, the cartoon, and that the musical and lyrical phrase "Who's afraid of the big bad wolf" came from that cartoon. Whatever Ronell added came later, and she was not involved in that first creative session in the Disney Studios, and thus the incident was rightfully portrayed in the kinescope without her. Moreover, though Ronell initially protested, she ultimately settled on the credits as rewritten and cashed the checks provided by Disney for the next twenty years. As for loss of reputation and income, defense held that no testimony was admitted into the trial from the people who might have been involved in denying Ronell work at the time or any of the personnel working on her life story, either on television or for the movies, when the productions were stalled.

The trial ended December 3, 1958, and post-trial memoranda were submitted the next day. The case was then turned over to Judge John Clancy, who submitted his decision five weeks later. Clancy noted that despite objecting to the revised credits at the time of publication, Ronell eventually collected the royalties and made no more complaints about the arrangement until 1954. The judge also found Disney's attitude toward Ronell in 1934 to be "kindly and understanding,"[74] and that on the broadcasts, the producer and his studio had "no intent to harm plaintiff."[75] Pointing out that like Disney, Ed Sullivan had not mentioned Ronell in his comments on *Toast of the Town* following the showing of the kinescope, Clancy held that the talk show host was as culpable as Disney and yet the suit did not involve Sullivan. The implication was that Ronell had had it in for Disney and his studio.

As for injury to her reputation and subsequent income, Clancy maintained that while it may have existed, no solid proof from third parties was ever introduced into trial, coming solely from "heavily interested witnesses"[76]— Ronell, Cowan, and friend Sigmund Spaeth. This part of the opinion had been foreshadowed during the trial in a brief exchange between the judge and plaintiff's attorney:

> SCHULMAN: Well, it seems to me that the effect of this broadcast upon the plaintiff is shown by the reaction of the people with whom she dealt.
>
> THE COURT: I know. But the question is, can you prove that?... I should think in a case like this you get one of the Mello-Larks here, if you can. And, if you can't, you can't prove it. Isn't that so?[77]

Clancy was not convinced of any part of plaintiff's claims, ending his nine-page decision: "The complaint is dismissed on the merits with costs."[78] Ronell and her team salvaged nothing.

18

Martha Revisited and the Metropolitan Opera: 1960–1961

"[T]he Ronell rhymes and patter ... are more original, fertile and
promising than the typical English libretti heard at the Met the last few years."

Because Ronell's movie work had dwindled after *Hondo* and *The Great Adventure,* she found herself in 1961 looking at Broadway again with a show based on a 1947 novel by Thomas B. Costain, *The Moneyman.* Costain, a Canadian, was one of the first popular historical fiction writers who was also comfortable in non-fiction, having had great success with a 1960 book about the invention of the telephone, *The Chord of Steel.* His best-known book was *The Last of the Plantagenets,* part of a series of books focusing on the English monarchy from 1145 through 1485.[1]

The title, *The Moneyman,* referred to Jacques Coeur, the moneyman (financial manager) for King Charles VII of France, and the female interest in the story was the king's mistress, Agnes Sorel.[2] Ronell was taken by the story, thought it would make a great musical, and began working on it. There are few details about the early production, and though it never seemed to go far, she did tell an interviewer in 1962 that *The Moneyman* was "a possibility for next season."[3] When this project faltered, she returned to one of her great loves, opera in English.

In 1950, Ronell had made a pitch to Earle Lewis at the Metropolitan Opera for his company to do *Martha*:

> Having read a glowing article on the American artists now starring the Met roster, I wondered if it weren't time to mention a certain operatic work "adapted for the American stage" by American lyricists, namely *Martha,* the Vicki Baum-Ann Ronell version published entirely in English by that esteemed house, G. Schirmer, Inc.
>
> Please let me call attention to our gaiety, our esprit de corps and successful youthfulness in this version....
>
> Would be *so* happy to show you the reviews, score, etc. anytime, if you believe there were any chance of projecting this property for performance.[4]

Whether or not this note prompted the Met to give *Martha* another look is open to conjecture, but if it did, it took several years to bear fruit. With advanced scheduling, numerous artists, and other considerations, the opera world moves slowly, so finally, in April of 1960, it was announced that *Martha* was on the Metropolitan Opera schedule for January of 1961.[5] It had not been seen on a Met program since the 1928-29 season.

Ronell was hired as a consultant for the libretto. It was the Met's intention to recapture the original German production with some changes and interpolation of composer Friedrich von Flotow's other music. But Ronell's designs were somewhat different. As she explained in the preface to her 1961 adaptation of *Martha*:

> [T]he case of so many classic operas is that the book and the sentiments of the original can become out of date in terms of modern story-telling to the point of being a handicap to performance....
>
> ... [T]he problem confronting me was to develop a libretto which would make the original story more credible in terms of today, while at the same time providing appropriate settings and dramatic situations for performance of the score.
>
> It is my hope that this adaptation of the score will bring fresh interest and new entertainment to *Martha* so that this tuneful work will be restored to its fitting place in the opera repertoire.[6]

These philosophies—conservation versus modernization of the original—were to clash by curtain time. Nonetheless, Ronell was eager to get started, as it was not every day that a Tin Pan Alley girl was able to work for the Metropolitan Opera.

At the time, communication among key personnel at the Met was less than perfect. During most of 1960, coordinating the efforts of Met personnel and Ronell was the task of Met assistant manager John Gutman. In one of his early letters regarding *Martha*, Gutman wrote to Hans Heinsheimer of G. Schirmer in late January of 1960:

> The fact is that the conductor is in Italy and all communication will have to be in writing which is a great nuisance, and the stage director, worse luck, has not even been appointed yet.
>
> In the absence of these two important personages, it would be utterly futile to go to work on rewriting of parts of the libretto, and I therefore must suggest that Miss Ronell be patient for quite a long while.[7]

Ronell complained a few months later, declaring to Gutman that "it is very difficult for me to start work on it without knowing exactly what you want."[8] Heinsheimer was on Ronell's side on the whole matter of completion of the libretto and in March wrote to Lester Cowan: "I might be wrong, but I have an uneasy feeling about this whole thing and I certainly don't want Ann to do any work before we know that the Metropolitan will really use our version."[9]

By May, however, Ronell was deep into the new libretto with frequent communications with Heinsheimer.[10] It was her task, as she saw it, to assimilate the various libretti that had been done on *Martha*, mostly in German, retaining Flotow's music but streamlining the plot. During these months, she worked with several people who had been involved with various productions of the opera. These included Emerson Buckley, the conductor of the New York City Center Opera, Estelle Liebling, who had sung a role in the 1928 production, and Richard Lert.[11]

Lert was an Austrian conductor who had come to the United States in 1938. He had been the conductor and orchestrator for the English version of *Martha* done in 1938 by Ronell and Vicki Baum, his wife. It was clear to Baum that "poor *Martha*" had undergone some "manipulations" over the years.[12] Baum and Lert felt that any plot changes made by them had been done so simply to move the sometimes plodding opera along and "served to dramatize a few points."[13] Baum concluded in a July 7, 1960, letter to Lester Cowan: "Just between you and me, whatever mise-en-scene we have seen in the Metropolitan up to now seem[s] a good deal less than admirable."[14]

Though Ronell finished the bulk of her work by mid–July, problems were ongoing. Nino Verchi, the conductor, and Carl Ebert, the director, were still in Europe, though not together. Beyond this, the set designer and costumer had been given the original German score and libretto with which to work, meaning that stage directions in Ronell's updated libretto might not necessarily correspond.[15]

The ongoing battle among the creators regarded how much of the original German plot and libretto were to be kept.[16] The majority, of which Ronell and Heinsheimer were not members, wanted to retain Flotow's opera as written. Though acknowledging the economy and stage appeal of the Baum-Ronell-Lert adaptation, the Metropolitan's hierarchy felt that retention of the original was artistically proper.

In reworking the libretto, Ronell had taken liberties not only with plot and lyrics, but also with the music, changing a few measures here and there. These musical changes were particularly unacceptable to both maestro Nino Verchi and John Gutman. In a long September 9, 1960 letter to Ronell, Gutman detailed the problems with her version. While making a few concessions to her, he summarized the Metropolitan's philosophy toward Flotow's opera: "Please believe me that we are not trying to be unnecessarily stubborn, but the score of *Martha*, while certainly not one of the musical masterpieces of operatic literature, is a well-known and well-established minor work which the Metropolitan does not wish to present in a widely divergent version."[17]

Over the next several days, Ronell and Gutman and his staff exchanged several letters, discussing changes of specific words and measures and at the same time, bickering as to how they had all gotten into such a quagmire.[18] By September 13, 1960, the situation boiled over, and Gutman gave Ronell an ultimatum:

> I am sorry that it seems that I have not made myself clear so far. The Metropolitan has not asked you, nor is asking you now, to rewrite the score of *Martha* in the way you see fit.
> I must ask you urgently and definitely to proceed with the writing of the additional pages and if you are unwilling to do so, please inform me right away since time is of the essence, and I would in that case have to try to make other arrangements.
> ... I must take an extremely serious view of the situation.[19]

After a meeting of the principals in the dispute, limited rapprochement was achieved, though several points remained unsettled. In a conciliatory letter after their meeting, Gutman agreed that they had "made progress," then detailed twenty-five separate points of contention regarding the libretto.[20]

Still, at the end of September, in letters to Nino Verchi and Carl Ebert, Ronell continued to plead her case for a streamlined version of *Martha*, in keeping with the Baum-Ronell-Lert edition. She explained that many of the cuts she had made from the original were important to an improved libretto and complained that Gutman had restored many of them. She regretted that due to Verchi and Ebert's European travels, she had not been able to confer with them regarding their vision of the libretto, stating, "Under ordinary circumstances, I would have discussed each cut with you for your approval, but this was not possible."[21]

But then, almost unable to help herself, she again stated her case: "Also, I am sure that neither of you have [*sic*] any illusions about the strengths and weaknesses of *Martha*—the fact that it has not been performed by the Metropolitan in the U.S. for 33 years speaks for itself."[22] She continued to dig in and even a month later, was still butting heads with Gutman. In a letter yet again discussing her cuts and their restoration, Gutman made a final plea to her:

> I am outlining below what we still need from you and I beg and urge you not to enter into another protracted discussion with us. In fact we are in the most serious trouble for this entire show on account of your reluctance to oblige us in the way we have so often suggested....
> Please, dear Ann Ronell, do take me seriously when I say that I am not prepared to enter into further discussions, and that there is a great hurry about all this.[23]

The director, Carl Ebert, had been doing some work on *Martha* while in Vienna during that summer. He, too, wanted to undo many of Ronell's cuts, but he also sympathized with anyone attempting to forge a "new" libretto for *Martha*. In a letter to Ronell on November

6, 1960, in which he discussed several changes in detail, Ebert prefaced her in a reassuring tone: "Let me first say how pleased I was to read your translation. It gave me back some of the courage which I had gradually lost working on the terrible stupid and mendaciously sentimental German text of the otherwise lovely little opera.... Am I right to say that I see some touches of a similar intention in your version?"[24] To this, Ronell replied: "Your understanding and enthusiasm for what I tried to do in the new libretto gives me confidence that you will create a fresh and entertaining production...."[25]

By the end of November, there appeared to be some agreement among the principals. Though most of her cuts had been ignored, some of Ronell's bigger suggestions were being included in the final version. However, as late as mid–December she was complaining to Richard Lert that "the Met plays havoc with my time as no one is efficiently in charge there."[26]

Her complaints to Lert, as usual, revolved around her desire to keep the libretto lively, a story in which the audience would stay interested. Most of the Metropolitan people felt the music was paramount, and the story be damned. One of her allies, as she wrote Lert, told her to "fight for THE STORY, and not give in to the singers on restoring cuts for they don't care about the story ... and the audience does."[27] And in a related comment, she added: "I have never met Mr. Bing [Met general manager], and gather that he couldn't care less about authors, especially American ones, or their work."[28]

Despite attempts at reconciliation, Ronell was not in agreement with the final version of the Met's libretto. What ultimately transpired was explained in a letter Ronell wrote to Rudolph Bing late into the production process. Director Carl Ebert had wanted to cut out a *Martha* subplot that was referred to as the ring story, involving the principal leads, Lionel and Martha. John Gutman had written Ronell concerning the ring subplot, "Allow me to make my modest contribution to the great ring controversy which, I understand, is still raging. By now I feel that the four dramas of Richard Wagner's Ring were simple compared to this problem which, frankly, I cannot even recognize as such."[29]

Ronell explained to Bing that the ring story was "integral and fundamental" to the opera's plot. She averred that although a director had final say on "minor language changes and musical cuts," he had "absolutely no right to change an author's work."[30] Ebert had accepted several other "additions and innovations made by me to revitalize the work." These, along with the ring story, constituted "her work,"[31] and he was not free to pick and choose which major contributions would be used. For Ebert to accept most of her additions and not the ring story was "inconsistent and defeats the very purpose for which I wrote."[32] After a lengthy letter of explanation, she left Bing with an ultimatum:

> Moreover, unless the ring story is retained as I wrote it in all details *for all performances*, your license is hereby terminated forthwith, and you are advised that such a presentation would cause serious damage to the property I have created and to my name and reputation. If, despite this formal notice to you, you persist in presenting the performance as Dr. Ebert insists it be presented rather than as I wrote it, I must insist that my name be removed from all program credits relative to performance under Dr. Ebert's direction.[33]

In a telegram to Ebert, she expressed her frustrations over his libretto changes:

> I UNDERSTAND THAT ADDITIONAL CHANGES ARE BEING MADE.... IF ANY AWKWARD WORDS OR SENTENCES ARE INSERTED WHICH ARE OUT OF CONTEXT OR RHYME I ALONE WILL BE PROFESSIONALLY DAMAGED FOR NEITHER THE CRITICS OR THE AUDIENCE WILL KNOW THAT OTHERS HAVE BEEN PERMITTED TO TAMPER WITH THE LYRICS AND RHYMING PATTERN[34]

Ronell finally asked that her name be removed from the credits. In a statement one week before the opening, Rudolph Bing responded:

The stage of the Metropolitan Opera during dress rehearsal for *Martha* in late January 1961. *Left to right:* unidentified man, Georgio Tozzi, Lorenzo Alvary, Carl Ebert (director), Ronell, Rosalind Elias, Victoria de Los Angeles, and Richard Tucker.

> Miss Ronell endeavored to make a basic change in the story, while the Metropolitan prefers to remain faithful to the original as devised by the composer and his librettist. Consequently Miss Ronell has asked that her name be withdrawn from the production, and the Metropolitan Opera will comply with her request.[35]

When *Martha* opened on January 26, 1961, her name did not appear on the program credits.[36] However, several of the reviews acknowledged her for having done the English libretto, and a few even gave reasons for her absence in the credits.[37] Explanations in the various reviews included "Miss Ronell got mad at Rudolph Bing over something," "the Met and Ann Ronell came to blows over her English translation," and "a wrangle over changes." One of the reviews referred to her libretto as "notably singable and smooth."[38] The most favorable comments came from the review in *Variety*: "[T]he Ronell rhymes and patter of the updated libretto are more original, fertile and promising than the typical English libretti heard at the Met the last few years."[39]

But what the public likes, the critics might not. If, as Louis Biancolli of the *New York World-Telegram* and *Sun* put it, "only a heart of stone could resist its bland charms,"[40] then it was stone hearts guiding the critics' typewriters that evening. *Variety* put it: "Seldom have the New York critics been so condescending. They did not sneer but sniffed."[41]

The staunchest traditionalist of the group was Harold C. Schonberg of the *New York*

Times. In contrast to the Ronell-Baum philosophy of opera in English, Schonberg did not believe in meddling with a minor classic: "The only way to revive a faded opera like *Martha* is to present it frankly as a period piece, and to present it honestly and lovingly, without vulgarisms and without an attempt to 'pretty' it up."[42] He objected to the translation, and in an obvious swipe at Ann Ronell, referred to the libretto's style as a "combination Hollywood and Tin Pan Alley."[43] Schonberg was extreme in his crusade against opera in English, writing a long essay in the *Times* a week later.[44] In close agreement was Harriett Johnson of the *New York Post*. She referred to the production as a "mishmash," surmising that at the Met, "those in authority are ashamed of the original and are trying to disguise it as much as possible."[45] Paul Henry Lang, in the *New York Herald Tribune*, simply called Ronell's libretto "undistinguished."[46]

The irony of the Met's *Martha* in English was that it was difficult to understand. Apparently the foreign accents of the two female leads, most notably Victoria de Los Angeles, rendered the English unclear. However, Georgio Tozzi and Richard Tucker were cited for their clarity.[47] Also criticized among the new scenes and libretto was a quasi-striptease, referred to as a "preposterous anachronism" in an opera set in the eighteenth century "during the reign of Queen Anne."[48]

But not all the critics sided against opera in English. The review in *Variety* was far more sympathetic though with reservations as to some of her phrases:

> A superficial scanning of the libretto, as printed, suggests that it is a good deal better than the critics conceded. Unhappily a few of her phrases stand out like a bandaged thumb. Such modernisms as "Oh, Brother!" and "Poor Fish!" give away Miss Ronell's screen and Tin Pan Alley antecedents.[49]

Ronell continued her crusade for opera in English, never being awed by the Met and its handling of *Martha*. In a long letter to friend and drama critic of the *Boston Herald*, Elinor Hughes, Ronell vented her frustrations and offered solutions:

> I don't intend to correct him [Tozzi] anymore, or take any more valuable time fighting dead-end streets in the opera world. It is a world apart, and tho the Met has a Broadway address, it knows very little of professional theater or professional workers.
>
> Every singer has either a "problem" or doesn't care what the words mean, so the writer can never find out unless he has time to experiment, and that's impossible. We need workshops—for writers—as well as performers. We need tryouts in every kind of theater, but opera disdains this. I've tried to advance the notion to the Met to have a workshop theater for their younger brood who never get a chance to perform, tho under contract, and for writers of English texts as well as for new original works of native composers....[50]

Performances of *Martha* were well-attended, and the production was considered a success, the critics notwithstanding. Paul Henry Lang surmised: "The public evidently liked *Martha*, and for harmless, good, clean fun, there is nothing like it."[51] The production was then taken on tour with essentially the same cast with performances in several major cities east of the Mississippi.

It was Richard Tucker, on closing night at the Met, who brought the opera in English controversy to a head. The most popular aria in *Martha* is sung by Lionel, Tucker's character, and is known well in the Italian version as "M'appari." To everyone's surprise, including conductor Nino Verchi and other Met personnel, Tucker sang the aria in Italian, receiving an ovation on its conclusion.[52] Apparently spurred by fan mail, Tucker had decided that "I'd give the old opera buffs out front a treat and let them hear the aria the way Caruso and Gigli used to sing it."[53]

The tenor's bilingual display upset both Ronell and Sir Rudolph Bing. Bing referred to the ploy as "highly inartistic" and was "disappointed that a serious artist should stoop to such a publicity stunt."[54] Shortly after, Ronell wired the Met's general manager:

> DEAR MR BING, AFTER ALL WE'VE BEEN THROUGH WITH MARTHA, I WAS HARDLY SURPRISED TO READ THAT MR TUCKER WAS NOW SINGING IN ITALIAN. I APPRECIATE YOUR CALLING HIM TO TASK ON THIS PUBLICLY. I SHALL WRITE HIM A NOTE ADVISING THAT HE IS IN VIOLATION OF THE LICENSE TO PERFORM MY ENGLISH LIBRETTO OF THE OPERA.[55]

Because Ronell held the copyright and license to the libretto, she warned Tucker that she would withdraw permission to perform her translation if he did this again on the Met's spring tour. Tucker was amused by the incident, claiming: "I never know when the mood may strike me."[56] The tour was a success with frequent, favorable reviews. As in New York, critics were split on the matters of the libretto and opera in English.[57] The audiences in the Eastern cities on the tour, however, only heard Lionel's "M'appari" in English, and the dust settled.

19

Meeting at a Far Meridian and the Cold War: 1963–1965

"When a musician meets a musician from another country,
they're in the same world."

The Cold War between the United States and the USSR started at the end of World War II and ended with the collapse of Soviet Russia in 1989. Though primarily political, the Cold War also stifled cultural and scientific exchange between the two post-war superpowers. In his novel of the era, *Meeting at a Far Meridian*, writer Mitchell A. Wilson addressed these conflicts, developing his plot around a love story between a Russian performing artist and an American scientist. Before becoming a novelist, Wilson had been a physicist, teaching at the university level, and had been a laboratory assistant to Enrico Fermi.[1] With a scientific background and writing sympathetic to détente, Wilson had become popular in the USSR, more so than in his native America. This novel of cultural exchange, *Meeting at a Far Meridian*, interested both Cowan and Ronell.

Cowan's plan for the story, one endorsed by President John Kennedy who believed strongly in cultural exchange, was to co-produce a movie of the book with Mosfilm Studios, the largest studio in Russia. With Fay Kanin and author Wilson as screen writers, Cowan made several trips to Russia, working on numerous aspects of the film, including a finished screenplay acceptable to both sides. As Cowan explained in a letter to an ABC Television executive, "The screen play, in effect, represents an ideological agreement between our people and the Russian people dramatizing the fact that our common interests and beliefs far exceed the differences."[2]

As Cowan worked on production details, Ronell traveled to Russia a few times as well and worked with Russian composers from the Union of Soviet Composers and Mosfilm Studios. She believed that music and other arts transcended political differences and felt that the film would "dramatize music's immunity to the U.S.–U.S.S.R. cold warfare."[3] She further explained to a *New York Post* reporter in an interview in 1965, "When a musician meets a musician from another country, they're in the same world. A good feeling is established right off."[4]

On her first visit to Russia in 1963, she gave recitals at both the American Embassy and the Soviet Composers Union and was surprised to find how much Western music had infiltrated Russia. She found that "Yank tunes were in abundant supply via Muzak-style dissemination, café bands, etc."[5] As Jack Pitman recorded in *Variety* after his 1965 interview with her:

Ronell and Cowan (holding bag) at airport with Russian delegation and author Mitchell Wilson, second from left, during an early work on *Meeting at a Far Meridian*, 1963.

> Nothing startled her so much among the familiar melodies, however, as her own "Who's Afraid of the Bid Bad Wolf?" (circa early Disney) which, she was even more abashed to learn, the Russians innocently insisted was a native folk tune. (They in turn were abashed when Miss Ronell disabused them of the notion.)
>
> Anyway, there's much Yankee music over there, and on the increase, as witness for instance the popularity of such plagiarisms as "Porgy" and "My Fair Lady." Ditto for Latino music.[6]

Ronell found common ground with composer Tikhon Khrennikov, with whom she wrote a song. At the time, Khrennikov was secretary (director) of the Union of Soviet Composers, a position to which he had been appointed by the communist regime in 1948. Within the artistic community of Soviet Russia, this post was powerful, and in being appointed, Khrennikov was instructed to assert rigid Party control of Soviet music. In this capacity over the years, he was openly critical of numerous Russian composers including Sergei Prokofiev and Dmitri Shostakovich.[7]

Despite this political position, which he held until the Soviet Union collapsed in 1989, Khrennikov was also a successful classical performer and composer, having written three symphonies and numerous concertos.[8] One of his concertos for violin was recorded by violinist Leonid Kogan with Mstislav Rostropovich conducting.

Ronell's collaboration with Khrennikov produced "Take Me, Take Me to the Moon,"[9] a ballad which had copyright protection in both Russia and the U.S., an uncommon practice at the time. Initially, Ronell had been given music to a song by Khrennikov, "Moscow Windows," and was asked to add a lyric. She did that and added some further music. As she explained to Herman Finkelstein at ASCAP in a letter from Russia:

When I saw Khrennikov next, I gave him the new version of his song which was now 36 bars and new lyrics. In the American fashion, I said, we need a "middle part," and a culminating lyrical form. He was delighted with the music I'd added, and said he wouldn't change it for the world, but would have it played here [Russia] as I brought it to him on TV and radio.[10]

The song, subtitled "The Moon Song," is credited as "Words by Ann Ronell" and "Music by Tikhon Khrennikov and Ann Ronell." It begins with a plain, eight-bar verse, but then a haunting melody emerges in the chorus. It is long at sixty measures, with an A-A$_1$-B-A$_2$ pattern, with two surprising twists in the melody in the last section, A$_2$.[11] Which of the two composers was responsible for all this is unclear, though in true American Popular Song style, Ronell created the eight-bar release section, B.

The song was also known as "The Windows of Moscow" with an alternative lyric. The song was not recorded in America, but it was used in the 1963 tour of Russia by the Bill and Cora Baird Marionette Theater.[12] The song, as performed by the puppets, was warmly received by Soviet audiences, especially on the evening of June 16, 1963. That was the night that cosmonaut Valentina Tereshkova made the first flight of a Soviet woman in Vostok 6, a moment of great pride for the Soviets.

The movie went into production in 1963, but filming was halted after a series of setbacks to American-Russian peace efforts, including the assassination of President John Kennedy, America's growing involvement in Vietnam, and later, the ouster of Nikita Khrushchev, led by Soviet hardliner Leonid Brezhnev in the fall of 1964.

In 1966, director King Vidor became interested in the project. He had read Wilson's novel and the screenplay and, like Cowan and Ronell, felt that such a film could help bridge the gap created by the Cold War. As he told Cowan:

> I believe the communication of making a co-production film with the Russians can be of tremendous importance in our harmonious relationship with them. As we well know, there is something of the articulated nature in the production and distribution of motion pictures that can do more to wipe out ideological differences than any other medium.... There is no doubt but that together we can do something very important for peace and understanding.[13]

In that same year, Ronell and Cowan were planning a Broadway musical entitled *Spasso House*, the name of the American ambassador's Moscow residence.[14] The plot of the show's book was a love story between a Russian ballerina and an American journalist. Ronell was to do both music and lyrics. A year later, they also worked with director Vidor on a documentary, *Warm Sounds in the Cold War*.[15] This also dealt with the gap bridged by musicians and artists during the political standoff of the Cold War and included some details of the work done earlier for *Meeting at a Far Meridian*. Unfortunately, none of the projects— movie, Broadway musical or documentary—ever came to fruition.

Ronell at a luncheon with Soviet composer Tikhon Khrennikov, discussing music for the film *Meeting at a Far Meridian* and their song, "Take Me, Take Me to the Moon."

The "Big Bad Wolf" had reared

its head in another form in 1962 when a controversial play opened on Broadway, *Who's Afraid of Virginia Woolf?*, written by Edward Albee. The comedic drama focused on the crumbling marriage of a couple in academia and starred Uta Hagen and Arthur Hill. It was satiric with a biting humor and took a step forward in profanity and sexual themes for the legitimate theater. Because of this, it was ultimately denied the Pulitzer Prize for Drama that year by the trustees of Columbia University, despite the advice of the school's award's committee.[16]

In two different scenes of the play, the battling couple, George and Martha, parody the Disney song lyrics, singing "Virginia Woolf" in lieu of "Big Bad Wolf." To Albee's characters, "Who's afraid of Virginia Woolf" meant "Who's afraid of living life without false illusions," and the question is eventually answered by Martha that she was.[17] Though the lyrics were a paraphrase of the Churchill-Ronell song, the melody used was not, but that of "Here We Go Round the Mulberry Bush," and therein was the problem.

Who's Afraid of Virginia Woolf? had opened off-Broadway on a tight budget. Albee had wanted to use the original song — words and music — and just modify the one phrase. When his producers sought permission from publisher Bourne, Inc., they were given a price of two hundred dollars per week for use of the song, too high for a fledgling production. Neither Disney Studios nor Ann Ronell was consulted, though each should have participated in such a decision because of publishing and artistic rights.[18]

At this time, Ronell and Cowan were traveling much, working on *Meeting at a Far Meridian*. Because of this, they were not on top of the problem as they usually would have been and did not see the play until February of 1963. They spoke with their legal counsel, and then Ronell wrote Albee regarding both the monetary issue and the fact that she had received adverse publicity as one of the parties wanting to charge the prohibitive weekly rate. She told Albee:

> I would be pleased to have the music from the song used in the play and would see that the license charge be reduced to the minimum of $25.00 per week.... Bourne, Inc. does not have the sole right to license the song. I have authority to license it to you through my own publishing firm, Picture Music, Inc....
>
> However, through your publicity the impression has been created that I was party to holding you up for a prohibitive price when in reality your producer is unwilling to pay even the minimum $25.00 per week. This disturbs me and I hope that you will do whatever is necessary to clarify and settle the matter.[19]

By this time, four months into the Broadway run, the issue of the melody being used was a moot point as Albee and his producers had already switched to the tune of "Here We Go Round the Mulberry Bush," an old nursery rhyme song which fit the meter of the words surprisingly well.[20] More importantly, the song had long been in the public domain, and no royalties were payable. Still, Ronell took issue with the playwright's use of her and Frank Churchill's lyrics. She felt that such use was an infringement on her copyright and warned Albee regarding the matter: "I am writing you personally to be certain that you are aware of the facts and of my attitude in the matter. I would like to cooperate with you as author to author and hope that it will not become necessary to unleash the lawyers for this would cost each of us more than the total involved."[21] Despite the legal saber-rattling so frequent in Ronell's career, it was decided that use of the short line of lyric was acceptable and not compensable.[22] Surprisingly, the Disney organization had not protested any of this from a legal standpoint. They had mostly ignored the play, but had objected to use of the song as they found the dramatic work "immoral and shocking."[23]

Matters quieted down during the summer of 1963 but then heated up again when composer Frank Loesser became involved. Ronell heard that "Frank Loesser Music Co. had applied for a license from the producers of *Who's Afraid of Virginia Woolf?* to publish a song by that title."[24] She decided to go see the lyricist-composer, famous for *Guys and Dolls* and also well-known on Broadway for a keen business sense. Before the visit, practicing a bit of one-upmanship, she wrote a song entitled "Who's Afraid of Virginia Woolf?" and had it registered with ASCAP and the Register of Copyrights. When she visited Loesser, whom she referred to as "an old friend of mine," she explained, "I told him I had brought him the song he was looking for."[25] While he was upset at having been beaten to the punch on the song, it turned out that he was more concerned about the "shabby treatment" she had received from the play's producers: "He reminded me that I was an author, and that every author suffers damage if precedents are accomplished which danger creative works, and that if I allowed this 'outrageous and parsimonious—chintzy' was his word for it, action on the part of a dramatic work, I'd have to allow the use of a newer parody on the same title such as a song from the play would obtain."[26] From Ronell's account of the incident, it sounded as if Loesser was shocked at the abuse of her rights as an author and thereby the rights of every author, but that he wanted her to go alone to do battle for all of them. But no battle lines were drawn and the issue faded away on the advice of Ronell's counsel.

Three years later when various productions had opened in Europe, she learned that while different lyrics were being used, the European versions had reverted to the original melody. She wrote to her attorney, William Krasilovsky:

> [T]he Cultural Attache at the London Czech Embassy thought my fame as the "song's composer" rested on my connection with "Al-Beeee." Naturally, I was upset to find that no foreign policing of my song's usage on dramatic productions has brought assets, even through ASCAP.[27]

Because of various legal technicalities, Ronell's claims of artistic infringement were never sustained, and she collected no further payments on the play's use of the song.

In the late sixties, Ronell and Krasilovsky became involved in a legal dispute between themselves. Ronell felt that he was not properly representing her interests regarding song renewal rights and royalties. She was especially annoyed over these foreign productions of *Who's Afraid of Virginia Woolf?* earning no royalties for her.[28] Krasilovsky, in turn, claimed several instances of nonpayment by Ronell on cases over the years.[29] The disagreement got so far that Krasilovsky filed a civil action against her in New York to recover $6,000.[30] The summons to her was dated November 7, 1969. Eventually, Ronell retained another attorney, Milton Rosenbloom, and the matter was settled by arbitration in 1970.[31]

In 1964, Republican presidential candidate Barry Goldwater was conservative but no moderate, and Ronell found his politics offensive. Goldwater was in his second term as U.S. Senator from Arizona and greatly wanted to reduce the powers and programs of the Federal government.[32] Moreover, his strong stand against communism in Vietnam and elsewhere made him the tacit leader of the hawks in Congress. Though Ronell had sworn off politics after the Adlai Stevenson presidential campaign, Goldwater's candidacy drew her back. She had been deeply involved in the 1956 presidential campaign of Adlai Stevenson, not only campaigning for the Democratic nominee but also writing a song, "Too Big a Price,"[33] which received some play at party functions.

She explained to New York City Mayor Robert Wagner what had drawn her back into the political fray to work for the Lyndon Johnson campaign: "Working in Hollywood lately, I saw a poster drawn by a teenager showing a covered wagon, Goldwater at the reins, and the sign 'Backward Ho!' over it.... The sight of this young boy working his head off with the same fear of the Goldwater campaign as I felt so deeply, was a goad to me to do the only thing I can do at the moment."[34]

Ronell believed strongly that a candidate needed his own original song — melody and lyric — if it "was to be effective and remembered."[35] At the time, she had completed a song for the candidacy of Robert Kennedy. He was running for the U.S. Senate seat from the State of New York held by his opponent, Senator Kenneth Keating. Born and raised in Massachusetts, Robert Kennedy had to defend his "carpetbagger" label, similar to that put on Senator Hilary Rodham Clinton in her 2002 winning campaign for the Senate seat from New York. Ronell felt strongly about Kennedy's candidacy and wanted to help with a campaign song. However, it got little play and was never used in the winning campaign.

As Ronell explained in a September, 1964 letter regarding campaign songs, "[T]he familiar melody used does not relate personally to the candidate — as a song written especially for him would do. In my song, the melody is catchy ... so that after exploiting the song frequently the listener would automatically sing the message with the tune."[36] The Kennedy song, "Put Kennedy in the Senate Now,"[37] had plenty of rhymes but no real identification with the candidate. Any candidate's name could have been substituted into the song, and nothing would have been lost. Not so with the Goldwater song.

"Backward Ho! with Barry" opens with a 2-bar introduction meant to be spoken: "Whoa! Back up the Old Gray Mare! Whoa!"[38] The chorus is only 18 measures long in a "Moderate March Tempo," and skewers his nearly reactionary views of government and his hawkish stance on the Vietnam War.

Members of the Democratic Party hierarchy loved it, calling it "catchy," "humorous," "truthful," and "delightful."[39] Richard Rodgers called it "terribly amusing" in a note to her, late in the campaign, adding that it "should have done a great deal of good."[40] Unlike the Stevenson song, "Backward Ho! with Barry" had more limited exposure and was included in the campaign too late to be of much help. President Lyndon Johnson won handily, carrying forty-four states.

20

Later Life and Career: 1965–1993

"Ann Ronell, who was writing popular songs and film scores when women were not writing much American music at all, has died."

Ann Ronell was a member of and served on boards of various organizations including the National Association of Popular Music (NAPM)/Songwriter's Hall of Fame (SHOF), American Guild of Authors and Composers, the Dramatists Guild, the Song Writers' Guild, and the American Society of Composers, Arrangers & Producers. Ever busy, she also helped initiate a project of recording the recollections of the great composers and lyricists of American Popular Song.

Friends and relatives all agreed that she was always working on something, usually several things. Her composing went on well into the 1970s, though little was published. A friend wrote to her during these years: "You're a wonder. Buzz-Buzz-Buzzing all over the place and at the same time dreaming up projects *all* the time."[1] A family friend from her days in Omaha corroborated Ronell's constant activity: "She was always writing something for something. Nobody could've been busier than she."[2] When not working, she liked to meet friends for lunch or coffee at her regular booth at The Flame, 58th Street and 9th Avenue, near her apartment on 60th Street, between Broadway and 9th Avenue.[3]

She had diverse musical interests and had always been open to new genres, but the era of rock 'n' roll had passed her by. Early on she had considered it a "fad,"[4] as many of her generation had. Fellow lyricist Alan Jay Lerner liked its "vitality" and "new sound" but felt that the lyrics were a "revolt against language."[5] It was a new sound, and this new music was definitely cutting into their royalties. But rather than dismissing it completely, she recognized it as a musical art form and took a stand on it: "[T]he only 'levels' I admit to are 'good' and 'bad' ... both good and bad rock and roll."[6] She became resigned to much of it, admitting in the early sixties:

> Today they want rock 'n' roll. That's the fast seller. But the record business still depends on old standards for the steady business. Not the crash sales. Those are rock 'n' roll.
> But the good singers still sing the old hits. And thank goodness, I have some.[7]

In 1981, Ronell was on the board of directors of the National Association of Popular Music, the parent organization of the Songwriter's Hall of Fame. Their ongoing mission is to "safeguard a special part of our American heritage and honor the men and women who helped create it."[8] To that end, in 1979 the NAPM organized an exhibit devoted to distaff songwrit-

At the Overseas Press Club, September 29, 1964. *Left to right:* two unidentified men, Ronell, David Ewen (music historian and biographer), Sigmund Spaeth (musicologist and historian)(Nebraska Jewish Historical Society).

ers—"Women Who Wrote the Songs." To honor the ladies, the NAPM displayed their photographs, music, and memorabilia from their careers. A ghusli [gusle], a single-stringed fiddle from Yugoslavia, given to Ronell by George Gershwin, was among the items displayed.[9]

The NAPM newsletter at the time explained the intent of the show and gave some specifics:

> Who wrote *The Student Prince*? Practically any red-blooded American will immediately answer "Sigmund Romberg." But Sigmund Romberg didn't write *The Student Prince*, he *composed The Student Prince*. The book and lyrics for that remarkable show came from the pen of Dorothy Donnelly. Let me ask further, "Who wrote *Naughty Marietta*?" The answer, of course, will be "Victor Herbert." I said "of course" because very few people realize that the lyrics were written by Rida Johnson Young, and that she also wrote *Maytime* for Sigmund Romberg. And while Chauncey Olcott and Ernest R. Ball were usually credited with "Mother Machree," the lyric was written by the same Rida Johnson Young.
>
> There are hundreds of American women whose contributions to song should have brought them public acclaim, but very few have been celebrated in the fashion which they deserve.[10]

The curator of the NAPM at the time, Oscar Brand, summed it up: "I was ashamed of our male sexism."[11]

The women honored in the NAPM exhibit included[12]:

Marilyn Bergman	Anne Caldwell	Dorothy Donnelly
Carrie Jacobs-Bond	Betty Comden	Maria Grever

Mildred Hill	Peggy Lee	Ann Ronell
Patty Hill	Ruth Lowe	Dana Suesse
Julia Ward Howe	Joni Mitchell	Kay Swift
Janis Ian	Dolly Parton	Clara Ward
Elsie Janis	Helen Reddy	Rida Johnson Young
Carole King	Mary Rodgers	

Ronell was honored in 1991 by the SHOF as an annual Song Citation winner for "Willow Weep for Me." Other winners that year were Cab Calloway for "Minnie the Moocher," Sidney Lippman for "Too Young," and Henry Tobias for "Miss You." In the program for the awards dinner, the name of Ann Ronell was absent from the list of inductees from 1969 to 1991. Only a Song Citation award had been given to her.[13]

She never dwelled on the difficulty and lack of recognition women encountered in the songwriting world, but from time to time she definitely felt resentment at how she had been treated.[14] Occasionally an issue would arise that necessitated comment. In 1988, it was suggested to composer Morton Gould, president of ASCAP, that Ronell be recognized with one of their theatre awards. While she was among the first to honor and credit talented male composers, she felt that distaff members of ASCAP were overlooked. She expressed this to Gould in a letter following an ASCAP awards ceremony:

> Having recently discovered I am listed in "Notable Names in the American Theater," I am enclosing a copy, though I doubt women writers have ever received attention equal to men at ASCAP. An example of this was obvious at the Wolf Trap concert where no woman composer was represented, in spite of having Dana Suesse alive and well at the time to perform superbly. If she had

Left: Ronell and Cowan, circa 1965. *Right:* Ronell at leisure, circa 1965.

played that ever familiar "You Ought to Be in Pictures," the house would have come down. There are other examples.... I am only happy to think at this late date that I may have encouraged others to enter as I did an artistic world completely dominated by men at that time.[15]

As recently as 2000, a compendium of Broadway songs, *Show Tunes*, mentioned the usual female songwriters and mentioned Ann Ronell as the composer of "Who's Afraid of the Big Bad Wolf?," never crediting her 1942 Broadway effort *Count Me In*, for which she did both words and music.[16]

More acclaim to female songwriters came along in the 1999 Public Broadcasting System special, *Yours for a Song: The Women of Tin Pan Alley*, part of public television's *American Masters* series. The show, hosted by Broadway and cabaret star Betty Buckley, focused on four women: Dorothy Fields, Ann Ronell, Dana Suesse, and Kay Swift. The latter three all wrote music, and their hits were from the 1930s. Of the four, lyricist Fields was most successful, having her first hit in 1928 with composer Jimmy McHugh, "I Can't Give You Anything But Love." She wrote into the 1960s, her last major work being the Broadway hit *Sweet Charity* with composer Cy Coleman, twenty-five years her junior.[17] Ronell was given a prominent position as well in *Yours for a Song* with "Willow Weep for Me" and "Who's Afraid of the Big Bad Wolf?" featured.

Into the decade of the eighties, Ronell and Lester Cowan, both well into their seventies, lived in their Upper West Side apartment, still meeting with old friends and

Top: Ronell (Song Citation Winner for "Willow Weep for Me") at the Songwriters' Hall of Fame induction ceremony (May 29, 1991) with Gene Autry (left, Lifetime Achievement Award) and Barry Manilow (center, Hitmaker Award). *Bottom:* Ronell (left) at Songwriters' Hall of Fame ceremony (May 29, 1991) with lyricist Betty Comden (Johnny Mercer Award).

associates from the music and movie worlds. Cowan died in 1990 of a heart attack at age eighty-three. With his death, she lost her husband and companion, someone with whom she had discussed big projects and small details for over fifty-five years.

A fall in 1992 left Ann confined to a wheelchair and exacerbated her arthritis. Cardiac and renal complications ensued following surgery for a hernia, and she died on December 25, 1993, eighty-eight years after her birth.[18] The *New York Times* allotted only three column inches to her obituary. The *Los Angeles Times* began theirs: "Ann Ronell, who was writing popular songs and film scores when women were not writing much American music at all, has died."[19]

APPENDIX A
Chronology

Date / Year	Occurrence
December 25, 1905	Born in Omaha, Nebraska, 401 South 38th Avenue
1911–1919	Attends and graduates elementary and Hebrew schools in Omaha
1919–1923	Attends and graduates Omaha Central High School
1923–1926	Attends Wheaton College, Norton, Massachusetts, majoring in liberal arts
1926–1927	Transfers to Radcliffe College in Boston, majoring in music and English, and graduates in spring of 1927
	Interviews George Gershwin for college magazine, *The Radcliffe*, striking up friendship
	Composes words and music of *College Is the Place for Me*, published in *Radcliffe Songbook*
1927–1929	Returns to New York after time in Omaha, seeks out George Gershwin, who introduces her around and helps her find work
	Works as rehearsal pianist for Broadway shows including *Whoopee, The New Moon, Show Girl*, and *Great Day!*
	Writes special material for various artists and coaches singers, including Marilyn Miller
1929	Words and music for "Down by de Ribber" for Radio City Music Hall show
	Words and music for "Love and I" for Ziegfeld Roof show, her first song published as a professional
1930	Words and music for "Baby's Birthday Party" for Famous Music, sells over 100,000 sheet music copies, recorded by Rudy Vallee and Guy Lombardo
1931	Words and music for "Let's Go Out in the Open Air," sung by Imogene Coca in Broadway revue produced by Heywood Broun, *Shoot the Works!*
	Words and music for "Rain on the Roof" recorded by Paul Whiteman and His Orchestra
1932	Words and music for "Willow Weep for Me" published by Irving Berlin, Inc., and recorded by Irene Bailey with Paul Whiteman and by Ruth Etting
	Takes first trip to Europe, traveling to France, Italy, and Switzerland
	Receives ASCAP membership, one of the few women at the time
1933	Words and music for "Mickey Mouse and Minnie's in Town" published by Disney to commemorate fifth anniversary of creation of Mickey Mouse
	Words and music for "In a Silly Symphony" for Disney Studios in Hollywood
	Writes additional lyrics for "Who's Afraid of the Big Bad Wolf?" music by Frank Churchill, published by Irving Berlin Music, Inc., for Disney Studios cartoon, *Three Little Pigs*
1934	Meets Lester Cowan, executive secretary of the Academy of Motion Picture Arts & Sciences, while both are in Washington, D.C., for hearings on motion picture review code

Date / Year	Occurrence
	Appears on stage in hometown of Omaha, Nebraska, at Paramount Theater, performing her own songs
	Works on RKO Pictures movie, *Down to Their Last Yacht*, including words and music for songs "Funny Little World" and "Beach Boy" and music for "South Sea Bolero"
1935	Composes music and libretto for ballet-operetta for prima ballerina Patricia Bowman and producers Fanchon & Marco, performed in Los Angeles and several cities of the Midwest
November 5, 1935	Marries Lester Cowan, by then an independent Hollywood producer, on ocean liner *Santa Elena*, traveling from San Francisco to New York
1936	Living at 2026 Vine Street, Hollywood
	Works on movies for Paramount Pictures, *The Big Broadcast of 1936* and *Champagne Waltz*, writing words and music for song, "The Merry-Go-Round"
1937	Begins adapting opera in English for conductors-professors Hugo Streilitzer and Richard Lert for Los Angeles high schools and colleges
1938	Works with composer Ralph Benatzky and writer Samuel Raphaelson on musical *King with the Umbrella*, never produced due to political climate
	Works on movie *Blockade*, including lyrics for songs "The River Is Blue," music by Kurt Weill (cut) and "Beloved, You're Lovely," music by Werner Janssen
	Works on movie *Algiers* for producer Walter Wanger, writing English lyrics and incidental songs for stars Charles Boyer and Nina Koshetz
	Adapts Friedrich von Flotow opera *Martha*, for American stage in English with writer Vicki Baum and conductor Richard Lert; it premieres at Hollywood Bowl
	Works with soprano Deanna Durbin on songbook of English translations of classical songs, *Deanna Durbin Album of Favorite Songs and Arias*, published by G. Schirmer, Inc.
1939	Adapts Johann Strauss opera *The Gypsy Baron* for English, working with author George Marion, Jr., and baritone John Charles Thomas
1940	American score of *Martha* published by G. Schirmer & Co., Inc.
1941	Hired as musical director and composer for movie *Magic in Music*, starring Susanna Foster, writing words and music for song "Fireflies on Parade"
	Living at 6826 Odin Street, Hollywood
	Works as musical production assistant with Ernst Toch on movie *Ladies in Retirement* and contributes to the efforts of recording the film's soundtrack, the first time ever done
	Applies for Guggenheim grant to work on three operas in English, but grant denied
	Collaborates with composer Oscar Straus on reworking of *The Chocolate Soldier*, his light opera, to which she contributes lyrics for four songs
1941–1942	Writes book and incidental lyrics for ballet-sing, *Ship South*, with music by composer-violinist Nicolai Berezovsky
	Composes words and music for Broadway show *Count Me In*, dealing with the home front in World War II, opening in New York, and becoming the first woman to write both words and music for an entire Broadway show
1942	Composer for music and songs for movie *Commandos Strike at Dawn*, including songs "Commandos March" and "Out to Pick the Berries"
1943	Reworks *The Gypsy Baron* for production with Irra Petina and John Tyers
1944	Modifies *The Gypsy Baron*, for production done by St. Louis Municipal Opera Company, re-titled *Open Road*, with Dorothy Sarnoff and John Tyers
	Serves as music director-composer for United Artists movie, *Tomorrow, the World!*

Date / Year	Occurrence
1945	Moves to ranch at 12220 Saticoy Street, Canoga Park, Los Angeles, but keeps apartment in Hollywood at 5959 Franklin Street
	Composes music for *The Story of G.I. Joe.*, based on war experiences of correspondent Ernie Pyle.
	Writes words and music for songs "I'm Coming Back," "Linda," and "The Ernie Pyle Infantry March," the last adopted as the "unofficial" march for the U.S. Army ground troops
1946	Receives Academy Award nomination for Best Song, "Linda," both words and music, and for Best Musical Score for *The Story of G.I. Joe* with Canadian Louis Applebaum
1947	Collaborates with writers Florence Ryerson and Colin Clements on musical life story of composer Stephen Foster, entitled *Oh! Susanna* and premieres at Pasadena Playhouse
1948	Works with Kurt Weill on movie *One Touch of Venus*, writing new lyrics to two of Weill's songs, "(Don't Look Now) But My Heart Is Showing" and "My Week"
1949	*Oh, Susanna!* is published for performance by Samuel French and receives productions by amateur theatres across the U.S. over the next several years
	Writes score for Marx Brothers movie *Love Happy*, and words and music for the title song and two others, "Harpo's Rumba" and "Who Stole the Jam?"
	"Willow Weep for Me" recorded by Stan Kenton Orchestra, becomes jazz classic
1951	Moves to Manhattan apartment at 41 East 75th Street
1951–52	Acts as musical director and composes score and songs for *Main Street to Broadway*, including "Just a Girl," sung by Herb Shriner
1952	Words and music for "The River," based on folk themes from India, the locale of the Jean Renoir film of the same name
1953	With Lester Cowan, works on autobiographical television series, *Tin Pan Alley Girl,* to no avail
	Words and music for lullaby "Sleep My Babe, My Darling" for *The Crucible* by Arthur Miller
	"Willow Weep for Me" recorded by both Frank Sinatra and Art Tatum and eventually becomes an American Popular Song standard
	Works with composer Hugo Friedhofer on John Wayne Western *Hondo* and writes lyrics to title song "Hondo, Hondo"
1955	Sues Walt Disney and Walt Disney Productions for denying her credit on creation of "Who's Afraid of the Big Bad Wolf?" thus damaging her reputation and potential income
	Words and music of title song for Swedish nature film, *The Great Adventure*, recorded by Hildegarde
1956	Words and music for campaign song, "Too Big a Price," for presidential campaign of Adlai E. Stevenson
1957–58	Disney suit goes to trial, but all claims and damages are denied by Judge W. John Clancy
1961	Works on new Metropolitan Opera adaptation of *Martha* starring Victoria de Los Angeles and Richard Tucker though program credit withdrawn at her request over creative differences
1962–1965	Works on music for *Meeting at a Far Meridian*, co-produced by Lester Cowan and Mosfilm Studios, including song "Take Me, Take Me to the Moon," with music by Russian composer Tikhon Khrennikov, though film never completed due to Cold War considerations
1964	Moves to apartment on West Side of Manhattan at 101 W. 55th Street

Date / Year	*Occurrence*
	Words and music for political campaign songs, "Backward Ho with Barry" and "Put Kennedy in the Senate Now" for the campaigns of President Lyndon Johnson and Robert F. Kennedy, respectively
1977	Living in Manhattan apartment, 30 W. 60th Street, doing occasional compositions
1979	Suffers injuries from auto accident which ultimately confine her to a wheelchair
	Honored in exhibition, "Women Who Wrote the Songs," at National Academy of Popular Music / Songwriters' Hall of Fame, New York
1981	Serves on board of directors of National Academy of Popular Music
1990	Lester Cowan, husband of fifty-five years, dies of heart attack.
1991	Song Citation winner for "Willow Weep for Me" presented by the Songwriters' Hall of Fame
December 25, 1993	Dies in Manhattan, eighty-eight years after her birth, from respiratory and cardiac complications after surgery to repair a hernia

APPENDIX B

Rosenblatt Family Tree

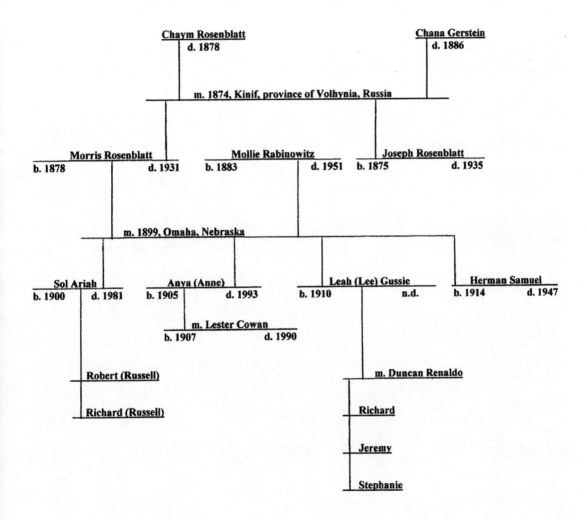

APPENDIX C
Songs

Year	Song	Collaborator[1]*	Publisher
1927	College Is the Place for Me (When We're Foolish and Young)		Radcliffe College
1928	Sweetie Pie		Irving Berlin Music, Inc.[2]
1929	Down by de Ribber		---[3]
1930	Baby's Birthday Party		Famous Music Corp.
	Just One Adventure		Santly Bros., Inc./ Famous Music Corp.
1931	The Candy Parade		Miller Music Corp.
	Give Me Your Love	Muriel Pollock (m)	Famous Music Corp.
	I'd Rather Have Him Than "It"	Lucy Bender Sokole (w, m)	---
	Love and I		Miller Music/G. Schirmer Inc.
	Molly and Me	Muriel Pollock (m)	Irving Berlin
	Rain on the Roof		Famous Music Corp.
	Sleepy-Bye		Famous Music Corp.
	There's a Woman with the Man in the Moon	Lu C. Bender (w)	Remick Music Corp.
	When You Say "Please"	Lu C. Bender (w, m)	Irving Berlin, Inc.
1932	A Cosmopolitan Woman	Lucy Bender Sokole (w, m)	---
	Give Me Back My Heart		Irving Berlin, Inc.
	Gonna Take My Time Down South		Irving Berlin, Inc.
	I Thought You Were Different	Lucy Bender Sokole (w, m)	---
	Just a Little Present	Lucy Bender Sokole (w, m)	---
	My Sweet	Lucy Bender Sokole (w, m)	---
	Take It with a Grain of Salt	Lucy Bender Sokole (w, m)	---
	Willow Weep for Me		Irving Berlin, Inc.
	What the Dickens Do We Care		DeSylva, Brown & Henderson, Inc.
	Shoot the Works! (musical revue)		
	Let's Go Out in the Open Air		Famous Music Corp.
1933	Brief Moment	Hilda Gottlieb (m)	Irving Berlin, Inc.
	Dark Moon (Come Out from the Clouds Above)	Moises Simons (m)	Edward B. Marks Music Corp.
	I Can't Even Cry	Lucy Bender (w, m)	---
	(I'm Gonna Hurry to) Take My Time Down South		Irving Berlin, Inc.
	In a Silly Symphony		Irving Berlin, Inc.
	Lullaby of Love		Irving Berlin, Inc.

References are to Notes to be found at the end of this appendix.

Year	Song	Collaborator	Publisher
	Mickey Mouse and Minnie's in Town		Irving Berlin, Inc.
	Tango Lover	Helmy Kresa (m)	Edward B. Marks Music Corp.
	There's Work to Be Done		Irving Berlin Music, Inc.
	What the Dickens Do We Care		Irving Berlin Music, Inc.
	Who's Afraid of the Big Bad Wolf?	Frank Churchill (w, m) AR (additional words)	Irving Berlin Music, Inc.
	Zelda by the Zuider Zee	Lu C. Bender (w), AR (m)	Irving Berlin Music, Inc.
	Palooka (movie)		
	Palooka (It's a Grand Old American Name)	Johnny Burke (w), AR (m)	Irving Berlin Music, Inc.
1934	An Elephant Never Forgets		---
	Twinkle, Twinkle WAMPAS Star		---
	Down to Their Last Yacht (movie)		
	Beach Boy		Irving Berlin Music, Inc.
	Funny Little World		Irving Berlin Music, Inc.
	South Sea Bolero (instrumental)	Max Steiner (m), AR (m)	Irving Berlin Music, Inc.
1935	Early Bird	Edward Eliscu (w)	Movietone Music Corp.
	Pretty Polly (Sea Chanty)	Edward Eliscu (w)	Movietone Music Corp.
	Magic of Spring (ballet-sing)		Ann Ronell Music, Inc.
	The Bugle Waltz		
	Sweet Magic		
	Only Once		
1936	*The Big Broadcast of 1936* (movie)[4]		
	Beep Beep Beep		---
	Listen in on My Heart		---
1937	*Champagne Waltz* (movie)[5]		Paramount Music, Inc./ Popular Melodies Inc.
	The Lorelei		
	Merry-Go-Round		
	The Music of My Heart		
	Say It with Handies		
	Singin' with the Band		
	Some Fun, Hey Kid		
	You're the You		
1938	The One Indispensable Man	Gioachino Rossini (m)[6]	G. Schirmer, Inc.
	Blockade (movie)		
	Beloved, You're Lovely	Werner Janssen (m)	Chappell & Co., Inc.
	The River Is (So) Blue[7]	Kurt Weill (m)	Walter Wanger Productions
	March-Finale[7]	Kurt Weill (m)	Walter Wanger Productions
	That Certain Age (movie)		
	Daydreams (Ah! Je Veux Vivre)	Charles Gounod (m)	G. Schirmer, Inc.
	The Girls of Cadiz (Les Filles de Cadix)	Leo Delibes (m)	G. Schirmer, Inc.
	Martha (opera)[8]	Friedrich von Flotow (m)	G. Schirmer, Inc.
	The Drinking Song		
	The First Rose of Summer		
	Here's (a) Goodnight		
	('Tis) the Last Rose of Summer		
	One Lonely Night		
	Over Hill, Over Dale		
	Round and Round		
	The Spinning Quartet		
	(Martha, Martha) Sweet as a Dream		
	Well, Now What?		
	While My Heart Has Trusted		
	Algiers (movie)		
	C'est la Vie (That's the Life)	Vincent Scotto (m)	Choudens, Editeur, Paris

Year	Song	Collaborator	Publisher
	Where Is Home? (Pepe Le Moko)	Vincent Scotto (m)	Robbins Music/Ann Ronell Music, Inc.
1939	Andy Panda		Nathaniel Shilkret Music/ W.A. Quincke & Co.
	Deanna Durbin Album of Favorite Songs and Arias (songbook)[9, 10]		G. Schirmer, Inc.
	Allelujia	Wolfgang Amadeus Mozart (m)	
	Country Song (Chanson Provencale)	E. dell' Aqua (m)	
	Daydreams (Je Veux Vivre)	Charles Gounod (m)	
	Girls of Cadiz (Les Filles de Cadix)	Leo Delibes (m)	
	I Vow to Do All in My Power (Micaela's Aria)	Georges Bizet (m)	
	The Kiss Waltz (Il Bacio)	L. Arditi (m)	
	The Last Rose of Summer	Friedrich von Flotow (m)	
	Yours the Dearest Name I Know (Cara Nome)	Giuseppe Verdi (m)	
1940	Blue Lie the Hills	Johann Strauss (m)	G. Schirmer, Inc.
	Forever But a Dream	Franz Liszt (m)	G. Schirmer, Inc.
	Love in Sorrento	C. A. Bixio (m)	Boston Music Co.
	The Gypsy Baron (operetta)[9]	Johann Strauss, Jr. (m)	G. Schirmer, Inc.
	Flirtation Intermezzo		
	Love Can Be Dreamed		
	Love Deals the Cards Tonight		
	Open Road, Open Sky		
	When Lovers Meet		
	The World Is Wide Open to Me		
	Your Eyes Shine in My Own		
	In the Judy Garland Manner (songbook)[9]		G. Schirmer, Inc. Based on:
	The Barca-Rhumba-Rolle	Jacques Offenbach (m)	Barcarolle
	Brother Jackie	French traditional folk song (m)	Freres Jacques
	Love's Violin	Anton Rubinstein (m)	Melody in F
	A Lover's Dream	Franz Liszt (m)	Liebestraum
	One Heart Was Yearning	Franz Schubert (m)	Schubert waltzes
	The Song My Mother Loved	B. Godard (m)	Berceuse
	A Song Out of Heaven	Frederic Chopin (m)	E Flat Nocturne
	Twilight, Twilight	Jules Massenet (m)	Elegy
	You Came, You Saw, You Wrote It Mr. Strauss	Johann Strauss (m)	Blue Danube Waltz
	You Can Waltz Beethoven's Minuet	Ludwig van Beethoven (m)	Minuet in G
1941	**There's Magic in Music** (movie)		
	Fireflies on Parade		Famous Music Corp.
	The Mountain Song	Edvard Grieg (m)	---
	The Chocolate Soldier (operetta)	Oscar Straus (m), AR (w)[11]	Oscar Straus/AR
	Love Comes Easy to Me		
	To Be in Love Is to Be		
	Soldier Ballet		
	Where Do We Go from Here		
1942	**Count Me In** (musical)[12]		
	The All Out Bugle Call		
	Bess—Arabia CUT		
	Boodle Is Cake CUT		Ann Ronell Music, Inc.
	Five Little Sparrows CUT		
	Grand Old Custom CUT		

Year	Song	Collaborator	Publisher
	It's a Funny Thing CUT		
	Let the Wind Blow CUT		
	Life Goes to Washington CUT		
	On Leave for Love		
	Papa's Lament CUT		
	Someone in the Know		Chappell & Co, Inc.
	A Stranger Lullaby CUT		
	There's Work to be Done CUT		
	Ticketyboo		Chappell & Co., Inc.
	The Way My Ancestors Went		
	We're Still on the Map		
	Who Is General Staff?		Chappell & Co., Inc.
	Why Do They Say They're the Fair Sex		Chappell & Co., Inc.
	The Woman of the Year		Chappell & Co., Inc.
	You've Got It All		Chappell & Co., Inc.
	April Nostalgia	Oscar Straus (m)	Ann Ronell Music., Inc.
	Ship South (ballet-sing)	Nicolai Berezovsky (m)	Nicolai Berezovsky/AR
1943	*Commandos Strike at Dawn* (movie)		
	The Commandos March	Louis Gruenberg (m)	Mills Music, Inc.
	Out to Pick the Berries	Norwegian folk song (m)	Mills Music, Inc.
	The Gypsy Baron (operetta revised)	Johann Strauss, Jr. (m)	Ann Ronell Music, Inc.
	The Grass Is Always Greener Somewhere Else		
	Gypsy Feast		
	Gypsy Temp'rament		
	The Model Farm		
	Soon As a New Man Appears		
1944	*Open Road* (operetta)[13]		Ann Ronell Music, Inc.
	Ding Dong! The Little Bell		
	The Grass Is Greener		
	I Want to Look Around Some More		
	Why Bother		
1945	Who's Walking in My Shoes		Desylva, Brown & Henderson, Inc.
	The Story of G.I. Joe (movie)		Picture Music., Inc./Leeds
	The Ernie Pyle Infantry March		
	I'm Comin' Back		
	Linda		
1947	*Oh! Susanna* (musical)[14]		Ann Ronell Music, Inc.
	Clean As April Day		
	Doo-Dah-Day (Camptown Races)		
	Godey's Lady's Book		
	Ho! for Lou'sianna #		
	I Dream of Jeannie		
	Kissing in the Dark		
	Minstrelsy #		
	My Forever Love		
	No Matter Where You Roam		
	No One to Love		
	Not for a Moment		
	O'er the Green		
	Oh! De Shanghai Chicken #		
	Oh! Susanna		
	Ring De Banjo Parade		
	The River's Song #		
	The Sewing Bee		

Year	Song	Collaborator	Publisher
	Sing Me a Lovesong Tonight		
	Some Folks Say		#
	Songs from the Heart		
	Watch the Folks Go By		
	'Way from Michigan to Mexico		
	Wear a Moustache		
	When De Glendy Burk Comes Down		
	Where the Waters Meet the Shore		
	Who'll Serenade You #		
1948	*One Touch of Venus* (movie)[15]	Kurt Weill (m)	Chappell & Co., Inc.
	(Don't Look Now) But My Heart is Showing		
	My Week		
1949	*Love Happy* (movie)		
	Harpo's Rumba		Ann Ronell Music, Inc.
	Love Happy		Jewel Music Publishing
	Who Stole the Jam?		Ann Ronell Music, Inc.
1951	Round and Round	Friedrich von Flotow (m)	G. Schirmer, Inc.
	To Dance, to Dream	Johann Strauss (m)	G. Schirmer, Inc.
	Too Soon	Leon Leonardi (m)	---
	Wear a Buddy Poppy		---
1952	The Five-Penny Whistle		Robert Music Corp.
	Happy Happy Wedding		Ann Ronell Music, Inc.
	The River (movie)		
	The River	Indian folk song (m)	G. Schirmer, Inc.
1953	*Main Street to Broadway* (movie)		
	Blue New York		Ann Ronell Music, Inc.
	Just a Girl		Ann Ronell Music, Inc.
	Hondo (movie)		
	Hondo, Hondo	Hugo Friedhofer (m)	Ann Ronell Music, Inc.
	The Crucible (drama)		
	Sleep, My Babe, My Darling (Lullaby)		Ann Ronell Music, Inc.
1955	The Ice Vogues		---
	The Great Adventure (movie)		
	The Great Adventure		Ann Ronell Music, Inc.
1956	Anatole	Jean and Rodolphe Legros (m)	Ann Ronell Music, Inc.
	The La-La Song (The Little Musicians)	Francesca Paolo Frontini (m)	Ann Ronell Music, Inc.
	The Little Musicians		Ann Ronell Music, Inc.
	Too Big a Price		Ann Ronell Music, Inc.
	Stop and Go on a Bike		Ann Ronell Music, Inc.
1957	Dear Miss Lonelyhearts		Ann Ronell Music, Inc.
	Happy, Happy Wedding		Ann Ronell
	Happy Birthday All Year Long		Ann Ronell Music, Inc.
	Hungry for Love		Ann Ronell Music, Inc.
1958	Across the Everglades		Ann Ronell Music, Inc.
1959	Henry Hudson-Hudson		Ann Ronell Music, Inc.
	Meranga		Ann Ronell Music, Inc.
1960	Morgen Auf Wiedersehen	Louis Applebaum (m)	Ann Ronell Music, Inc.
	The St. Thomas Carnival		Ann Ronell Music, Inc.
1961	Gay Adventure	Friedrich von Flotow (m)	---
	If You Listen	Friedrich von Flotow (m)	---
	One Lonely Night	Friedrich von Flotow (m)	Ann Ronell Music, Inc.
1962	Take Me, Take Me to the Moon	Tikhon Khrennikov (m)	Ann Ronell Music, Inc.
1963	Who's Afraid of Virginia Woolf?		Ann Ronell Music, Inc.

Year	Song	Collaborator	Publisher
1964	Backward Ho with Barry		Ann Ronell Music, Inc.
	Put Kennedy in the Senate Now		Ann Ronell Music, Inc.
1965	Kookie Kook		Ann Ronell Music, Inc.
1966	In Karlovy Vary		Ann Ronell Music, Inc.
	Unfinished project	Dejean Bontempelli (m)	Ann Ronell Music, Inc
	Angela's Wedding		
	How Do You Say?		
	If You Speak French		
	The Little Mascot		
	The Man Rimbaud		
	The River Seine		
	A Song for Juliet		
	What a Rendezvous		
	Where Were You Then, Madrid?		
	Why Not Begin Again		
	The Young Debs		
1968	Love Is in My Heart	Philip Ginder (w, m)	Ann Ronell Music, Inc.
1970	Le Shanah		Ann Ronell Music, Inc.
	My Friend John		Ann Ronell
1972	My Second Chance		Ann Ronell
1985	Meditations	Moshe Davis (w)	Ann Ronell
2002	The Picture on the Wall	Kurt Weill (m)	European American Music Corp.
	Your Technique	Kurt Weill (m)	European American Music Corp.

Copyrighted Songs with Uncertain Dates[16]

Song	Collaborator	Purpose
Alert America		American Legion Convention
At the ANTA Ball		American National Theater
Association show		
Awake and Sing		Film music[17]
Beethoven Specialty		For Hildegarde
Buy a Buddy Poppy		Veterans of America show
Cable Car Song (Cable Car Click-a-Choo)		Citizens Committee to Save the Cable Cars
Canzone Del Porter from Mar		#
Carmen, Carmen, You're Too Charmen	George Bizet (m)	For Irra Petina for Metropolitan Opera New Years' Concert
Champagne Lady (Valse Bluette)	Riccardo Drigo (m)	For Anna Maria Alberghetti
Cuban Echo		
Dear Miss Emily Post		
The Do-Re-Mi		Film music
Evening Bells (Dream-time Bells)	Anton Rubinstein (m)	# Production number[18]
The Eyes of You	Dejean Bontempelli (m)	
Give Me a Lesson in Love		Film music
Happy Holiday		
He Loves Me "Yes" (The Daisies Ought to Tell)	Leo Delibes (m)	# For Mary Martin
Hi, There, Charlie McCarthy		Film music
If You Whistle		Film music
In California		Film music
It Had to Be		
Je Dis que Rien ne m'Eprouva		#
Let Me Live Lazy with You		Production number
Let the Wind Blow		Production number
Let's Go to Church		Production number

Copyrighted Songs with Uncertain Dates[16]	Collaborator	Purpose
Like a Little Bird		Special material
Little Silver Bells	Johann Sebastian Bach (m)	#
Love's the Beginning		Film music
Lovin' Arms		
The Lullaby of Love		
Memphisizing Tennessee		Tennessee Cotton Festival
Music Master		Film music
The Music of My Heart		Film music
My Fortune Is in Your Hand		
My Kingdom for Your Kiss		
My Opium Dreams		
A Night for Love		#
Oh, Where Is the Star		
The One Indispensable Man	Gioachino Rossini (m)	# Production number
Opium Dreams		Production number
Our Childhood Days		
Playtime		Film music
Presto Presto	Treharne Bryceson (m)	#
Propaganda	Gioachino Rossini (m)	Production number
The Rising Tide		Film music
A Rumba for the Harp		Film music
Shadow Lace	Fredric Chopin (m)	#
Sleeping Heart of Mine	Peter Ilich Tchaikovsky (m)	# Film music
Sold on Love		
The Song of De Skoit		Production number
Stars and Stripes Forever	John Philip Sousa (m)	Production number
The Storm Is Gone	Frederic Chopin (m)	# Production number
Streamlined		
Sunny Bunny in His Gunny Sack		Film music
This One Man		
To Hear Your Voice Again	Anton Rubinstein (m)	# Film music
When Lights Are Low	Robert Schumann (m)	# Production number
When the Night Is Over		
The Wishing Song		*Wizard of Oz* radio project
The World's in Love		Film music
The Yearning Waltz	Franz Schubert (m)	#
You Fill Me with Delight		#
You Give Me a Lift		Film music
You Used to Love Me		

Unpublished Songs with No Dates[19]	Collaborator	Purpose
Alice in Wonderland		Film music
Be Very Saks–Fifth Avenue		
The Cowardly Lion		*Wizard of Oz* radio project
The Customer Is Always Right		
Darkie Debbil		
An Elephant Never Forgets		Production number
Eyes of Love Light		
Five Little Sparrows		
Hail to Thee, Chocolate Eclair		
Hungry for Love		
I Wish I Could		
I'd Spend the Day with You		
If		
I'll Sing a Song	Edward Horan (m)	Operetta

Unpublished Songs with No Dates[19]	Collaborator	Purpose
Invitation to the Dance	Carl Maria von Weber (m)	Arrangement for voices
Is It Lovelight? (Dark Eyes)	Russian folk song (m)	Production number
The Judge Can't Get Off the Bench to Chase Chickens		For Breakfast Club, Los Angeles
Just Like a Little Bird		For Helen Morgan
The Land of Oz		*Wizard of Oz* radio project
Let Your Red Shoes Dance	Henryk Wieniawski (m)	
The Little Do Do Clown		For New York toy companies
The Little Tailor		For New York toy companies
Lonesome Prairie		*Wizard of Oz* radio project
Love Plays Solitaire	Ann Leaf (m)	
Lover, I Am Leaving		
Low, Like the Gentle Lark (Listen to the Lark)	Henry R. Bishop (m)	For Mary Martin
The Mazurka Ensemble	Edward Horan (m)	Operetta
Moon Magic		Production number
My Dream Girl		Zeta Beta Tau convention
My Hai Resh Daddy		
A Night Like This	Ann Leaf (m)	
Now Goodnight (Cradle Song)	Johannes Brahms (m)	
One Year Younger		For Sigmund Romberg's 70th
Only Once		Operetta
Play the Song My Heart Is Singing	Edward Horan (m)	
The Rio-Coco		
Rommy Dance		
The Scarecrow		*Wizard of Oz* radio project
Shadow Lace	Frederic Chopin (m)	
Sipping a Soda		
Sleep My Baby (Falla Bambino)		For Anna Maria Alberghetti
Song of the Skirt		
Star of the Sea	Georges Bizet (m)	
The Storm Is Gone	Frederic Chopin (m)	For Jan Kiepura
Such a Crazy Romance		
The Sunshine Bugle Call		Novelty
Sweet Little Silver Bells	Johann Sebastian Bach (m)	
Take the Well to the Bucket		
That Theme (That Haunting Theme)		
Then Will I Dream Again		
This is My Home	Goldmark	
The Tin Woodman Song		*Wizard of Oz* radio project
To Be or Not to Be a Muff		*Puss in Boots* project
Too Soon		
A Tune from Tunisia	Cesar Cui (m)	
Twilight	Edward Horan (m)	Operetta
Velvet		Special material
The Voices of Spring	Johann Strauss (m)	
Vote for Emmett Lavery		Political campaign song
Waltzing Moonlight		
Was It the Kiss?		
The Weatherman Song	Ann Leaf (m)	
The Wedding Song		For Hildegarde
Where Is Home?		Film music
Who Put the Good in Goodbye?		Lyrics for Meredith Willson
Who's Got the Best of the Bargain		*Puss in Boots* project
Wishing Dishes		*Wizard of Oz* radio project
You Can't Be a Friend of Mine		
You're the You		

Notes

1. Both words (w) and music (m) done by Ann Ronell unless the name of a composer, e.g., Oscar Straus (m), is shown, indicating that Ronell wrote only the words. Any other exceptions to this are indicated with an AR ( ) designation and with that of another composer and/or lyricist ( ).

2. Irving Berlin Music, Inc. later became Bourne Music, Inc.

3. --- indicates date is known, but publisher of song is uncertain.

4. These two songs were written by AR prior to employment by the producer, Paramount, and were never used in the film.

5. AR was the principal song composer for *Champagne Waltz*, but of all these songs, only "The Merry-Go-Round" was used.

6. Ronell did numerous arrangements of compositions by classical composers, often adding English lyrics. Several classical composers will thus appear in this appendix.

7. Cut from final version of movie.

8. Words and libretto translated by Vicki Baum and Ann Ronell.

9. English words and libretto by Ann Ronell.

10. Compiled and edited by Andres de Segurola.

11. AR wrote words to the music of Oscar Strauss for these four new songs for the reworking of the operetta.

12. Songs marked CUT were dropped from the show before it's Broadway opening.

13. Music based on that from opera *The Gypsy Baron*, composed by Johann Strauss, Jr. AR modified words and libretto to create this musical work.

14. All words and music by Stephen Foster with piano and choral arrangements by Ann Ronell as well as occasional changes in the words to accommodate the new version. For purposes of the musical, Ronell altered many of the titles. Songs marked # were published by G. Schirmer, Inc., as piano-choral arrangements. Of all these, "Some Folks Say" was the song Ronell most altered and could claim as her own.

15. The original words to these two songs written by Ogden Nash, but words and titles changed by AR to conform to scenes in movie.

16. All songs copyrighted by Ann Ronell Music, Inc., unless marked # denoting G. Schirmer, Inc.

17. Film music refers to those songs written or arranged for a film, though in many cases, were not used.

18. Production numbers are those AR created for particular singers for their solo acts, concerts, or recitals.

19. These songs were written mostly for special occasions or as unique materials for various singers. Ronell kept files on these songs but they were not published or copyrighted, as far as can be ascertained from available records. Some of these are complete songs, while other may just be sketches of lyrics and/or a melody, never completed.

APPENDIX D

Singers and Artists Affiliated with Ronell

The following is a list of persons Ronell worked with as coach, arranger, and composer of special materials, lyrics, and songs.

Anna Maria Alberghetti	Evelyn Herbert	Helen Morgan
Louis Armstrong	Hildegarde	Jan Peerce
Baccaloni	Helen Jepson	Irra Petina
Charles Boyer	Howard Keel	John Raitt
Eddie Cantor	Jan Kiepura	Robert Rounseville
Vivian Della Chiesa	Nina Koshetz	Rise Stevens
June Christy	Steve Lawrence	Dorothy Stone
Eugene Conley	Brenda Lewis	Brian Sullivan
Nadine Connor	Diana Lynn	Gladys Swarthout
Nina Crimi	Gordon MacRae	Richard Tauber
Deanna Durbin	Mary Martin	John Charles Thomas
Marta Eggerth	Robert Merrill	John Tyers
Ruth Etting	Marilyn Miller	Karl Weis
Ella Fitzgerald	Grace Moore	Andy Williams
Judy Garland	Dennis Morgan	Earl Wrightson

APPENDIX E

Film Credits

Year	Film (Production Company)	Song	AR Role	Collaborator (Role)
1934	*Palooka* (Edward Small–Reliance)	"Palooka"	W/M	Johnny Burke (W/M)
1934	*Down to Their Last Yacht* (RKO)	"Beach Boy"	W/M	
		"Funny Little World"	W/M	
		"South Sea Bolero"	M	Max Steiner (M/MD)
1936	*Big Broadcast of 1936* (Paramount)[1*]	"Listen In on My Heart"	W/M	
		"Beep Beep Beep"	W/M	
	Captain January (Fox)[2]		W/M	
	Poor Little Rich Girl (Fox)[2]		W/M	
1937	*Champagne Waltz* (Paramount)[3]	"The Merry-Go-Round"	W/M	
		"The Lorelei"	W/M	
		"Twilight, Twilight"	W	
		"Music of My Heart"	W/M	
		"Singin' with the Band"	W/M	
		"You're the You"	W/M	
		"Some Fun, Hey Kid"	W/M	
		"Say It with Handies"	W/M	
1938	*Algiers* (United Artists)	"C'est la Vie"	W/Sc	Vincent Scotto (M)
		"Algiers"	W/Sc	Vincent Scotto (M)
1938	*Blockade* (United Artists)	"Beloved, You're Lovely"	W/AMD	Werner Janssen (M/Sc)
		"The River Is Blue" (cut)	W	Kurt Weill (M)
1939	*You Can't Cheat an Honest Man* (Universal)		AMD	
1941	*There's Magic in Music* (Paramount)	"Fireflies on Parade"	W/M/St	
1941	*Ladies in Retirement* (Columbia)		AMD	Ernst Toch (Sc)
1942	*Commandos Strike at Dawn* (Columbia)	"Out to Pick the Berries"	W/M	Louis Gruenberg (Sc)
		"Commandos March"	W	Louis Gruenberg (M)
1944	*Tomorrow, the World!* (Lester Cowan Productions/ United Artists)		MD	Louis Applebaum (Sc)
1945	*The Story of G.I. Joe* (United Artists)	"Linda"	W/Sc	Louis Applebaum (M/Sc)
		"I'm Coming Back"	W	Louis Applebaum (M)
		"The Ernie Pyle Infantry March"	W	Louis Applebaum (M)
1948	*One Touch of Venus*[4] (Universal/Artists Alliance)	"My Week"	W	Kurt Weill (M)
		"Don't Look Now But My Heart Is Showing"	W	Kurt Weill (M)
		"Speak Low"	W	Kurt Weill (M)

*References are to Notes on the following page.

166

Year	Film (Production Company)	Song	AR Role	Collaborator (Role)
1950	*Love Happy* (United Artists)	"Love Happy"	W/M/Sc	
1951	*The River* (United Artists)	"The River"	W/M	
1953	*Main Street to Broadway* (MGM)	"Just a Girl"	W/M/ MD/Sc	
		"Blue New York"	W/M	
1955	*Hondo* (Warner Bros.)	"Hondo, Hondo"	W/M	Hugo Friedhofer (Sc)
1955	*The Great Adventure* (Rochemont)	"The Great Adventure"	W/M	
1962	*Meeting at a Far Meridian*[5] (Mosfilm)	"Take Me, Take Me to the Moon"	W/M	Tikhon Khrennikov (M)

Key:

```
AMD . . . . . . Associate music director
C . . . . . . . . . Conductor
M . . . . . . . . Music
MD . . . . . . . Music director
Sc . . . . . . . . Score
St . . . . . . . . Story
W . . . . . . . . Words
```

Notes

1. These two songs were written by AR prior to employment with Paramount and could not be used.

2. AR appears to have worked on the music and songs for this film, but was uncredited.

3. AR was the principal song composer for *Champagne Waltz*, but of all these songs, only "The Merry-Go-Round" was used.

4. Original words of these three songs by Ogden Nash with all modified for movie by Ann Ronell.

5. Movie never completed.

APPENDIX F

Opera in English: Translations and Adaptations

Year	Opera	Work	For
1937	The Magic Flute	co-lyricist	Los Angeles Junior College
1937	La serva padrona	co-lyricist	Los Angeles Junior College
1938	The Merry Wives of Windsor	co-lyricist	Los Angeles Junior College
1938	The Barber of Seville	co-lyricist	Los Angeles Junior College
1938	Tales of Hoffmann	co-lyricist	Los Angeles City College
1939	Martha	co-librettist and musical adaptation	Hollywood Bowl and Richard Lert
1941	The Chocolate Soldier	lyrics for additional songs	Los Angeles Light Civic Opera
1943	The Gypsy Baron	lyrics, music, and libretto	Los Angeles Light Civic Opera
1944	Open Road	lyrics, music, and libretto	St. Louis Park Theatre
1961	Martha	libretto and musical adaptation	Metropolitan Opera

APPENDIX G

Memberships, Awards, and Honors

Memberships

American Guild of Authors and Composers (AGAC)
American Society of Composers, Arrangers and Publishers (ASCAP)
Dramatists Guild
National Association of Popular Music/Songwriters Hall of Fame
National Council of Women of the United States
National Music Camp Arts Academy/Member National Advisory Board
Radcliffe Club of New York
Songwriters' Guild of America (previously AGAC)

Awards and Honors

Academy Award Nomination — Best Music Score for *The Story of G.I. Joe* (1945)
Academy Award Nomination — Best Song "Linda" from *The Story of G.I. Joe* (1945)
Song "The Ernie Pyle Infantry March" from *The Story of G.I. Joe* adopted as Official Song of the United States Army Ground Forces (1945)
Best Film Score for *Love Happy* awarded by *Film Music* magazine (1949)
Songwriters Hall of Fame/National Academy of Popular Music Song Citation award for "Willow Weep for Me" (1991)

APPENDIX H

Other Artists Recording "Willow Weep for Me"

Addis & Crofut
Ames Brothers
Gene Ammons
Louis Armstrong
Eden Atwood
Count Basie
George Benson
Ruby Braff & Roy Eldridge
Herbie Brock
Tally Brown
Ray Bryant
Joe Bushkin
Camarata Orchestra
Chad & Jeremy
Frank Chaksfield Orchestra
Pearl Chertok
June Christy
Kenny Clark
Bud Cole
Nat "King" Cole
Johnny Costa
Carol Creveling
Sonny Criss
Bob Davis Quartet
Buddy DeFranco
Wynton Delly Trio
Harry "Sweets" Edison
Roy Eldridge, Sonny Stitt, & Jonah Jones
Duke Ellington
Havelock Ellis
Ruth Etting
Frances Faye
Ferrante & Teicher
Ted Fio Rito
First Nighters
Ella Fitzgerald
Tommy Flanagan
Fontana Sisters
John Fox & His Orchestra

Laura Fygi
Red Garland Trio
Erroll Garner
Stan Getz
Jackie Gleason Orchestra
Larry Goldings
Dexter Gordon
Conley Graves Trio
Grant Green
Vince Guaraldi Trio
Lionel Hampton
Coleman Hawkins
Naura Hayden
Woody Herman Herd
Earl Hines
Art Hodes & Milt Hinton
Billie Holiday (4)
Leroy Holmes Orchestra
Rupert Holmes
Lena Horne
Milt Jackson
Harry James
Jazz Couriers
Jack Jones
Tom Kellock Strings
Stan Kenton Orchestra
Kern & Sloop & Mitchell
Gene Krupa Quartet
John Lewis & Sacha Distel
Living Jazz
Henry Mancini with Doc Severinsen
Herbie Mann & Bill Evans Trio
Muzzy Marcellino
Mary Mayo
Howard McGhee
Hal McKusick
Marian & Jimmy McPartland
Red Mitchell
Modern Jazz Quartet

Wes Montgomery
Now Brass
Oscar Peterson
Bud Powell
Boyd Raeburn Orchestra
Lou Rawls
Buddy Rich
Lita Roza
David Sanborn
Stefan Scaggiari Trio
David Seville Orchestra
Serena Shaw
Nina Simone
Zoot Sims
Frank Sinatra
Jimmy Smith
Dakota Staton
Sonny Stitt
Les Strand
Art Tatum (5)
Billy Taylor
Three Sounds
Cal Tjader
Joe Turner
Stanley Turrentine
McCoy Tyner
Sarah Vaughan
Dinah Washington
Ernie Watts
Ben Webster
Lawrence Welk
Paul Whiteman Orchestra with Irene Taylor
Joe Wilder
Andy Williams
Mary Lou Williams with Bobby Hackett
Nancy Wilson
Phil Woods
Lester Young

APPENDIX I

"A Dissertation on What's It All About"

Radcliffe Magazine, January, 1927

"What is it all about?" The inevitable endless question sidles up to the older generation with all the seduction of a demi-monde, and pokes the sensibilities of the younger generation with all the importance of an ancient sooth-sayer. What *is* it all about?—This daring, this probing, this searching into the depths of the old ivy-laden well Realism, whose waters once tasted by Talent produce a variated hysteria named Modernism.

"It's the work of the Devil!" cry out the old humbugs. "Can't you see the cloven foot stalking through our literature, horn-curves crooking our art, and pitchforks pricking the meters of our music?— Yes, pitchforks, piling up a mass of notes to throw upon our sacred hearths, and idiots calling the result 'red-hot'!"

While the young humbugs shout, "It's the spirit of the age! Freedom is life! no rules, no ancestors, no qualms! Rip up the classics, stir up the melting pot! All for originality—individuality or death!" And so on the exclamation points;—and fewer dots at the close of chapters.

New books, new plays, new magazine competition, new song-hits; everything must be new. No matter if nothing's new under the sun: paint it with silver gilt and it shines in the moonlight. And the sibilant contest finds a hallelujah: "On with the subway stand, the science of psychology, and the subtleties of Schonberg."

The Little Theatres which flourish in both the lighted and darkened scurryways of cities, make constant stir with plays of modern color: Freudian splashes and Arlenesque streaks, Chekhovish shadows and Guitrian silhouettes. The large orchestras which play in carpeted halls, monthly create new reputations with music of the latest ink. Mengelberg gives a labeled day of "Pleasant and Unpleasant Music" of the young fledgling moderns. Koussevit-

zky goes to New York to present an entire program of the aesthetic ultra-moderns. Where Honegger, others of the French Six, and the American Copland distract the vibrations of one concert-hall, Krasa, Webern, and Gruenberg both limpidly and cadaverously claw the senses of the other concert-hall.

Music as a polite subject is smiled upon by the penny-point bridge fiends who take their music *a la* radio; music as a bone of contention is wrangled over by countless conservatory pupils; music as a cure for boredom is advertised by the owners of European-furnished homes of both continents:— "Are you invited to the tea Mrs. Bank is giving for Soandso, the composer who was commended in the recent reviews for writing a sonata with no themes?"—"No, I am going to Mrs. Roll's afternoon for that young fellow whose picture was in the paper—I forgot his name—who, when he was greeted by hisses at the performance of his Concerto for two Kettledrums, shouted 'Eureka!' at the audience."—"Well, I like Soandso's music best. He is so English-looking, and never asks for onions with the cheese."

The real arguments pro and con are kept in circulation by frequent repetition on the part of the conservatory students,—God save them! Who the originators of any keen criticism are, no one can tell in this day of free thinking, but we have a suspicion that they may be some of the old intelli-gents who were too versatile to write valuable music. To discuss modern music one must have at his fingertips such terms as *atonality, impressionism, pianissimo espressivo, saxophone, rhythmic atmosphere,* and *Rhapsodie in Blue.* If one cannot distinguish between the musical expression of the flutter of an enchanted bird's wings and human heart-beats, he is forever lost to the cause of the Critics. His fate is one of program-notes.

To preserve the effect suggested by the above italicized words, we must continue to talk around them. The reader has probably heard of the noun *atonality*; it is the subject of the Stravinsky predicate (or should we say predicament? On second thought, no, for we would be accused of wearing monocles. Also, a predicate is a verb, — a verb does things, — so does Stravinsky, — refer to geometric laws, — Q.E.D.). Anyway, there is no key whatever to this atonality situation.

Concerning *impressionism* and *pianissimo espressivo*, the former is the more faded word. Debussy, as you are aware, was the impressionist *par excellence*, but Milhaud assures us that the style is spineless and the entirety of impressionism is naught but a blind alley. We observant ones have realized for long that a complete abstraction in musical sound is the newest mark of genius; for has not Paul Stefan declared that the writing of "a shadow of a tune" is one of the noblest gifts given to a composer? The elusive wisps of Hungarian sounds are opposed in ideals to the sensuous French harmonies. One must have much imagination to appreciate their evasive beauty; and on the other hand, but little imagination is needed to understand the total abstraction of their aim. With all due homage to Anton Von Webern, we adopt the *pianissimo espressivo* as a test of the modern composer's abilities; — can he produce "a genuine sigh"?

Coming to the more tangible idea of *saxophone*, we can state that this phenomenon appears in the composer's score, but rarely in the conductor's. The latter religiously substitutes the clarinet in the "highbrow orchestra"; possibly, it has been suggested, for no other reason than to leave saxophonists free to make up the annual saxophone assemblies (we have too much respect for the title "symphonies"). This instrument heads the list of "low-brow" orchestral members used only in the spirit of victory, surrender, or abandon. So one may be certain that any composer asking for saxophone, mandolin, banjo, harmonica, or non-skid chains is perfectly modern.

Hearing music of *rhythmic atmosphere*, one will comprehend the meaning by the sensations which urge him to waltz, commit setting-up exercises, Charleston, sway the body — or do all of them. The sound waves hit the senses with pleasant, if shocking, persuasion.

And finally, we arrive at the end of our vocabulary explanations with the statement that the *Rhapsodie in Blue* is a term used when the music reminds one of something he had heard before, but he is not absolutely sure when or how much; so he remarks, "There is a touch of the *Rhapsodie* in this, don't you think? A decided Gershwinian flavor to this work, I'll be blowed!" And so they blue the piccolos.

No matter what we joke about, however, and no matter what we fight about, this Modern business cannot be shrugged off the mind with a classical frown. The drawings in the drama today, the rhythms in our present art, and the gestures of our twentieth-century music are all various masks of the artist Modernism, whom some worship as a god, with whom some scorn to fraternize, and from whom others borrow ideas to enhance their own feeble glory. Nothing is worthless which has power to attract the attention of worth; it has value even for naught else but adding a link to the chain of development. The trouble with railers and scorners is poor eye-sight. They see only the outer shine and superficialities of novelty; they cannot perceive what lies beneath. Nor can they conceive the whole line of labor through the ages taking several steps through this one. The paths of the forest are hidden always from the plain.

That's *what it is all about*! It's all about a growing tree, proverbially called Progress, that is decked out by foresters with all the artificialities of the Xmas spirit to appear as unfamiliar as possible to the old woods birds, who keep to their haunts only to see their offspring pecking at the fascinating tinsel to find out what's underneath.

And what *is* there? New shoots and strong branches, — just a bit silvery from star-dust.

Anne Rosenblatt, '27

APPENDIX J
Ann Ronell Firsts

First woman to:

- score a Hollywood film, *Algiers*, 1938
- conduct a soundtrack for a Hollywood film
- earn an Academy Award nomination for Best Song, "Linda," 1945
- earn an Academy Award nomination for Best Film Score, *The Story of G.I. Joe*, with Louis Applebaum
- write words and music for songs in a Hollywood film, *Down to Their Last Yacht* (1934): "Beach Boy" and "Funny Little World"
- compose film score for feature Hollywood films, *One Touch of Venus*, 1948, *Love Happy*, 1949, and *Main Street to Broadway*, 1953
- compose words and music for a Broadway show, *Count Me In*, 1942
- serve as music director for a Hollywood feature film, *Tomorrow, the World!*, 1944
- do the English libretto for a European opera, *Martha*, 1938, with Vicki Baum

First Hollywood composer to:

- be involved, among other personnel, with recording of the complete film score recorded for sale to the public, *Ladies in Retirement*, 1942
- have song, "Ernie Pyle Infantry March," sung over title credits of film, *The Story of G.I. Joe*, 1945

Chapter Notes

Abbreviations are as follows:

NJHS .... Ann Ronell Papers—Nebraska Jewish Historical Society, Omaha
ARA ..... Ann Ronell Archive—Collection of the author, Chicago
NYPL .... Ann Ronell Special Collections—Music Division, New York Public Library for the
Performing Arts, Astor, Lennox and Tilden Foundations, New York
MHL..... Lester Cowan Papers—Margaret Herrick Library, Academy of Motion Picture Arts
and Sciences, Special Collections, Beverly Hills

Chapter 1

1. Julia Blanshard, "She Crashed Tin Pan Alley," *NEA News Service*, January 23, 1933.
2. *The Columbia Encyclopedia*, 6th ed., ed. Paul Lagasse (New York: Columbia University Press, 2000), s.v. "pogrom"; *Encyclopedia American: International Edition* (Danbury, CT: Scholastic Library Publishing, 2006), s.v. "pogrom"; *The New Encyclopedia Britannica*, 15th ed., s.v. "pogrom."
3. P.J. Rosenblatt to Ronell, August 21, 1975, Nebraska Jewish Historical Society (NJHS); Robert Russell, nephew, phone discussion with author, February 16, 2004; Robert Russell to NJHS, n.d., NJHS.
4. Ronell to Peter Rosenblatt, nephew, August 25, 1976, ARA.
5. Ronell, "Notes on Ann Ronell's Life," unpublished, circa 1985, 1, NJHS.
6. Ronell to Peter Rosenblatt.
7. Edward Jablonski, "Ann Ronell—Omaha's Musical Trailblazer," *Nebraska Life* (Fall 1997), 16.
8. "Little Lady of Song: An Interview with Composer Ann Ronell," *American Illustrated*, United States Information Agency magazine, draft copy, Story #335-63, 1963, 2, ARA.
9. *Omaha Daily News* [uncertain date, c. 1921], MHL.
10. Yearbook entry, Central High School, Omaha, Nebraska, 1932, NJHS.
11. Scrapbook #1, unpublished, MHL.
12. *Ibid.*
13. Margaret Matson, "Page for Women," unidentified newspaper, circa 1932, NJHS.
14. "The Fiddler Announces: Music Club Shows Relation of Science and Music," *The Radcliffe News*, April 8, 1927.
15. *The Yardstick* (Cambridge, MA: Radcliffe College, 1927), s.v. "Ronell, Anne."
16. Jablonski, 17.
17. Anne Rosenblatt, "A Dissertation on What's It All About," *Radcliffe Magazine* (January 1927), 26–27 (Appendix I).
18. "Little Lady of Song," 3.
19. Steven Suskin, *Show Tunes: 1905–1985: The Songs, Shows and Careers of Broadway's Major Composers* (New York: Dodd, Mead, 1986), 104–24; Stanley Green, *Encyclopedia of the Musical Theatre* (New York: Dodd, Mead, 1976), s.v. "Gershwin, George."
20. "Notes on Ann Ronell's Life," 4.
21. "From Radcliffe to Tin Pan Alley," *Boston Globe*, January 22, 1933.
22. "Notes on Ann Ronell's Life," 6.
23. Joan Peyser, *The Memory of All That: The Life of George Gershwin* (New York: Simon and Schuster, 1993), 149.
24. Lucia Perrigo, "Girl Composer of Hits Some Day to Do Score of U.S. Film Opera," *Wisconsin State Journal*, September 14, 1950.
25. "Little Lady of Song," 4.
26. Ronell, "Account of Creative Work," unpublished working notes, n.d., 2, NJHS.
27. Betty Walker, "Hollywood's No. 1 Woman Composer Knows Score," *Chicago Sun-Times*, June 23, 1950.
28. *Ann Ronell v. Walt Disney Productions, Inc., and Walt Disney*, U.S. District Court, Southern District of New York, Civil Action No. 101-179, "Deposition of Plaintiff, Ann Ronell," September 8, 1955, 9.
29. *Omaha World-Herald*, "She Trade-Marks Crooners," February 23, 1932.
30. Blanshard.
31. William Hinckle to Ronell, April 3, 1941, MHL.
32. "Ann Ronell Unafraid of Bad Wolf or Hard Work," *Omaha World-Herald*, July 4, 1934.
33. Ronell to unidentified family member, circa 1975, NJHS.
34. Wilfrid Sheed, *The House That George Built* (New York: Random House, 2007), 49; Howard Pollack, *George Gershwin: His Life and Work* (Berkeley, CA: University of California Press, 2006), 157–58.

35. Sandra K. Gorney, *Brother, Can You Spare a Dime?: The Life of Composer Jay Gorney* (Lanham, MD: Scarecrow Press, 2005), 9.

36. Walker.

37. Sheed, 49.

38. George Gershwin to Ronell, June 5, 1934, NYPL.

39. George Gershwin to Ronell, December 6, 1934, NYPL.

40. Peyser, 264–65.

41. Ronell to Robert Kimball, May 17, 1973, ARA.

42. Peyser, 149–50.

Chapter 2

1. Jessie Ash Arndt, "Songwriter as Plucky as Three Little Pigs," *The Christian Science Monitor*, January 3, 1955, 10.

2. Jerene Claire Cline, "Ann Ronell's Songwriting Dynamo," *Omaha World-Herald Sunday Magazine*, November 28, 1948, C-4.

3. "Ann Ronell Unafraid of Bad Wolf or Hard Work," *Omaha World-Herald*, July 4, 1934.

4. "Little Lady of Song: An Interview with Composer Ann Ronell," *American Illustrated*, U.S. Information Agency magazine, draft copy, #335-63, Washington, D.C., 1963, 3, ARA.

5. "Ann in Jig Time Spun 'Bad Wolf,'" unidentified newspaper, October 16, 1933, NYPL.

6. Arndt.

7. J. Benito Rica, "Who Says Women Can't Write Songs," *Popular Songs* (October 1934), 17, 33; Dick Jacobs and Harriet Jacobs, *Who Wrote That Song?*, 2nd ed. (Cincinnati, OH: Writer's Digest Books, 1994), 316, 397.

8. Phyllis Battelle, "Royalties are 'Fine and Dandy': Composer Has Had a Noteworthy Career," *Long Island Press*, August 10, 1976, 10.

9. Patricia Peale, "Those Songwriter Blues," *The New Yorker*, January 27, 1951, 49.

10. Julia Blanshard, "She Crashed Tin Pan Alley," *NEA News Service*, January 23, 1933.

11. Joan Peyser, *The Memory of All That: The Life of George Gershwin* (New York: Simon and Schuster, 1993), 149–50.

12. "From Radcliffe to Tin Pan Alley," *Boston Globe*, January 22, 1933.

13. Elinor Hughes, "Radcliffe Honors Graduate Composer," *The Boston Herald*, September 21, 1942.

14. Douglas Gilbert, "Girl Succeeds at Writing Songs After Getting Start on a Fluke," *New York World Telegram*, October 15, 1942.

15. Ronell, "Baby's Birthday Party" (New York: Famous Music Corporation, 1932).

16. Benjamin Sears, "Ann Ronell," unpublished manuscript, April 29, 2005, collection of E.A. Kral, 5.

17. Gilbert.

18. *The World Book Encyclopedia*, 2006, s.v. "Phonograph."

19. Gerald Bordman, *Jerome Kern: His Life and Music* (New York: Oxford University Press, 1980), 49.

20. *Ibid.*, 94.

21. Richard Buell, "Music Review: Slice of Americana Served Up with Style," *Boston Globe*, July 4, 1997.

22. Robert Baral, *Revue: A Nostalgic Reprise of the Great Broadway Period* (New York: Fleet Publishing Corporation, 1962), 193.

23. Ronell, "Let's Go Out in the Open Air" (New York: Famous Music Corporation, 1932).

24. Donald J. Stubblebine, *Broadway Sheet Music: A Comprehensive Listing of Published Music from Broadway and Other Stage Shows, 1918–1993* (Jefferson, NC: McFarland, 1996), s.v., "*Shoot the Works*"; Sondra K. Gorney, *Brother Can You Spare a Dime?: The Life of Composer Jay Gorney* (Lanham, MD: Scarecrow Press, 2005), 12.

25. Bob Grimes, to author, August 29, 2006, ARA.

26. Steven Suskin, *Show Tunes: 1905–1985* (New York: Dodd, Mead, 1986), 96, 277.

27. Ronell, "Rain on the Roof" (New York: Famous Music Corporation, 1932).

28. Olive Melville Brown, "News Especially for Women: She's Not Afraid of the Big Bad Wolf!," unidentified newspaper, circa 1934, ARA.

29. *Washington Daily News*, "Young Girl Composer Puts the Simple Things of Life into Successful Music," September 1, 1934.

30. Lucy Key Miller, "Front Views & Profiles," *Chicago Daily Tribune*, August 10, 1953, part 3, 5.

31. Ronell, New York City Royalty Agreement regarding "Rain on the Roof," Famous Music Corporation, January 24, 1931, Vol. 931, 242, ARA.

32. Ronell to Charles Hutaff, Cleveland, December 20, 1949, ARA.

33. *Variety*, "Lovin' Spoonful's New 'Rain on Roof' Springs 'Unfair Competish' Leak," October 19, 1966.

34. *Variety*, "Cues Ann Ronell Protest; She Used Same Tag in '33," April 21, 1971.

35. Stuart Kahan, Famous Music Corporation to MGM Records and Kama-Sutra Productions, October 13, 1966, ARA.

36. Sidney Herman, Stuart Kahan, Edmund Grainger, Jr., John M. Gross, Miles J. Laurie, multiple letters, 1966–1967, ARA.

37. Lester Cowan to Edmund C. Grainger, January 7, 1967, ARA.

38. John M. Gross, Kama-Sutra Productions to Stuart Kahan, February 13, 1967, ARA.

39. Sidney Herman, Famous Music Corporation to Hal Prince Productions, March 9, 1971, ARA.

40. Robert H. Montgomery to Sidney Herman, April 5, 1971, ARA.

41. Ronell, notes on unpublished radio script, 1941, 10, ARA.

42. Ronell, "Give Me Back My Heart" (New York: Bourne, 1932).

43. Ronell to Artie Shaw, March 2, 1951, NYPL.

44. Ann Ronell, passport, United States of America, April 27, 1932, NYPL.

45. *Notable Names in the American Theatre* (Clifton, NJ: James T. White, 1976), s.v. "Ronell, Ann."

46. Ken Bloom, *Hollywood Song: The Complete Film and Musical Companion* (New York: Facts on File, 1995), s.v., "Champagne Waltz."

47. "Soundtracks for 'Champagne Waltz,'" http:///www.imdb.com/title/tt0028705/soundtrack (accessed November 25, 2007); Donald J. Stubblebine, *Cinema Sheet Music* (Jefferson, NC: McFarland, 1991), s.v. "Champagne Waltz."

48. Ronell, "The Merry-Go-Round" (New York: Popular Melodies, 1936).

49. Bloom.

50. Frank Veloz to Ronell, June 9, 1936, ARA.

51. Ronell, "The Merry-Go-Round."

52. Ronell to George Gershwin, June 22, 1936, NYPL.

53. J.C. Copeland to Ronell, February 13, 1937, MHL.

54. Wilfrid Sheed, *The House That George Built* (New York: Random House, 2007), 57–58.

55. Lester Cowan to Sol Rosenblatt, telegram, June 7, 1936, ARA.

56. William Jaffe to Ronell, telegram, July 7, 1936, ARA.

57. Ronell to Lou Diamond, Famous Publishing Company, telegram, December 5, 1936, NJHS.

58. Program, Radio City Music Hall, New York, week beginning June 30, 1949.

59. "The Theater: Shoot the Works," *Time*, July 4, 1949, 41.

60. Barney Rossen, Artists Alliance, Inc., to Herman Rosenblatt, July 15, 1949, NJHS.

61. Bloom, s.v., "The Parson of Panamint."

Chapter 3

1. Edward Jablonski, "Ann Ronell — Omaha's Musical Trailblazer," *Nebraska Life* (Fall 1997), 17.

2. Joseph Mitchell, "Songwriter Discovered Repeatedly," *New York World-Telegram*, October 16, 1932.

3. Douglas Gilbert, "Girl Succeeds at Writing Song After Getting Start on a Fluke," *New York World-Telegram*, October 15, 1942.

4. Gershwin Memorial Program, YMCA, New York, July 14, 1937.

5. Ronell, "Willow Weep for Me" (New York: Irving Berlin, 1932).

6. *American Popular Songs: From the Revolutionary War to the Present*, ed. David Ewen (New York: Random House, 1966), 443.

7. Frank Brookhouser, "Man About Town: Little Lady of Words and Music," *Philadelphia Sunday Bulletin*, February 4, 1962.

8. *Washington Daily News*, "Young Girl Composer Puts the Simple Things of Life into Successful Music," September 1, 1934.

9. *St. Louis Star and Times*, "Obscure Omaha Girl Crashes Tin Pan Alley" [1933], MHL.

10. Nels Nelson, "Composer Ronell's 'Willow' Will Weep Forever," *Philadelphia Daily News*, January 7, 1994.

11. *Ibid*.

12. Ronell to Saul H. Bourne, Bourne Music, Inc., February 17, 1950, ARA.

13. Charles J. Schreiber, "Records: Album Makes a Rave Hit," *New York World-Telegram & Sun*, September 30, 1953.

14. *Phonolog Reports*, July 28, 1958; Howard Colson to Ronell, December 15, 1985, ARA; ACE Title Search, The American Society of Composers, Authors and Publishers, http://www.ascap.com/ace/search.cfm?requesttime out=300 (accessed September 24, 2004).

15. Billboard Hot 100, *Billboard*, weeks ending December 5 and 19, 1964.

16. Bourne, Inc., accounting statement for six-month period ending June 30, 1966, NYPL.

17. Donald Clarke, *Wishing on the Moon: The Life and Times of Billie Holiday* (New York: Viking Press, 1994), 373–74; Stuart Nicholson, *Billie Holiday* (Boston: Northeastern University Press, 1995), 203, 275–76, 279.

18. Bill Dufty to Ronell, July 29, 1965, ARA.

19. Arnold Laubich to Ronell, March 11, 1956, NYPL.

20. Earl Wilson, "It Happened Last Night: Love Songs by the Ladies," *New York Post*, July 27, 1976.

21. American Society of Composers, Authors and Publishers, "ASCAP Honors Women Songwriters at Champagne Fete," news release, June, 1976.

22. Program, Rialto Theatre, New York, *Blues in the Night*, opening night, June 2, 1982.

23. Clive Barnes, "Three Ladies Sing the Blues, Smok-

ily," *New York Post*, June 3, 1982; Douglas Watt, "We Gotta Right to Sing the Blues," *New York Daily News*, June 3, 1982; Townsend Brewster, "Enthusiastic 'Blues in the Night' Audience," *New York Amsterdam News*, June 12, 1982.

24. Alec Wilder, *American Popular Song: The Great Innovators: 1900–1950* (New York: Oxford University Press, 1972), 480.

25. Alec Wilder to Ronell, March 1, 1977, NJHS.

26. Meredith Willson to Ronell and Lester Cowan, December 22, 1947, ARA.

27. *The Complete Encyclopedia of Popular Music and Jazz: 1900–1950*, ed. Roger D. Kinkle (New Rochelle, NY: Arlington House, 1974), s.v. "Martin, Hugh"; Stanley Green, *Encyclopaedia of the Musical Theatre* (New York: Dodd, Mead, 1976), s.v. "Martin, Hugh."

28. Hugh Martin to Ronell, May 16, 1990, ARA.

29. Tim Golden, "Eulogy in Jazz Is Held in Harlem for Dexter Gordon, Saxophonist," *New York Times*, May 12, 1990, B14.

30. John S. Wilson, "Cabaret: Sylvia Sims Sings," *New York Times*, March 26, 1982.

31. Corinne J. Naden, "Noteworthy Requests," crossword puzzle, *New York Times Magazine*, May 25, 1986.

Chapter 4

1. Prunella Hall, "Radcliffe Grad Writes Movie Musical Scores," *New York Post*, February 10, 1950.

2. David Tietyen, *The Musical World of Walt Disney* (Milwaukee: Hal Leonard Publishing Corporation, 1990), 24.

3. Ronell, "Mickey Mouse and Minnie's Back in Town" (New York: Irving Berlin Music, 1933).

4. Prunella Hall, "Has No Formula for Success," *Boston Post*, August 19, 1945.

5. Tietyen, 24.

6. *Ibid.*, 25.

7. Neil Gabler, *Walt Disney: The Triumph of the American Imagination* (New York: Vintage Books, 2006), 182

8. Frank Churchill and Ronell, "Who's Afraid of the Big Bad Wolf?" (New York: Irving Berlin Music, 1933).

9. Edward Jablonski, "Ann Ronell — Omaha's Musical Trailblazer," *Nebraska Life* (Fall 1997), 16.

10. Elinor Hughes, "Radcliffe Honors Graduate Composer," *Boston Herald*, September 21, 1942.

11. Tietyen, 30.

12. "Little Lady of Song: An Interview with Composer Ann Ronell," *American Illustrated*, U.S. Information Agency magazine, draft copy, #335-63, Washington, D.C., 1963, 3, ARA.

13. Jablonski.

14. Gabler, 185.

15. "Ann Ronell," http://www.imdb.com/name/nm 0740056/ (accessed November 30, 2004).

16. "Little Lady of Song," 8.

17. "Andy Panda," http://www.toonopedia.com/andy-pand.htm (accessed May 13, 2008).

18. Ronell to Vyvyan Donner, October 16, 1939, MHL.

19. "Andy Panda," http://en.wikipedia.org/wiki/Andy _Panda (accessed May 12, 2008).

20. Bill Peirce, Cinema Productions, Hollywood, "Biography of Ann Ronell," circa 1953, ARA; *The Biographical Dictionary and Who's Who of the American Theatre* (New York: Heineman Publishing, 1966), s.v. "Ronell, Ann."

21. Ronell to Jack Karp, Paramount Pictures, January 22, 1951, ARA; "Anna Maria Alberghetti," http://www.annamariaalberghetti.com//Biography.htm (accessed April 10, 2007).

22. *Omaha World-Herald*, advertisement for Paramount Theater, July 5, 1934.

23. Jack Reel, "Ronell Sings, Plays Lyrics at Paramount," *Omaha Bee-News*, July 5, 1934.

24. Ronell, "Account of Creative Work," unpublished, 1941, 2–3, ARA.

25. Ronell, *Like Magic: A Ballet with Songs* (New York: Ann Ronell, 1936, 1984).

26. *Ibid.*

27. Ronell, "Sweet Magic Spring," unpublished lyrics, 1936, ARA.

28. "Ronell's Dance Fantasy Unique," *Hollywood Reporter*, March 15, 1935.

29. *Ibid.*

30. *Variety*, "Paramount, L.A.," March 20, 1935.

31. Irene Cavanaugh, "Her Mother Knew Best: Piano-Playing Helped," *Los Angeles Illustrated Daily News*, March 16, 1935.

32. Larry Spier to Ronell, telegram, May 8, 1934, NYPL.

33. Darryl F. Zanuck to Ronell, November 22, 1934, NYPL.

18. "Girl Author of 'Big Bad Wolf' and Other Hit Songs Weds at Sea," *Boston American*, October 7, 1935.

19. Julia Blanshard, "She Crashed Tin Pan Alley," *NEA News Service*, January 23, 1933.

20. "Applause," *Washington, D.C. Pathfinder*, October 17, 1945.

21. Jerene Claire Cline, "Ann Ronell's Songwriting Dynamo," *Omaha Sunday World-Herald Magazine*, November 28, 1948, C-4.

22. "Music in Motion Pictures," Ronell, lecturer, course prospectus, University of Southern California, circa 1937, NYPL.

23. Ronell to Edna Gladney, Fort Worth, Texas, August 2, 1946, ARA.

24. Ronell to Bertha Corman, July 26, 1946, MHL.

25. Jessie Ash Arndt, "Songwriter as Plucky as Three Little Pigs," *The Christian Science Monitor*, January 3, 1955, 10.

26. Cline.

27. Arndt.

28. Lester Cowan to John Schulman, November 30, 1958, ARA.

29. Ronell to Louis Applebaum, November 26, 1946, MHL.

30. Anonymous, interview with author, January 21, 2004.

Chapter 5

1. Louella Parsons, *Hollywood Reporter,* November 5, 1935.

2. Paul Yawitz, "New York Uncensored," *New York Sunday Mirror,* October 1, 1933.

3. Lester Cowan to George Volck, Columbia Pictures Corporation, December 30, 1934, ARA.

4. Lester Cowan, "Lester Cowan's Record of Service to the Motion Picture Industry," n.d., unpublished, 1–2, ARA.

5. *Ibid.*, 2.

6. Glenn Fowler, obituary of Lester Cowan, *New York Times,* October 23, 1990.

7. Ronell, "Ann Ronell — Personal Notes," unpublished, 1941, 2, ARA.

8. Ronell, "Funny Little World" (New York: Irving Berlin, 1934); "Soundtracks for *Down to Their Last Yacht*," http://www.imdb.com/title/tt0025066/soundtrack (accessed, November 25, 2007).

9. Ronell, "Beach Boy" (New York: Irving Berlin, 1934); "Soundtracks."

10. Ronell to Lou Brock, July 7, 1936, NYPL.

11. Ronell, "Personal Notes," 2.

12. *Hollywood Reporter*, "Ann Ronell Will Write Songs for *January*," August 24, 1935.

13. Louella Parsons, "Shirley Temple Will Have Star Role in *Poor Little Rich Girl*," *Hollywood Reporter*, June 26, 1935.

14. *Captain January* and *Poor Little Rich Girl*, http://imdb.com/title (accessed May 18, 2008); Donald J. Stubblebine, *Cinema Sheet Music: A Comprehensive Listing of Published Film Music from* Squaw Man *(1914) to* Batman *(1989)* (Jefferson, NC: McFarland, 1991), s.v. *Captain January, Poor Little Rich Girl.*

15. Alma Whitaker, "Women Songwriter Rates High in Field," *Los Angeles Times*, September 17, 1935.

16. Anonymous, phone discussion with author, April 26, 2004.

17. Ronell to Tamara Geva, April 15, 1936, NJHS.

Chapter 6

1. David Drew, *Kurt Weill: A Handbook* (Berkeley: University of California Press, 1987), 282–83.

2. *American National Biography*, eds. John A. Garraty and Mark C. Carnes (New York: Oxford University Press, 1999), s.v. "Odets, Clifford."

3. Charles Isherwood, "Go East, Young Writers, For Theater!," *New York Times*, November 13, 2007.

4. Ronald Sanders, *The Days Grow Short: The Life and Music of Kurt Weill* (New York: Holt, Rinehart and Winston, 1980), 262–63.

5. "Spanish Civil War," http://www.sispain.org/english/history/civil.html (accessed November 19, 2002); Nancy Lynn Schwartz, *The Hollywood Writers' Wars* (New York: Alfred A. Knopf, 1982), 127.

6. "Spanish Civil War."

7. Kurt Weill to Lotte Lenya, January 28, 1937, *Speak Low (When You Speak Love): The Letters of Kurt Weill and Lotte Lenya*, eds. Kim H. Kowalke and Lys Symonette (Berkeley: University of California Press, 1995), 196.

8. *Speak Low*, Weill to Lenya, March 3, 1937, 211.

9. Ronell, "Document composed by Ann Ronell for Werner Janssen to be included in his book," September, 1979, 1, unpublished, ARA.

10. Ronell to Sam and Lil Jaffe, May 21, 1938, MHL.

11. Paul Buhle and David Wagner, *Blacklisted: The Film Lover's Guide to the Hollywood Blacklist* (New York: Palgrave Macmillan, 2003), XVIII.

12. Ronell, "Document for Janssen," 2.

13. *Ibid.*

14. Leslie Anderson, "Women Film and Television Composers in the United State," in *The Musical Women: An International Perspective* (Westport, CT: Greenwood Press, 1991), 3:1–2.

15. Elinor Hughes, "Radcliffe Composer Does Music for Ernie Pyle Film," *Boston Herald*, August 8, 1945.

16. *Ibid.*

17. Marjory M. Fisher, "She's Not Afraid of 'Big Bad Wolf'; She Wrote It," *San Francisco Chronicle*, October 14, 1949.

18. Anderson, "Women Film and Television Composers," 3:2.

19. Ronell, "Document for Janssen," 2–4; Jurgen Schebera, *Kurt Weill: An Illustrated Life* (New Haven: Yale University Press, 1995), 256–57; Weill to Lenya, April 19, 1938, *Speak Low,* 250–51.

20. Ronell, "Document for Janssen," 3.

21. Ronell and Kurt Weill, "The River Is So Blue" and "Finale — March (The River Is Blue)," applications for copyrights, Register of Copyrights, March 9, 17, 1938, ARA.

22. Ronell and Kurt Weill, "The River Is So Blue" (Hollywood: Walter Wanger Productions, 1938); Donald J. Stubblebine, *Cinema Sheet Music: A Comprehensive Listing of Published Film Music from* Squaw Man *(1914) to* Batman *(1989)* (Jefferson, NC: McFarland, 1991), 37.

23. Weill to Lenya, March 3, 1937, *Speak Low,* 212.

24. Weill to Lenya, April 19, 1938, *Speak Low,* 250.

25. Lenya to Weill, April 21, 1938, *Speak Low,* 252.

26. Ronell, "Document for Janssen," 3–4.

27. *The New Grove Dictionary of Music and Musicians* 2nd ed., ed. Stanley Sadie (London: Grove Press, 2001), s.v. "Janssen, Werner"; *The International Cyclopedia of Music and Musicians* 11th ed., ed. Bruce Bohle (New York: Dodd, Mead, 1985), s.v. "Janssen, Werner"; Alva Johnson, "Profiles: American Maestro," *The New Yorker,* October 20, 1934, 26–30, October 27, 1943, 23–26; Claire R. Reis, *Composers in America: Biographical Sketches of Contemporary Composers with a Record of Their Works* (New York: Macmillan, 1947), s.v. "Janssen, Werner"; Gene Lees, *The Musical Worlds of Lerner and Loewe* (Lincoln, NE: University of Nebraska Press, 1990), 329; *The Complete Encyclopedia of Popular Music and Jazz: 1900–1950,* ed. Roger D. Kinkle (New Rochelle, NY: Arlington House, 1974), s.v. "Janssen, Werner."

28. Frank S. Nugent, "Blocking *Blockade,*" *New York Times,* June 26, 1939; *Los Angeles Examiner,* "Blockade, War Film, Protested As Propaganda," June 28, 1939.

29. Frank S. Nugent, review of *Blockade,* directed by William Dieterle, *New York Times,* June 17, 1938; Pauline Kael, *5001 Nights at the Movies* (New York: Henry Holt, 1991), 81–82; Maurice Kann, "The Blockade Against *Blockade,*" editorial, *Box Office: The National Film Weekly,* July 30, 1938.

30. Ronell, "Account of Creative Work," unpublished, 1941, 5, ARA.

31. Ann Ronell and Werner Janssen, "Beloved, You're Lovely" (New York: Miller Music, 1938).

32. Weill to Ronell, November 29, 1938, NYPL.

33. Gerard Raoul-Duval, Acting French Consul to Joseph Breen, June 14, 1938, MHL.

34. Walter F. Wanger to Raoul-Duval, June 23, 1938, MHL.

35. Ronell, "Document for Janssen," 2.

36. Rocco Vocco to Ronell, June 29, 1938, MHL; Stubblebine, *Cinema Sheet Music,* 6; "Soundtrack for *Algiers* (1938)," http://www.imdb.com/title/tt0029855/soundtrack (accessed November 25, 2007).

37. Steven Suskin, *Show Tunes: 1905–1985* (New York: Dodd, Mead, 1986), 305.

38. Ronell to Cheryl Crawford, May 20, 1938, MHL.

39. Crawford to Ronell, April 19, 1938, MHL.

Chapter 7

1. Ronell, "Account of Creative Work," unpublished, 1941, 3, ARA.

2. Ronell, "Ann Ronell — Prestige Work," unpublished notes, circa 1961, 1, ARA.

3. Deanna Durbin and Ronell, *The Deanna Durbin Songbook of Favorite Arias* (New York: G. Schirmer, 1938).

4. Ronell, "Prestige Work," 2.

5. Lester Cowan to William Hinckle, December 27, 1939, MHL.

6. Ronell to Ida Koverman, May 27, 1941, MHL.

7. Nelson Eddy to Ronell, July 7, 1941, MHL.

8. Ronell to Nelson Eddy, August 19, 1941, MHL.

9. Obituary of Vicki Baum, *New York Times,* August 31, 1960.

10. Vicki Baum to Ronell [circa 1948], MHL.

11. Vicki Baum and Ronell, preface, American libretto, *Martha* (Los Angeles: Presmel Publishing, 1938), 2.

12. Ronell to [Frank] Orsatti, November 21, 1939, ARA.

13. *Ibid.*

14. Program, *Martha,* Hollywood Bowl, opening night, August 30, 1938.

15. *The New Grove Dictionary of Opera,* ed. Stanley Sadie (London: Macmillan Reference Limited, 1997), s.v. "Translation," 787.

16. Sigmund Spaeth, "Translating Music," *Music Quarterly* 1 (1915): 191–98, in *The New Grove Dictionary of Opera,* s.v. "Translation," 788.

17. *The New Grove Dictionary,* 788.

18. *Ibid.,* 787.

19. *Ibid.,* 787.

20. Program, *Martha.*

21. *The New Grove Dictionary of Music and Musicians,* 2nd ed., ed. Stanley Sadie (London: Grove Press, 2001), s.v. "Von Flotow, Friedrich"; Phil G. Goulding, *Ticket to the Opera* (New York: Fawcett Columbine, 1996), s.v. "Martha."

22. Baum and Ronell, preface.

23. Frank Mittauer, "Evidence That People Enjoy What They Can Understand," *Los Angeles Evening News,* August 31, 1938.

24. Dr. Bruno David Ussher, "Music," *Los Angeles Daily News,* September 1, 1938.

25. Richard D. Saunders, "Acclaim Given Opera Sung in Translation," *Hollywood Citizen,* September 3, 1938.

26. *Ibid.*

27. *Music Leader,* Chicago, November 9, 1940.

28. "The Arts: Chicago Opera Routs Tradition," *San Francisco Chronicle,* November 25, 1940, 24.

29. *Ibid.*

30. W.E.J. Martin, "Ann Ronell Stands Alone Among Composers for Films," *Buffalo Courier Express,* August 9, 1953; Ronell, "Record of the Published and Performed Works of Ann Ronell: Popular and Classic," 3, unpublished, n.d., MHL.

31. Ronell, "Account of Creative Work," 5–6.

32. Ronell to Albert Bender [circa 1940], MHL.

33. Edwin Lester, Jr., to Ronell, December 6, 1940, MHL.

34. Ronell to Bender.

35. Ronell, "Account of Creative Work," 5.

36. Ronell, "Concise Statement of Project," grant application to John Simon Guggenheim Foundation committee, October 31, 1941, ARA.

37. Ronell (speech, National Federation Music Clubs Bicentennial Convention, June, 1941), ARA.

38. Ronell, "Concise Statement of Project."

39. Robert Lawrence, "For Opera in English," *New York Herald Tribune,* November 9, 1941.

40. Ronell, "Description of Project," grant application

to John Simon Guggenheim Foundation committee, October 31, 1941, 1–5, ARA.

41. *Ibid.*

42. *Ibid.*

43. *Ibid.*

44. *Ibid.*

45. Ronell to Nat Shilkret, February 15, 1950, ARA.

46. Ronell, "Description of Project."

47. *Ibid.*

48. Ronell, "Ultimate Purpose," grant application to John Simon Guggenheim Foundation committee, October 31, 1941, ARA.

49. Walter Piston to Ronell, February 3, 1941, NYPL.

50. Ronell to Walter Piston, late February, 1941, ARA.

51. *Ibid.*

52. Ronell to Earle Lewis, August 24, 1941, 1, MHL.

53. *Ibid.*, 2.

54. *Ibid.*, 2.

55. Tom Trenkle, publicist, "Ann Ronell, A Triple-Threat Author and Composer," New York, 1961, ARA.

Chapter 8

1. *The Metropolitan Opera Encyclopedia: A Comprehensive Guide to the World of Opera*, ed. David Hamilton (New York: Simon and Schuster, 1987), s.v. "Strauss, Johann, Jr."; *The New Grove Dictionary of Opera*, ed. Stanley Sadie (London: Grove Press, 1997), s.v. "Zigeunerbaron, Der"; *The Viking Opera Guide*, ed. Amanda Holden (New York: Viking Press, 1993), s.v. "Strauss, Johann, Jr."

2. Agreement among Ann Ronell, George Marion, Jr., and Los Angeles Civic Light Opera Association, regarding *The Gypsy Baron*, April 4, 1939, ARA.

3. *The New Grove Dictionary of Music and Musicians*, 2nd ed., ed. Stanley Sadie (London: Grove Press, 2001), s.v. "Thomas, John Charles"; *American National Biography*, ed. John C. Garraty and Marc C. Carnes (Oxford: Oxford University Press, 1999), s.v. "Thomas, John Charles"; Michael J. Maher, *John Charles Thomas: Beloved Baritone of American Opera and Popular Music* (Jefferson, NC: McFarland, 2006), 88–89.

4. Agreement between Ronell and G. Schirmer, Inc. regarding songs from *The Gypsy Baron*, May 18, 1940, ARA; Ronell to Gustave Schirmer, April 13, 1943, ARA.

5. *The Playgoer* program, *The Gypsy Baron*, Los Angeles Civic Light Opera, June 5, 1939.

6. Maher, 89.

7. Reviews of *The Gypsy Baron*, directed by Edwin Lester, Los Angeles Civic Light Opera, June 19, 1939: Frank Mittauer, *Los Angeles Evening News*, Harrison Carroll, *Los Angeles Evening Herald and Express,* Harry Mines, *Los Angeles Daily News*, staff writer, *Variety,* June 20, 1939; *Los Angeles Herald Express*, June 21, 1939; *Los Angeles Daily News*, June 22, 1939.

8. Mines, *Los Angeles Daily News.*

9. Anonymous family member, in-person interview with author, January 21, 2004.

10. Edwin Lester to Ronell, telegram, June 23, 1939, NYPL.

11. Edwin Lester to Ronell, February 18, 1942, ARA.

12. Maher, 172.

13. Ronell to John Charles Thomas, March 6, 1942, ARA.

14. Nadine Cohodas, *Queen: The Life and Music of Dinah Washington* (New York: Pantheon Books, 2004), 43–44; *The Complete Encyclopedia of Popular Music and*

Jazz: 1900–1950, ed. Roger D. Kinkle (New Rochelle, NY: Arlington House, 1974), s.v., "Petrillo, James C."

15. Marjory M. Fisher, "She's Not Afraid of 'Big Bad Wolf'; She Wrote It," *San Francisco Chronicle*, October 14, 1949.

16. Bosley Crowther, "*There's Magic in Music* Picture Now Showing at Loew's Criterion," review of *There's Magic in Music, New York Times*, June 5, 1941; IMDb review of *There's Magic in Music*, http://imdb.com/title/tt0034275/combined (accessed March 6, 2007), 1–6.

17. Oscar Straus to Ronell, April 12, 1941, ARA.

18. *The New Grove Dictionary*, s.v. "Straus, Oscar"; *The International Cyclopedia of Music and Musicians*, 11th ed., ed. Bruce Bohle (New York: Dodd, Mead, 1985), s.v. "Straus, Oscar."

19. Steven Suskin, *Show Tunes: 1905–1985* (New York: Dodd, Mead, 1986), 373.

20. Gene Lees, *The Musical Worlds of Lerner & Loewe* (Lincoln, NE: University of Nebraska Press, 1990), 13.

21. Gerald Bordman, *Jerome Kern: His Life and Music* (New York: Oxford University Press, 1980), 51.

22. *Ibid.*, 95.

23. Straus to Ronell, April 2, 1942, NYPL.

24. Edwin Lester, "Foreword," *The Playgoer* program, *The Chocolate Soldier*, Los Angeles Civic Light Opera Festival, June 2, 1941.

25. Review of *The Chocolate Soldier*, directed by Zeke Colvan, Los Angeles Civic Light Opera, June 2, 1941, Harrison Carroll, *Los Angeles Evening Herald and Express*, June 3, 1941.

26. Constantin Bakaleinikoff to Ronell, June 6, 1941, MHL.

27. Maher, 173–74.

28. *The Playgoer* program, *The Gypsy Baron*, Los Angeles Civic Light Opera, May 10, 1943.

29. Ronell to Carl Engel, G. Schirmer, Inc., April 13, 1943, ARA.

30. Dolores Hayward to Ronell, April 15, 1943, ARA.

31. Lester Cowan to Edwin Lester, telegram, n.d., ARA.

32. Rosenblatt family members to Ronell, telegram, May 24, 1943, ARA.

33. Reviews of *The Gypsy Baron*, directed by Edwin Lester, Los Angeles Civic Light Opera, May 24, 1943: Virginia Wright and Harry Mines, *Los Angeles Daily News*, Harrison Carroll, *Los Angeles Evening Herald and Express*, Florence Lawrence, *Los Angeles Examiner*, May 25, 1943.

34. Robert Cowan to Ronell, May 5, 1943, MHL.

35. Jack Kapp to Ronell, April 26, 1943, MHL.

36. Lester Cowan to Edwin Lester, telegram, February 4, 1943, ARA.

37. Lester Cowan to Edwin Lester, telegram, February 13, 1943, ARA.

38. Charles V. Clifford, *St. Louis' Fabulous Municipal Theatre: Fifty Seasons of Summer Musicals* (St. Louis: St. Louis Municipal Theatre, 1969), 117–18.

39. Ronell to Lorna Jeanne Cochran, January 30, 1952, ARA; Ronell to Charles V. Clifford, March 11, 1952, ARA.

40. Itemized invoice detailing arrangers, work done, and rates, n.d. [June, 1944], ARA.

41. Ronell to Lester Cowan, n.d. [summer,1944], ARA.

42. Ronell to Paul Beisman, June 13, 1944, MHL.

43. Beisman to Ronell, August 24, 1944, MHL.

44. Laurence Schwab to Cowan, September 2, 1944, MHL.

45. Ronell to Jack Sheehan, August 10, 1944, ARA.

46. Agreement between Rise Stevens and Lester Cowan, regarding *The Gypsy Baron* to be used for photoplay, November 1, 1944, ARA.

47. Agreement between Ronell and G. Schirmer, Inc., regarding *The Gypsy Baron*, April 27, 1950.

48. Ronell to Hans Heinsheimer, G. Schirmer, Inc., March 13, 1951, ARA; Ronell to George Marion, Jr., March 19, 1951, ARA; Ronell to Miriam Howell, April 2, 1951, ARA.

49. Ronell to Gustave Schirmer, April 15, 1951, ARA.

50. Howard Taubman, "MET to Enter TV and Seek Sponsors," *New York Times*, April 3, 1951.

51. *Ibid.*

52. Ronell to Hans Heinsheimer, April 3, 1951, ARA.

53. Ronell to George Marion, Jr., April 8, 1951, ARA.

54. *Ibid.*

55. Ronell to Milton Pickman, RKO Studios, February 21, 1952, ARA.

56. Ronell to Olin Clark, MGM, New York, March 13, 1952, ARA.

57. Ronell, outline for *Josephine*, n.d. [1956], unpublished, ARA.

58. Lester Cowan to Max Benoff, April 18, 1956, ARA.

59. Cowan to Richard Pinkham, National Broadcasting Company, April 2, 1956, ARA.

60. Cowan to Arthur L. Park, MCA Artists, Ltd., April 17, 1956, ARA.

61. Laura Lee, "Lively Blond Writes Movie Mood Music," *Philadelphia Evening Bulletin*, February 27, 1950.

62. *Ibid.*

63. Ira Wallach to Ronell, July 8, 1960, ARA.

64. Maurice Valency, English libretto, *The Gypsy Baron*, Ed. 2364 (New York: G. Schirmer, 1959).

65. *The New Grove Dictionary of Opera*, s.v. "Offenbach, Jacques," "Orphee aux enfers."

66. Ronell to Jules Rudel, October 13, 1955, ARA.

67. *The New Grove Dictionary of Opera*, s.v. "Rudel, Julius"; *The Oxford Dictionary of Opera*, ed. John Warrack and Ewan West (Oxford: Oxford University Press, 1992), s.v "Rudel, Julius."

68. Ronell to Simon Boosey, August 25, 1955; David S. Adams to Ronell, August 30, 1955; Boosey to Ronell, September 2, 1955; Ronell to Boosey, September 12, 1955, ARA.

Chapter 9

1. Ronell to Robert Presnell, Sam Goldwyn Studios, June 21, 1941, ARA.

2. Ronell, "Account of Creative Work," unpublished, 1941, 2–3, ARA.

3. Ronell to Presnell.

4. Leon Barzin to Ronell, telegram, March 20, 1941, ARA; M.E. Hughes to Barzin, telegram, April 3, 1941, ARA.

5. *The New Grove Dictionary of Music and Musicians*, 2nd ed., ed. Stanley Sadie (London: Grove Press, 2001), s.v. "Berezovsky, Nicolai"; *The International Cyclopedia of Music and Musicians*, 11th ed., ed. Bruce Bohle (New York: Dodd, Mead, 1985), s.v. "Berezovsky"; *The Harvard Concise Dictionary of Music*, ed. Don Michael Randel (Cambridge, MA: Belknap Press of Harvard University, 1978), s.v. "Berezovsky."

6. *The World Book Encyclopedia*, 2006, s.v. "Pan-Americanism."

7. Ronell to Nicolai Berezovsky, May 20, 1941, ARA.

8. *Ibid.*

9. Berezovsky to Ronell, June 18, 1941, ARA.

10. *Ibid.*

11. Ronell to Berezovsky, June 20, 1941, ARA.

12. Elinor Hughes, "Radcliffe Honors Graduate Composer," *Boston Herald*, September 21, 1942.

13. Berezovsky to Ronell, telegram, June 26, 1941, ARA.

14. Berezovsky to Ronell, July 28, 1941, ARA.

15. Berezovsky to Ronell, telegram, August 2, 1941, ARA.

16. Ronell to Berezovsky, November 26, 1941, NYPL.

17. Berezovsky to Ronell, multiple letters, 1940–41, NYPL.

18. Ronell to Berezovsky, October 6, 1941, ARA.

19. *Ibid.*

20. *The New Grove Dictionary*, s.v. "Barzin, Leon"; *The International Cyclopedia of Music and Musicians*, s.v. "Barzin, Leon."

21. Ronell to Berezovsky, n.d., [October 1941], ARA.

22. *Ibid.*

23. Ronell to George Balanchine, February 8, 1942, ARA.

24. Ronell to Agnes de Mille, February 12, March 9, 1942, ARA.

25. Leon Barzin to Ronell, February 27, 1942, ARA.

26. Ronell to Board of Directors, National Orchestral Association, October 28, 1963, ARA.

Chapter 10

1. *Wikipedia*, s.v. "Benatzky, Ralph," http://en.wikipedia.org/wiki/RalphBenatzky (accessed April 22, 2007); *The New Grove Dictionary of Music and Musicians* 2nd ed., ed. Stanley Sadie (London: Macmillan, 2002), s.v. "Benatzky, Ralph."

2. Ronell, "Biographic Information Form," Department of State, 1960, ARA.

3. "Lyricist Doing Lederer Play," *Los Angeles Examiner*, circa 1937, ARA.

4. Program, *Count Me In*, University Theatre, The Catholic University of America, "A Note on This Production," May 10, 1942.

5. Gerald Bordman, *American Musical Theatre: A Chronicle* (New York: Oxford University Press, 1978), 526, 528, 532.

6. Bordman, 531; program, *This Is the Army*, Masonic Auditorium, Detroit, December 21, 1942.

7. Bordman, 531.

8. Walter Kerr, "Professional Meets Tributary, 1942," *Theatre Arts*, November, 1942, 458.

9. Reviews of *Count Me In*, Catholic University, Washington, D.C., directed by Dr. Josephine McGarry Callan and Alan Schneider, May 10, 1942: Richard L. Coe, *Washington Post*, May 11, 1942; Jay Carmody, *Washington Evening Star*, May 11, 1942; *Washington Daily News*, May 11, 1942; Bernie Harrison, *Washington Times-Herald*, May 12, 1942; *Catholic University Tower*, May 14, 1942; *Variety*, May 20, 1942.

10. Jay Carmody, "C.U. Works Woes of War into Gay Musical Show," *The Evening Star*, Washington, D.C., May 11, 1942.

11. Jake Rachman, "Stage and Screen," *Omaha World-Herald*, January 2, 1943.

12. Program, *Playbill, Count Me In*, Ethel Barrymore Theatre, New York, October 8, 1942.

13. Program, University Theatre.

14. Stanley Green, *Encyclopedia of the Musical Theatre* (New York: Dodd, Mead, 1976), s.v. "Abbott, George (Francis)."

15. Program, *Playbill, Count Me In*, Ethel Barrymore

Theatre, New York, October 8, 1942; George Abbott to Lester Cowan, June 4, 1942, ARA.

16. Ronell to Cowan, circa June 1, 1942, MHL.
17. Ibid.
18. Ronell to Cowan, June 11, 1942, 1, MHL.
19. Ibid., 2.
20. Ronell to Cowan, May 23, 1942, 1, MHL.
21. Ronell to Cowan, June 4, 1942, 3, MHL.
22. Abbott to Cowan, June 10, 1942, ARA.
23. John Stewart, Broadway Musicals: 1943–2004 (Jefferson, NC: McFarland, 2006), 441, 555.
24. Program, Count Me In, Shubert Theatre, Boston, September 21, 1942.
25. John Anthony Gilvey, Before the Parade Passes By: Gower Champion and the Glorious American Musical (New York: St. Martin's Press, 2005), 20.
26. Steven Suskin, Show Tunes: 1905–1985: The Songs, Shows and Careers of Broadway's Major Composers (New York: Dodd, Mead, 1986), 602–03.
27. Ibid., 59, 243.
28. Brooks Atkinson, review of Count Me In, directed by Robert Ross, Barrymore Theatre, October 8, 1942, New York Times, October 9, 1942.
29. Suskin, Show Tunes, 35, 216, 264, 331.
30. Ibid., 279.
31. Reviews of Count Me In, Shubert Theater, Boston, directed by Robert Ross, September 10, 1942: Elinor Hughes, Boston Herald; Helen Eager, Boston Traveler; Elliot Norton, Boston Post; unsigned, Boston Daily Globe; Peggy Doyle, Boston Evening American; L.A. Sloper, Christian Science Monitor, September 11, 1942; Leo Gaffney, Boston Daily Record, September 12, 1942; unsigned, Variety, September 16, 1942.
32. Bernie Harrison, "C.U. Revue to Feature 'Ticketyboo' Theme Song," Washington Times-Herald, January 21, 1942; New York Times, "Churchill Acted as Plane's Pilot," January 19, 1942; Jay Carmody, "Churchill's Flight Home Gives C.U. a Play Title," Washington Evening Star, January 21, 1942.
33. Ann Ronell, "Ticketyboo" (New York: Chappell Music, 1942).
34. Ann Ronell, "On Leave for Love" (New York: Chappell Music, 1942).
35. Mack Gordon and Harry Warren, "You Can't Say No to a Soldier" (New York: Mayfair, 1942); Tony Thomas, Harry Warren and the Hollywood Musical (Secaucus, NJ: Citadel Press, 1975), 190–91.
36. Harold Arlen and Johnny Mercer, "I'm Doing It for Defense" (New York: Famous Music, 1942).
37. Edward Jablonski, Harold Arlen: Rhythm, Rainbows, and Blues (Boston: Northeastern University Press, 1996), 157–58.
38. Eager, Boston Traveler.
39. Kerr, "Professional Meets Tributary," 459.
40. Hughes, Boston Herald.
41. Suskin, 543, 602, 607; The Complete Encyclopedia of Popular Music and Jazz: 1900–1950, ed. Roger D. Kinkle (New Rochelle, NY: Arlington House, 1974), s.v., "Caldwell, Anne," Donnelly, Dorothy," "Fields, Dorothy," "Swift, Kay," "Young, Rida Johnson"; Green, Encyclopedia of the Musical Theatre (New York: Dodd, Mead, 1976), s.v. "Caldwell, Anne," "Donnelly, Dorothy," "Fields, Dorothy," "Swift, Kay," "Young, Rida Johnson."
42. Suskin, Show Tunes, 542–43.
43. Program, Count Me In, Shubert Theatre, Boston; program, Playbill, Count Me In, Ethel Barrymore Theatre.
44. Program, Playbill.
45. Reviews of Count Me In, directed by Robert Ross, Ethel Barrymore Theatre, October 8, 1942:

Date	Periodical	Reviewer
10/9/42	New York Journal-American	John Anderson
10/9/42	New York Herald Tribune	Howard Barnes
10/9/42	New York World-Telegram	John Mason Brown
10/9/42	New York Post	Wilella Waldorf
10/9/42	New York Daily News	Burns Mantle
10/9/42	P.M. New York	Louis Kronenberger
10/9/42	Brooklyn Citizen	Edgar Price
10/9/42	New York Times	Brooks Atkinson
10/9/42	New York Morning Telegram	George Freedley
10/9/42	New York Sun	Richard Lockridge
10/9/42	New York Daily Mirror	Robert Coleman
10/9/42	Christian Science Monitor	John Beaufort
10/9/42	Newark Evening News	Rowland Field
10/14/42	Variety	Staff
10/17/42	The New Yorker	Wolcott Gibbs

46. Gibbs, The New Yorker.
47. Atkinson, New York Times.
48. Gilvey, Before the Parade Passes By, 20.
49. Ann Ronell, "You've Got It All" (New York: Chappell Music, 1942).
50. Mantle, New York Daily News.
51. Rachman, "Stage and Screen."
52. Ibid.
53. Beaufort, Christian Science Monitor.
54. Price, Brooklyn Citizen.
55. Atkinson, New York Times.
56. Advertisement, Count Me In, New York Times, October 19, 1942; Danton Walker, "Broadway," New York Times, October 17, 1942.
57. Obituary, Luella Gear, New York Times, April 5, 1980; The Encyclopedia of Popular Music, 4th ed., ed. Colin Larkin (New York: Oxford University Press, 2006), s.v. "Gear, Luella."
58. Walter Kerr to Ronell, January 12, 1943, NYPL.
59. Bernie Harrison, "Scene and Heard," Washington, D.C. Times-Herald, June 25, 1950, 27.
60. Jack E. Joy, Program Production Chief, Radio Branch, War Department to Ronell, May 29, 1942, MHL.
61. Anna Sosenko to Ronell, November 20, 1942, MHL.
62. Ibid.
63. Ronell, personal notes on Count Me In, circa 1950, unpublished, ARA.
64. Ibid.
65. Ronell to Kerr and Leo Brady, February 19, 1951; Ronell to the Rev. Gilbert Hartke, March 20, 1951, NYPL.
66. Ronell to Kerr, March 13, 1951, NYPL.
67. Ronell to Irving Kahn, March 13, 1951, NYPL.
68. Ronell to Kerr, April 18, 1951, NYPL, August 7, 1951, ARA.
69. New York Times, "Dubois Designs; Holiday Matinee," New York Daily News, June 23, 1954.
70. Sol A. Rosenblatt to Josh Baldwin and Chuck Olsen, Hampton Playhouse, June 28, 1954, ARA.
71. Notes regarding night letter, Ronell to Henry Kaplan, October 26, 1955, ARA.
72. Louis Gruenberg to Ronell, August 27, 1942, ARA.
73. Ann Ronell, "Out to Pick the Berries" (New York: Mills Music, 1943).
74. Ann Ronell and Louis Gruenberg, "The Commandos March" (New York: Mills Music, 1943).
75. Alice Hughes, "A Woman's New York: A Little Slip of a Girl Writes a March for the Doughboys," King Features Syndicate, New York, September 2, 1945, MHL.
76. Al Tamarin, "Ann Ronell Biography," United Artists press release, 1953, ARA.

Chapter 11

1. Virginia Wright, *Los Angeles Daily News,* January 15, 1945.
2. Program for *Tomorrow, the World!,* Hollywood Writers Mobilization premiere and town meeting, Fox Village Theatre, January 30, 1945.
3. Kenneth Macgowan for Writers Award Committee, program for *Tomorrow, the World!*
4. Fredric March, program for *Tomorrow, the World!*
5. William Krasilovsky to and from various personnel of Sam Fox Publishing Company, Leeds Music Corporation, and Music Holding Corporation, 1960–1965, ARA.
6. *Theatre Arts* (September 1945), 514–20.
7. *Turner Classic Movies Newsletter,* review of *The Story of G.I. Joe,* directed by William A. Wellman, http://turnerclassicmovies.com/ThisMonth/Article/0,,37500.html (accessed February 12, 2004).
8. *Turner Classic Movies Newsletter,* 1.
9. *The New Grove Dictionary of Music and Musicians,* 2nd ed., ed. Stanley Sadie (London: Grove Press, 2001), s.v., "Applebaum, Louis."
10. Elinor Hughes, "Radcliffe Composer Does Music for Entire Pyle Film," *The Boston Herald,* August 8, 1945.
11. Ronell to Lester Cowan, 1958, ARA.
12. Jerene Claire Cline, "Ann Ronell's Songwriting Dynamo," *Omaha Sunday World-Herald Magazine,* November 28, 1948.
13. Judith Klein, "Woman Scores a Hit Directing *G.I. Joe* Music," *New York Herald Tribune,* September 2, 1945.
14. Ronell to John Rosenfield, *Dallas News,* November 21, 1944, MHL.
15. Ann Ronell, "Ann Ronell — Prestige Work," unpublished, circa 1961, ARA.
16. "Little Lady of Song: An Interview with Composer Ann Ronell," *American Illustrated,* U.S. Information Agency magazine, draft copy, Story #335-63, 1963, 2, ARA.
17. Susan Sackett, *Hollywood Sings! An Inside Look at 60 Years of Academy Award-nominated Songs* (New York: Billboard Books, 1995), 77–88.
18. Wilfrid Sheed, *The House That George Built* (New York: Random House, 2007), 183.
19. Klein.
20. Ronell to Ernie Pyle, July 28, 1944, ARA.
21. Eileen Creelman, "Ann Ronell Discusses The Musical Score of 'Ernie Pyle's *Story of G.I. Joe,*'" *New York Sun,* October 10, 1945; Ken Johnson, "Fun Fare," *Toronto Telegram,* July 17, 1953.
22. *Boston Daily Globe,* "'Ernie Pyle Infantry March' Author Tells Here of Movie Songwriting," August 7, 1945.
23. Ann Ronell, "Linda" (New York: Leeds Music Corporation, 1945).
24. Creelman, "Ann Ronell Discusses."
25. Ann Ronell, "Linda," unpublished lyrics, n.d., Lester Cowan Collection, Harry Ransom Humanities Research Center, University of Texas at Austin.
26. Review of *The Story of G.I. Joe,* directed by William A. Wellman, *New York* Times, October 6, 1945.
27. *Ibid.*
28. *Turner Classic Movies Newsletter,* review of *G.I. Joe;* Lee Server, *Robert Mitchum: "Baby, I Don't Care"* (New York: St. Martin's Press, 2001), 83–89, 94–95; review of *The Story of G.I. Joe,* *Time,* July 23, 1945.
29. Rear Admiral J.J. Clark to Ronell, July 16, 1944, ARA.
30. Ronell to Jack Sheehan, August 10, 1944, ARA.
31. Staff member of American Society of Composers, Authors and Publishers to Ronell, telegram, February 28, 1947, ARA.
32. Dick Jacobs and Harriet Jacobs, *Who Wrote That Song?,* 2nd ed. (Cincinnati, OH: Writer's Digest Books, 1994), 147.
33. Julian B. Rosenthal to Ronell and Lester Cowan, February 26, 1947, ARA.
34. *Variety,* "Lester Cowan's *G.I. Joe* into 30 Texas Markets," July 15, 1970; *Dallas Morning News,* "Youngsters to See Old War Picture," July 15, 1970.

Chapter 12

1. Prunella Hall, "Screen Gossip," *Boston Post,* July 11, 1946.
2. *Ibid.*
3. Humphrey Burton, *Leonard Bernstein* (New York: Doubleday, 1994), 155–56.
4. Joan Peyser, *Bernstein: A Biography* (New York: Beech Tree Books, 1987), 154–55.
5. Burton, 156.
6. Peyser, 162; Burton, 157.
7. Peyser, 155.
8. Ronell to Leonard Bernstein, October 6, 1948, NYPL.
9. *Who Was Who in America: 1943–50* (Chicago: A. N. Marquis, 1950), s.v. "Clements, Colin"; *The Oxford Companion to American Theatre,* 3rd ed., eds. Gerald Bordman and Thomas S. Hischak (Oxford: Oxford University Press, 2004), s.v. "*Harriet.*"
10. *Variety,* "Inside Stuff — Legit," July 13, 1949.
11. *Ibid.*
12. Morrison Foster, *My Brother Stephen* (Indianapolis, IN: Hollenbeck Press, 1932), 51.
13. *The New Grove Dictionary of Music and Musicians,* 2nd ed., ed. Stanley Sadie (New York: Grove Press, 2001), s.v. "Foster, Stephen."
14. Morrison Foster, 55.
15. *The New Grove Dictionary.*
16. Ronell, "Composer's Notes," program, Pasadena Playhouse, *Oh! Susanna,* May 21, 1947.
17. Promotional card, *Oh! Susanna* (New York: Samuel French, 1950).
18. *Ibid.*
19. Ronell to Horace Peter Hunt, April 18, 1951, ARA.
20. Ronell to Floyd Crutchfield, Samuel French, April 18, 1951, ARA.
21. Reviews of *Oh! Susanna,* by Colin Clements, Ann Ronell, and Florence Ryerson, Pasadena Playhouse, May 21, 1947: Robert O. Foote, *Pasadena Star News,* May 22, 1947; Patterson Greene, *Los Angeles Examiner,* May 23, 1947; W. E. Oliver, *Los Angeles Herald-Examiner,* May 22, 1947; Katherine Von Blon, *Los Angeles Times,* May 27, 1947; *Variety,* May 23, 1947.
22. Ronell to Albert Taylor, May 28, 1947, ARA.
23. Oliver, *Los Angeles Herald-Examiner.*
24. Foote, *Pasadena Star News.*
25. Program, Pasadena Playhouse, *Oh! Susanna; The Concise Edition of Baker's Biographical Dictionary of Musicians,* 8th ed., ed. Nicolas Slonimsky (New York: Schirmer Books, 1994), s.v., "Nixon, Marni"; Stanley Green, *Encyclopedia of the Musical Film* (Oxford: Oxford University Press, 1981), 157; Marni Nixon with Stephen Cole, *I Could Have Sung All Night: My Story* (New York: Billboard Press, 2006), 86–95, 129–38, 144–54; Foote, *Pasadena Star News.*
26. Ronell to Vanette Lawler, Music Division, Pan-American Union, November 24, 1947, MHL.

27. K. Elmo Lowe to Garrett Leverton, November 12, 1949, ARA.

28. Review of *Oh! Susanna*, by Colin Clements, Ann Ronell and Florence Ryerson, directed by K. Elmo Lowe, Cleveland Playhouse, Omar Ranney, *Cleveland Press*, December 15, 1949.

29. William F. McDermott, review of *Oh! Susanna*, *Cleveland Plain Dealer*, December 15, 1949.

30. Ronell to Elsie Swanson, December 13, 1951, ARA.

31. Staff member, Samuel French to Harold Fendler, January 3, 1952, ARA.

32. Ronell to Florence Ryerson, February 18, 1951, ARA.

33. Ronell to Gustave Schirmer, February 7, 1951, ARA.

34. Ronell to Ryerson.

35. *Ibid*.

36. Ryerson to Ronell, March 27, 1951, NYPL.

37. Ronell to Martin Jurow, William Morris Agency, February 27, 1951, ARA.

38. Cheryl Crawford to Ronell, March 20, 1951, ARA.

39. Ronell to Ryerson, March 26, 1951, ARA.

40. Ronell, "What makes *Oh! Susanna* fresh and different material for a TV show serial?" n.d., unpublished notes, ARA; Ronell, "*Oh! Susanna*— Book-Musical TV Series," n.d., unpublished, ARA.

41. Ronell to Ryerson, April 10, 1951, ARA.

42. *Cambridge Guide to American Theatre*, ed. Don B. Wilmeth and Tice L. Miller (Cambridge: Cambridge University Press, 1993), s.v. "*Green Pastures, The*"; *The Oxford Companion to American Theatre*, s.v. "*Green Pastures, The*"; Gerald Bordman, *American Theatre: A Chronicle of Comedy and Drama, 1914–1930* (Oxford: Oxford University Press, 1995), 408.

43. *Cambridge Guide*.

44. Stockton Helffrich to Elliott Lewis, February 8, 1956, ARA.

45. Helffrich to Ronell, February 24, 1956, ARA.

46. Ronell, "RE:MENC Convention in St. Louis, 1956," unpublished notes, n.d., ARA.

47. Sam Saks to Robert Newman, September 5, 1950, ARA.

48. Ronell, unpublished notes, August, 1950, ARA.

49. Ronell and Ryerson to Herbert Yates, telegram, September 7, 1950, ARA.

50. Ryerson to Ronell, September 10, 1950, ARA.

51. Sol A. Rosenblatt to Robert V. Newman, draft copy, September 26, 1950, ARA.

52. Harold A. Fendler to Republic Productions, Inc., November 28, 1951, ARA.

53. IMDb review for *Oh! Susanna*, directed by Joseph Kane, http://www.imdb.com/title/tt0043874/ (accessed October 8, 2007).

Chapter 13

1. Steven Suskin, *Show Tunes: 1905–1985* (New York: Dodd, Mead, 1986), 307–08; *The Encyclopedia of Popular Music*, 4th ed., ed. Colin Larkin (Oxford: Oxford University Press, 2006), s.v. "Weill, Kurt."

2. David Drew, *Kurt Weill: A Handbook* (Berkeley: University of California Press, 1987), 347–48.

3. Ronell to Weill, January 22, 1948, Kurt Weill Foundation.

4. Ronell to Weill, December 18, 1947, NYPL.

5. Weill to Ronell, February 4, 1948, Kurt Weill Foundation.

6. Ronell to Weill, January 22, 1948.

7. *Ibid*.

8. Drew, 348.

9. Tom Donnelly, "Goodie! Here's Another Song We Can Leave Out!," *Washington Daily News*, June 23, 1950.

10. Ronell to Anya Berezovsky, November 29, 1948, NYPL.

11. Donnelly.

12. Ogden Nash and Kurt Weill, "The Trouble with Women" (New York: Chappell, 1943).

13. Gerald Boardman, *Jerome Kern: His Life and Music* (New York: Oxford University Press, 1980), 369.

14. Anonymous family member, interview with author, January 21, 2004.

15. Weill to Ronell, February 6, 1948, Kurt Weill Foundation.

16. Ann Ronell and Kurt Weill, "Don't Look Now, But My Heart Is Showing" and "My Week," Copyright Registration, U.S. Copyright Office, May 17, 1948.

17. Helen Van Dongen to Ronell, March 1, 1948, April 14, 1948, NYPL.

18. *Complete Encyclopedia of Popular Music and Jazz: 1900–1950*, ed. Roger D. Kinkle (New Rochelle, NY: Arlington House, 1974), s.v. "Haymes, Dick."

19. Ronell to Weill, March 1, 1948, Kurt Weill Foundation.

20. Ronell to Weill, February 6, 1948.

21. *Ibid*.

22. *Ibid*.

23. *Ibid*.

24. Ann Ronell, lyrics, Standard Uniform Popular Songwriters Contracts for "My Heart Is Showing" and "My Week," Chappell & Co., Inc., July 8, 1948.

25. Ronell to Max Dreyfus, Chappell & Co., Inc., September 23, 1948, NYPL.

26. *Ibid*.

27. *Ibid*.

28. *Ibid*.

29. Gene Buck to Ronell, October 10, 1939, MHL.

30. Buck to Ronell, December 21, 1933, MHL.

31. Buck to Ronell, April 6, October 10, November 4, 1939, MHL; Deems Taylor, ASCAP President to Ronell, April 1, 1943, MHL.

32. Ronell to Buck, November 4, 1939.

33. Ronell to Sylvia Rosenberg, ASCAP, September 30, 1948, ARA.

34. *Ibid*.

35. Ronell to ASCAP, November 29, 1949, NYPL.

36. *Ibid*.

37. John G. Paine, ASCAP to Ronell, November 12, 1946, MHL.

38. Ronell to Paine, January 1, 1947, MHL.

39. Ronell to Paine, January 13, 1947, MHL.

40. Ronell to Cheryl Crawford, October 28, 1948, NYPL.

41. Lester Cowan to Ray Anderson, Bankers Trust, New York, June 20, 1952, ARA.

42. Ronell, *A Song Out of Heaven*, typescript, unpublished, 1973, ARA.

43. Lester Cowan to Al Kingston, H. N. Swanson, Inc., March 11, 1973, ARA.

44. *Ibid*.

Chapter 14

1. Lester Cowan to Ben Hecht, July 3, 1947, MHL.

2. Frank Brookhouser, "Man About Town: Little

Lady of Words and Music," *Philadelphia Sunday Bulletin*, February 4, 1962.

3. W.E.J. Martin, "Ann Ronell Stands Alone Among Composers For Film," *Buffalo Courier-Express*, August 9, 1953, 4; Lucia Perrigo, Central Press, "Woman Composer May Try Score of First American Film Opera," *Terre Haute (IN) Tribune and Star*, August 27, 1950.

4. "Ernie Pyle Infantry March Author Tells Here of Movie Song-writing," *Boston Daily Globe*, August 7, 1945.

5. Ann Ronell, "The Score of the Month—*Love Happy*: Composer's Notes," *Film Music Notes* (March-April, 1950), 5.

6. *Ibid.*, 4.

7. *Webster's Third New International Dictionary*, s.v. "leitmotiv"; *The Harvard Dictionary of Music*, 4th ed., ed. Don Michael Randel (Cambridge, MA: Belknap Press of Harvard University Press, 2003), s.v. "leitmotif, leitmotiv"; *Oxford English Reference Dictionary*, revised 2nd ed., eds. Judy Pearsall and Bill Trumble (Oxford: Oxford University Press, 2002), s.v. "leitmotif."

8. Harry Geller, "An Article on *Love Happy*: Comments on Ann Ronell's Score," *Film Music Notes*, 5.

9. Paul Smith, "An Article on *Love Happy*: On Precision Timing," *Film Music Notes*, 12.

10. Ronell, "The Score of the Month," 4.

11. Smith, 10–11.

12. "Ann Ronell Visiting 'Home' Has Grand Career in Music," *Omaha Evening World-Herald*, August 5, 1953.

13. Smith, 11.

14. Review of *Love Happy*, directed by David Miller, Harry MacArthur, "Partly Happy," *Washington, D.C. Evening Star*, June 8, 1950.

15. Perrigo, "Woman Composer."

16. Ronell to Peter Artz, September 27, 1948, ARA.

17. Ronell to Lester Cowan, October 2, 1948, ARA.

18. Ronell, first draft lyrics for "Love Happy," to Peter Artz, September 27, 1948, ARA.

19. Ronell, "Love Happy" (New York: Jewel Music Publishing, 1949).

20. Geller, 9.

21. Lester Cowan to Mannie Sachs, Columbia Records, Inc., July 5, 1949, ARA.

22. Ronell to John H. Sarles, Knox-Reeves Advertising Co., unpublished lyrics, March 31, 1949, MHL.

23. Ronell to Lester Sacks, Jewel Music Co., July 15, 1949, ARA.

24. Ronell to Hal Dickinson, The Modernaires, July 29, 1949, ARA.

25. Compact disc, "The Complete Modernaires with Paula Kelly on Columbia, Volume 4 (1949–1950)," Sony Music Entertainment, 2002.

26. Lester Sacks to Ronell, September 13, 1949, ARA.

27. *Ibid.*

28. "Soundtracks for *Love Happy* (1949)," http://www.imdb.com/title/tt0041604/soundtrack (accessed November 25, 2007).

29. Reviews of *Love Happy*, directed by David Miller: Mildred Martin, "Marx Brothers at Karlton in Slap-Happy *Love Happy*," *Philadelphia Inquirer*, March 2,1950; Hortense Morton, "*Love Happy* Hits Classic Comedy Heights For Marx Bros.," *San Francisco Examiner*, October 13, 1949.

30. Lester Sacks to Ronell, October 25, 1949, ARA.

31. Ronell to Jesse Kaye, MGM Records, December 21, 1949, ARA.

32. Ronell to Peter Pryor, May 16, 1950, ARA.

33. Staff of "Betty Crocker: Magazine of the Air," Ronell, n.d., ARA.

Chapter 15

1. "Main Street to Broadway," *Theatre Arts* (July 1953), 17.

2. Arthur Schwartz, "*Main Street to Broadway*: Giving the Theatre a New Lease on Life," *Theatre Arts* (July 1953), 19.

3. Lester Cowan, "*Main Street to Broadway*: Stage and Screen Find Common Ground," *Theatre Arts* (July 1953), 20–21.

4. Schwartz, 19.

5. John Beaufort, "On and Off Broadway: A Girl from Main Street," *Christian Science Monitor*, n.d., 1953, ARA.

6. Lester Cowan to Ray Anderson, Bankers Trust, New York, June 20, 1952, ARA.

7. Cowan to Anderson, July 11, 1952, ARA.

8. Ann Ronell, "So You Want To Be a Music Director?: Notes on *Main Street to Broadway*," *Film Music* (May-June 1953), 4.

9. Mary Martin to Ronell and Cowan, December 23, 1952, ARA.

10. Ronell to Eleanor Lattimore, January 5, 1953, ARA.

11. Alex Barris, "On the Screen: Ann Ronell: The Only Woman Writing Music for Movies," *Toronto Globe and Mail*, July 18, 1953.

12. Ronell to Natalie Boardman, August 19, 1952, ARA.

13. Ronell, "So You Want To Be a Music Director?," 6.

14. Richard Rodgers and Oscar Hammerstein II, "There's Music in You" (New York: Rodgers & Hammerstein Foundation, 1953); Stanley Green, "Richard Rodgers' Film Music: Not a Few of His Songs Were Left on the Cutting Room Floor," *Films in Review* (October 1956), 398–405; David Ewen, *Richard Rodgers* (New York: Henry Holt, 1957), 293–94.

15. Ann Ronell, "Just a Girl" (New York: Ann Ronell Music, 1953).

16. Ann Ronell, "Theme from *Main Street to Broadway*: Blue New York" (New York: Ann Ronell Music, 1953).

17. Hye Bossin, "On the Square," *Canadian Film Weekly*, July 20, 1953; Barris, "On the Screen"; Ken Johnson, "Fun Fare," *Toronto Telegram*, July 17, 1953; *Stratford (Ontario) Daily*, July 20, 1953.

18. Ronell to Arthur Manson, July 21, 1953, ARA.

19. Manson to Ronell, July 22, 1953, ARA.

20. Reviews of *Main Street to Broadway*, directed by Tay Garnett: Mae Tinee, "Stars Pop In and Out of Benefit Film," *Chicago Daily Tribune*, July 29, 1953; Bosley Crowther, *New York Times*, October 14, 1953.

21. Crowther.

22. Alva Coil Denison and Ann Ronell, "*The River*," *Film Music* (January-February, 1952), 4–10.

23. Denison and Ronell, 4.

24. Ronell, "The River" (New York: G. Schirmer, 1952).

25. *Ibid.*

26. Ronell to Arthur S. Lall, Consul General of India, New York, March 6, 1952, ARA.

27. Letter, Arthur S. Lall to Ronell, March 7, 1952, ARA.

28. Ronell to Lall.

29. Ronell to Milton Krasne, May 19, 1952, ARA.

30. Ronell to Walter Lowenthal, May 20, 1952, ARA.

31. Ronell to M.A. Sreedhar, July 21, 1952, ARA.

32. Melvina McEldowney to Ronell, March 14, 1952, ARA.

33. Ronell to David Cavanaugh, March 25, 1952, ARA.

34. Ronell to George Avakian, April 11, 1952, ARA.

35. *The Encyclopedia of Popular Music*, 3rd ed., ed.

Colin Larkin (New York: Music Video Books, 1998), s.v. "Lieberson, Goddard."

36. Ronell to Gustave G. Schirmer, April 3, 1952, ARA.

37. Ronell to Morton Palitz, April 9, 1952, ARA; Ronell to Schirmer.

38. Ronell to Gustave G. Schirmer, July 23, 1952, ARA; Ronell to Walter Gould, July 28, 1952, ARA.

39. Ronell, "Notes on *Tin Pan Alley Girl* and *Words and Music: Ann Ronell Story*," unpublished, November 28, 1958, ARA.

40. Ronell, "Character Is Unique; Story Is Unique," circa 1953, unpublished, ARA.

41. Ronell, "Tin Pan Alley Girl: Personalities," circa 1952, unpublished, MHL.

42. Ronell, "Tin Pan Alley Girl: The Career of a Young Girl in a Man's World," circa 1953, unpublished, ARA.

43. Radie Harris, "Lester Cowan Film Being Made with Top-Bracket Cast," *Los Angeles Times*, December 14, 1952; Ronell "Notes from Meeting with De Rochement," circa 1952, unpublished, MHL.

Chapter 16

1. *Benet's Reader's Encyclopedia of American Literature* (New York: HarperCollins, 1991), s.v. "Crucible, The"; *Benet's Reader's Encyclopedia*, ed. Bruce Murphy (New York: HarperCollins, 1996), s.v. "McCarthy, Joseph R."

2. Ronell, "Sleep, My Babe, My Darling," musical manuscript, 1952, ARA.

3. Ronell to Kermit Bloomgarden, December 30, 1952, NYPL.

4. *Ibid.*

5. Ronell to Tony Randall, September 30, 1991, NYPL.

6. Jean Dalrymple to Ronell, February 19, 1953, ARA.

7. Arthur Miller, *The Crucible*, television production, 1967, #003805, collection of The Museum of Television and Radio, New York.

8. *The Complete Encyclopedia of Popular Music and Jazz: 1900–1950*, ed. Roger D. Kinkle (Westport, CT: Arlington House, 1974), s.v. "Friedhofer, Hugo."

9. Ronell and Hugo Friedhofer, "Hondo! Hondo!" (New York: Ann Ronell Music, 1953).

10. Ronell to William Hinckle, November 11, 1953, ARA.

11. Hugo Friedhofer to Ronell, October 7, 1953; Donald J. Stubblebine, *Cinema Sheet Music: A Comprehensive Listing of Published Film Music from* Squaw Man *(1914) to* Batman *(1989)* (Jefferson, NC: McFarland, 1991), s.v. "Hondo."

12. Ronell, "The Great Adventure" (New York: Ann Ronell Music, 1955).

13. Ronell to Edie and Rac, February 14, 1956, ARA.

14. Edmund Grainger, O'Brien, Driscoll, and Raftery to multiple parties, April 24, 1959, ARA; H. A. Ortiz to multiple parties, April 29, 1959, ARA; Irwin Snyder to H. A. Ortiz, May 1, 1959, ARA.

15. Ronell, *Very-Very Too-Too*, August 7, 1937, unpublished, ARA.

16. Ronell to Peter Lind Hayes, April 24, 1956, ARA.

17. *Encyclopedia Americana: International Edition* (Danbury, CT: Scholastic Publishing, 2005), s.v. "Nixon, Richard Milhous"; *Benet's Reader's Encyclopedia*, s.v. "Nixon, Richard."

18. *Encyclopedia Americana.*

19. *Ibid.*

20. Ronell, "Too Big a Price" (New York: Ann Ronell Music, 1956).

21. Ronell to Walter Craig, August 3, 1956; Ronell to Asher Lowich, August 3, 1956, ARA.

22. Ronell to Paul Ziffren, August 13, 1956, ARA.

23. Ronell to Paul Ziffren, September 13, 1956, ARA.

24. *The Complete Encyclopedia of Popular Music and Jazz: 1900–1950*, 680–81; *Wikipedia*, s.v. "Thelma Carpenter," http://en.wikipedia.org/wiki/Thelma_Carpenter (accessed 12/22/07).

25. Gene Lees, *The Musical Worlds of Lerner and Loewe* (Lincoln, NE: University of Nebraska Press, 1990), 91.

26. Ronell to Alan Jay Lerner, October 15, 1956, ARA.

27. Ronell to Dick Russell, May 30, 1960, ARA.

28. Adlai E. Stevenson to Ronell, August 10, 1960, ARA.

Chapter 17

1. *The Cambridge Biographical Encyclopedia*, ed. David Crystal (Cambridge: Cambridge University Press, 1994), s.v. "Sullivan, Ed(ward Vincent)."

2. *American National Biography*, eds. John C. Garraty and Mark C. Carnes (Oxford: Oxford University Press, 1999), s.v. "Sullivan, Ed."

3. Gene Lees, *The Musical Worlds of Lerner and Loewe* (Lincoln, NE: University of Nebraska Press, 1990), 202.

4. *American National Biography.*

5. *American National Biography*, s.v. "Disney, Walt."

6. David Smith, *Disney A to Z* (New York: Hyperion Press, 1996), 320–21.

7. *Time*, September 25, 1933, 30.

8. *The Cambridge Biographical Encyclopedia*, s.v. "Disney, Walt(er Elias)."

9. *Ibid.*

10. *Ann Ronell v. Walt Disney Productions, Inc., and Walt Disney*, U.S. District Court, Southern District of New York, Civil Action No. 101-179, "Plaintiff's Trial Memorandum — Preliminary Statement," December 1, 1958, 9.

11. *Ibid.*, 9.

12. *Ibid.*, 9–13.

13. *Ibid.*, 13.

14. *Ronell v. Disney*, "Original Complaint," April 11, 1955, 4, 7.

15. *Ibid.*, 9.

16. *Ronell v. Disney*, "Deposition of Plaintiff, Ann Ronell," September 8, 1955, 24, 22.

17. George Joy to Sol Bourne, January 9, 1934, ARA.

18. *The Complete Encyclopedia of Popular Music and Jazz: 1900–1950*, ed. Roger D. Kinkle (New Rochelle, NY: Arlington House, 1974), s.v. "Burke, Johnny"; Dick Jacobs and Harriet Jacobs, *Who Wrote That Song?*, 2nd ed. (Cincinnati, OH: Writer's Digest Books, 1994), 295, 394.

19. Donald J. Stubblebine, *Cinema Sheet Music: A Comprehensive Listing of Published Film Music from* Squaw Man *(1914) to* Batman *(1989)* (Jefferson, NC: McFarland, 1991), s.v. "*Palooka*."

20. *Time.*

21. "Deposition of Plaintiff," 68.

22. *Ibid.*, 345–46.

23. Lester Cowan to John Schulman, December 3, 1955, 2, ARA.

24. Cowan to Schulman, November 30, 1958, 1, ARA.

25. *Ronell v. Disney*, "Stenographer's Minutes: Opening Statement," John Schulman, December 1, 1958, 4–5.

26. "Stenographer's Minutes: Opening Statement," George S. Leisure, 10.

27. "Deposition of Plaintiff," 41–42.

28. "Deposition of Plaintiff," November 9, 1955, 240–41.

29. *The Complete Encyclopedia of Popular Music and Jazz*, s.v. "Spaeth, Sigmund."

30. *Ronell v. Disney*, "Stenographer's Minutes: Testimony," Sigmund Spaeth, December 2, 1958, 48, 50.

31. *Ibid.*, 69.

32. *Picture Music, Inc., v. Bourne, Inc.*, 457 F.2d 1213, *cert. denied*, 93 S. Ct. 320, 409 U.S. 99 L. Ed. 2d 262 (Southern District New York 1970), "Appendix," 58.

33. *Ronell v. Disney*, "Memorandum of Defendant," December 4, 1958, 1.

34. Neil Gabler, *Walt Disney: The Triumph of the American Imagination* (New York: Vintage Books, 2006), 183, 186.

35. "Testimony," Ann Ronell, from *New York Daily Mirror*, August 2, 1933, 138–39; *Detroit News*, June 15, 1933, 140–41.

36. "Testimony," Sigmund Spaeth, 49.

37. Cowan to Schulman, November 30, 1958, 1.

38. *Ronell v. Disney*, "Deposition of Defendant, Walt Disney," December 5, 1955, in "Stenographer's Minutes: Testimony," December 3, 1958, 198.

39. Elinor Hughes, "Radcliffe Honors Graduate Composer," *Boston Herald*, September 21, 1942.

40. Lester Cowan, "Lester Cowan's Record of Service to the Motion Picture Industry," n.d., unpublished, 1–2, ARA.

41. Cowan to Schulman, December 3, 1955, 2–3.

42. "Testimony," Ronell, December 2, 1958, 105.

43. *Ibid.*, 105.

44. *Ibid.*, 106.

45. Sol Bourne to Loyd Wright, May 11, 1934, ARA.

46. *Picture Music v. Bourne*, 58.

47. Loyd Wright to Irving Berlin, Inc. [Bourne Music], May 5, 1934, MHL.

48. George Joy to Sol Rosenblatt, June 21, 1934, ARA.

49. *Ronell v. Disney*, "Plaintiff's Trial Memorandum — Preliminary Statement," December 1, 1958, 14–15.

50. *Ibid.*, 1–2.

51. *Ibid.*, 18.

52. "Deposition of Plaintiff," September 8, 1955, 49.

53. *Ibid.*, 113.

54. "Deposition of Plaintiff," November 9, 1955, 321–22.

55. *Ronell v. Disney*, "Original Complaint," April 11, 1955, 4–5.

56. *Variety*, "Says Disney Cold Shoulder Has Hurt Her," December 4, 1958.

57. Cowan to Schulman, November 30, 1958, 3.

58. "Deposition of Plaintiff," October 18, 1955, 187–89.

59. "Preliminary Statement," 38.

60. "Deposition of Plaintiff," October 18, 1955, 174, 178, 195.

61. Cowan to Schulman, December 3, 1955, 3.

62. "Deposition of Plaintiff," 89.

63. "Deposition of Plaintiff," November 9, 1955, 271.

64. Stubblebine, 265, 313, 448.

65. Cowan to Schulman, 3.

66. "Testimony," Ronell, December 3, 1958, 163.

67. *Ibid.*, 168.

68. "Testimony," Lester Cowan, December 3, 1958, 192.

69. Cowan to Schulman, November 30, 1958, 3.

70. "Deposition of Plaintiff," October 5, 1955, 143, 151.

71. Stephen Suskin, *Show Tunes: 1905–1985* (New York: Dodd, Mead, 1986), 383; John Stewart, *Broadway Musicals, 1943–2004* (Jefferson, NC: McFarland, 2006), s.v. "Peter Pan."

72. "Deposition of Plaintiff," November 9, 1955, 324, 328.

73. *Ibid.*, 310.

74. *Ronell v. Disney*, John W. Clancy, U.S.D.J., "Opinion," January 12, 1959, 7.

75. *Ibid.*, 7.

76. *Ibid.*, 8.

77. "Testimony," December 2, 1958, 120–21.

78. Clancy, 9.

Chapter 18

1. *Wikipedia*, "Thomas B. Costain," http://en.wikipedia.org/wiki/Thomas_B._Costain#Novels (accessed April 12, 2007).

2. *Wikipedia*, "The Moneyman," http://www.fantasticfiction.co.uk/c/thomas-6-costain/moneyman.htm (accessed April 12, 2007).

3. Frank Brookhouser, "Man About Town: Little Lady of Words and Music," *Philadelphia Sunday Bulletin*, February 4, 1962, 11.

4. Ronell to Earle Lewis, February 2, 1950, ARA.

5. *New York Herald Tribune*, "Met to Create New Staging for 4 Works," April 7, 1960; *New York Post*, "Met Opera Lists '60-'61 Repertory," April 7, 1960.

6. Ronell, "Notes from the Preface to the Adaptation of *Martha*," 1961, ARA.

7. John Gutman to H. W. Heinsheimer, January 28, 1960, ARA.

8. Ronell to John Gutman, February 29, 1960, ARA.

9. Heinsheimer to Lester Cowan, March 16, 1960, ARA.

10. Ronell to Heinsheimer, May 25, 31, June 1, 6, 1960, ARA.

11. Ronell to Dr. Richard Lert, June 3, 1960, ARA.

12. Vicki Baum to Cowan, July 6, 1960, ARA.

13. *Ibid.*

14. *Ibid.*

15. Ronell to Baum, July 12, 1960, ARA.

16. Ronell to Baum, draft of letter, August 28, 1960, ARA.

17. Gutman to Ronell, September 9, 1960, ARA.

18. Gutman and staff to Ronell, September 9, 13, 19, October 26, 1960, ARA.

19. Gutman to Ronell, September 13, 1960, ARA.

20. Gutman to Ronell, September 19, 1960, ARA.

21. Ronell to Nino Verchi and Carl Ebert, September 30, 1960, ARA.

22. *Ibid.*

23. Gutman to Ronell, October 26, 1960, ARA.

24. Ebert to Ronell, November 6, 1960, ARA.

25. Ronell to Ebert, November 26, 1960, ARA.

26. Ronell to Lert, December 12, 1960, ARA.

27. *Ibid.*

28. *Ibid.*

29. Gutman to Ronell, January 10, 1961, ARA.

30. Ronell to Rudolph Bing, no date, ARA.

31. *Ibid.*

32. *Ibid.*

33. *Ibid.*

34. Ronell to Ebert, telegram, January 11, 1961, ARA.

35. "'Met' librettist won't be named," *New York Times*, January 20, 1961.

36. "*Martha* (Fact Sheet)," Press Department (New York: Metropolitan Opera, January, 1961); *Martha* program, Metropolitan Opera, 1960-61 Season.

37. Reviews of *Martha*, directed by Carl Ebert, Metropolitan Opera, January 26, 1961: John Chapman, "Met Opera Revives Old Tuner, *Martha*," *New York Times*, Jan-

uary 28, 1961; Louis Biancolli, "*Martha* Returns after 32 years," *New York World-Telegram and Sun*, January 27, 1961; Harriett Johnson, "Words and Music: A New *Martha* Returns to Met," January 27, 1961; Harold C. Schonberg, "Opera: *Martha* Revived," *New York Times*, January 26, 1961; Paul Henry Lang, "Music: *Martha*," *New York Herald Tribune*, January 27, 1961; Miles Kastendieck, "*Martha* at the Met: Sets to the Rescue on Opera Holiday," *New York Journal-American*, January 27, 1961; "Opera Reviews," *Variety*, February 1, 1961; "The Last Rose of Flotow," *Time*, February 3, 1961.

38. Biancolli.

39. *Variety*.

40. Biancolli.

41. *Variety*.

42. Schonberg.

43. *Ibid*.

44. Harold C. Schonberg, "Easy Way Out: Opera in English May Attract a Public, But Its Morality Is Open to Question," *New York* Times, February 5, 1961.

45. Johnson.

46. Lang.

47. *Variety*.

48. Johnson.

49. *Variety*.

50. Ronell to Elinor Hughes, March, 1961, ARA.

51. Lang.

52. "Tucker bursts into Italian for Met's English *Martha*," *New York Herald Tribune*, April 14, 1961; "Stage Talk," *New York Mirror*, April 15, 1961; "Tucker Disturbs 'Met' with Bilingual 'Treat,'" *New York Times*, April 15, 1961; Jack Klein, "Another 'M'Appari' in Italian May Upset *Martha* in English," *New York World-Telegram and Sun*, April 15, 1961.

53. *New York Herald Tribune*, April 14, 1961.

54. *New York Times*, April 15, 1961.

55. Ronell to Bing, telegram, April 14, 1961, ARA.

56. Klein.

57. Herbert Elwell, "Met's *Martha* Sparkles in New Finery," *Cleveland Plain Dealer*, May 1, 1961; Robert C. Marsh, "Met scores in *Martha* and *Turandot* here," *Chicago Sun-Times*, May 15, 1961; Hugh Thomas, "Met's Finale Here Has Zestful Pace," *Chicago Daily News*, May 15, 1961.

Chapter 19

1. "Mitchell A. Wilson," http://en.wikipedi.org/wiki/Mitchell_Wilson (accessed October 7, 2006).

2. Lester Cowan to ABC executive, circa 1964, ARA.

3. Jack Pitman, "With Joint U.S.–USSR Pic Still Pending, Cowan-Ronell Try TV Cold War Thaw," *Variety*, March 17, 1965.

4. Sally Hammond, "A Veteran of Cultural Exchange Will Write It Into a Film Script," *New York Post*, March 17, 1965.

5. Pitman.

6. *Ibid*.

7. "Tikhon Khrennikov," http://en.wikipedia.org/wili/Tikhon_Khrennikov (accessed October 7, 2006).

8. *The New Grove Dictionary of Music and Musicians*, 2nd ed., ed. Stanley Sadie (London: Macmillan, 2002), s.v. "Khrennikov, Tikhon"; "Tikhon Khrennikov," *The Voice of Russia*, http://www.vor.ru/VIS_A_VIS_new/TKhrennikov_arx.html (accessed October 7, 2006).

9. Tikhon Khrennikov and Ann Ronell, "Take Me, Take Me to the Moon" (New York: Ann Ronell Music, Inc., 1963).

10. Ronell to Herman Finkelstein, August 26, 1962, ARA.

11. Khrennikov and Ronell, "Take Me, Take Me to the Moon."

12. Stuart W. Little, "How Village Puppets Entered Russian Hearts the Easy Way," *New York Herald Tribune*, September 13, 1963.

13. King Vidor to Lester Cowan, December 22, 1966, ARA.

14. Louis Calta, "News of the Rialto: Lester Cowan Readies New Musical With Soviet Setting," *New York Post*, July 19, 1964.

15. Pitman; Hammond.

16. "*Who's Afraid of Virginia Woolf?*," http://en.wikipedia.org/wiki/Who's_Afraid_of_Virginia_Woolf%3F (accessed March 21, 2008), 1.

17. *Ibid*., 2.

18. Unidentified author, "'Who's Afraid of Virginia Woolf?' Events Re: Ronell," March 22, 1963, 1, ARA.

19. Ronell to Edward Albee, February 19, 1963, 1–2, ARA.

20. James Marshall, *James Marshall's Mother Goose* (New York: Farrar, Straus & Giroux, 1979), 4.

21. Ronell to Albee, 2.

22. Charles B. Seton to Lewis A. Dreyer, May 28, 1963, 1–2, ARA.

23. Ronell to Harold Fendler, November 11, 1963, 2, ARA.

24. *Ibid*., 1.

25. *Ibid*., 2.

26. *Ibid*., 2.

27. Ronell to William Krasilovsky, July 26, 1966, 1, ARA.

28. Ronell to Krasilovsky, November 18, 1963, July 15, 1968, February 23, 1970, ARA.

29. Krasilovsky to Ronell, July 18, 1968, February 10, 1970, March 2, 1970, ARA.

30. Krasilovsky to Milton Rosenbloom, November 6, 1969, ARA.

31. Rosenbloom to Ronell, April 7, 1970, April 20, 1970, ARA.

32. *The World Book Encyclopedia* (Chicago: World Book, 2006), s.v. "Goldwater, Barry."

33. Ronell, "Too Big a Price" (New York: Ann Ronell Music, 1956).

34. Ronell to Mayor Robert Wagner, August 18, 1964, ARA.

35. Ronell to Bernard Endelman, September 30, 1964, ARA.

36. *Ibid*.

37. Ronell, "Put Kennedy in the Senate Now" (New York: Ann Ronell Music, 1964).

38. Ronell, "Backward Ho! with Barry," unpublished lyrics, 1964, ARA.

39. Leonard Louis Levinson to Sam Brightman, August 29, 1964, ARA; Carolyn Gustafson to Ronell, October 27, 1964, ARA.

40. Richard Rodgers to Ronell, October 27, 1964, ARA.

Chapter 20

1. Gail Kubik to Ronell, May 8, 1968, NYPL.

2. Beatrice Sommer, interview with author at Nebraska Jewish Historical Society, Omaha, September 25, 2006.

3. Benjamin Sears, "Ann Ronell," unpublished manuscript, April 29, 2005, collection of E.A. Kral, 11.

4. "Little Lady of Song: An Interview with Composer Ann Ronell," draft copy, *American Illustrated,* U.S. Information Agency magazine, Story #335-63, 1963, 11, ARA.

5. Gene Lees, *The Musical Worlds of Lerner and Loewe* (Lincoln, NE: University of Nebraska Press, 1990), 249.

6. "Little Lady of Song," 11.

7. Frank Brookhouser, "Man About Town: Little Lady of Words and Music," *Philadelphia Bulletin,* February 4, 1962.

8. "They're Playing Our Song," program, National Association of Popular Music, Songwriters' Hall of Fame Awards Dinner, March 9, 1981.

9. *The New Grove Dictionary of Musical Instruments,* ed. Stanley Sadie (London: Macmillan, 1984), 206; *Musical Instruments of the World: An Illustrated Encyclopedia* (London: Paddington, 1976), s.v. "gusle."

10. National Association of Popular Music, newsletter, no.1 (1979), 1.

11. Donna Lawson, "Unsung Heroines No Longer," *New York Post,* June 29, 1977.

12. National Association of Popular Music, newsletter.

13. National Association of Popular Music, program, Songwriters' Hall of Fame Awards Dinner, 1991.

14. Anonymous, in phone discussion with author, April 26, 2004.

15. Ronell to Morton Gould, ASCAP, August 16, 1988, ARA.

16. Steven Suskin, *Show Tunes: The Songs, Shows, and Careers of Broadway's Major Composers,* rev. 3rd ed. (New York: Oxford University Press, 2000), 390.

17. *The Complete Encyclopedia of Popular Music and Jazz: 1900–1950,* ed. Roger D. Kinkle (New Rochelle, NY: Arlington House, 1974), s.v. "Fields, Dorothy"; Stanley Green, *Encyclopedia of the Musical Theatre* (New York: Dodd, Mead, 1976), s.v. "Fields, Dorothy."

18. Obituaries of Ann Ronell, *New York Times,* December 29, 1993; *Los Angeles Times,* December 30, 1993; *Hollywood Reporter,* January 4, 1994; *Variety,* January 5, 1994.

19. *Los Angeles Times.*

Bibliography

American Society of Composers, Authors and Publishers. *ACE Title Search.* "Willow Weep for Me." http://www.ascap.com/ace/search.cfm?request timeout=300 (accessed September 24, 2004).

Anderson, Leslie. "Women Film and Television Composers in the United States." Chapter 7 in *The Musical Women: An International Perspective: 1986–1990,* edited by Judith Lang Zaimont, 353–70. Westport, CT: Greenwood Press, 1991.

Ann Ronell v. Walt Disney Productions, Inc. and Walt Disney, Civil Action 101–179. New York: U.S. District Court, Southern District of New York, 1955.

Arndt, Jessie Ash. "Songwriter as Plucky as Three Little Pigs." *Christian Science Monitor* (January 3, 1955): 10.

Baral, Robert. *Revue: A Nostalgic Reprise of the Great Broadway Period.* New York: Fleet Publishing Corporation, 1962.

Benet's Reader's Encyclopedia of American Literature. New York: HarperCollins, 1991.

Biographical Dictionary and Who's Who of the American Theatre. New York: Heineman Publishing, 1966.

Bloom, Ken. *Hollywood Song: The Complete Film and Musical Companion.* New York: Facts on File, 1995.

Bohle, Bruce, ed. *The International Cyclopedia of Music and Musicians.* 11th ed. New York: Dodd, Mead, 1985.

Bordman, Gerald. *American Musical Theatre: A Chronicle.* New York: Oxford University Press, 1978.

_____. *American Theatre: A Chronicle of Comedy and Drama.* Oxford: Oxford University Press, 1995.

_____. *Jerome Kern: His Life and Music.* New York: Oxford University Press, 1980.

_____, and Thomas S. Hischak, eds. *The Oxford Companion to American Theatre.* 3rd ed. Oxford: Oxford University Press, 2004.

Brookhouser, Frank. "Man About Town: Little Lady of Words and Music." *Philadelphia Sunday Bulletin* (February 4, 1962): 11.

Buhle, Paul, and David Wagner. *Blacklisted: The Film Lover's Guide to the Hollywood Blacklist.* New York: Palgrave Macmillan, 2003.

Burton, Humphrey. *Leonard Bernstein.* New York: Doubleday, 1994.

Carnes, Mark C., and John A. Garraty, eds. *American National Biography.* New York: Oxford University Press, 1999.

Clarke, Donald. *Wishing on the Moon: The Life and Times of Billie Holiday.* New York: Viking Press, 1994.

Cline, Jerene Claire. "Ann Ronell's Songwriting Dynamo." *Omaha World-Herald Sunday Magazine* (November 24, 1948): C-4.

Cohodas, Nadine. *Queen: The Life and Music of Dinah Washington.* New York: Pantheon Books, 2004.

Crystal, David, ed. *The Cambridge Biographical Encyclopedia.* Cambridge: Cambridge University Press, 1994.

Drew, David. *Kurt Weill: A Handbook.* Berkeley: University of California Press, 1987.

Encyclopedia Americana: International Edition. Danbury, CT: Scholastic Publishing, 2005.

Ewen, David, ed. *American Popular Songs: From the Revolutionary War to the Present.* New York: Random House, 1966.

_____. *Richard Rodgers.* New York: Henry Holt, 1957.

Foster, Morrison. *My Brother Stephen.* Indianapolis, IN: Hollenbeck Press, 1932.

Gabler, Neil. *Walt Disney: The Triumph of the American Imagination.* New York: Vintage Books, 2006.

Gilbert, Douglas. "Girl Succeeds at Writing Songs After Getting Start on a Fluke." *New York World-Telegram* (October 15, 1942).

Gilvey, John Anthony. *Before the Parade Passes By: Gower Champion and the Glorious American Musical.* New York: St. Martin's Press, 2005.

Gorney, Sandra K. *Brother Can You Spare a Dime?: The Life of Composer Jay Gorney.* Lanham, MD: Scarecrow Press, 2005.

Goulding, Phil G. *Ticket to the Opera.* New York: Fawcett Columbine, 1996.

Green, Stanley. *Encyclopedia of the Musical Film*. Oxford: Oxford University Press, 1981.

_____. *Encyclopedia of the Musical Theatre*. New York: Dodd, Mead, 1976.

_____. "Richard Rodgers' Film Music: Not a Few of His Songs Were Left on the Cutting Room Floor." *Films in Review* (October 1956): 398–405.

Hamilton, David, ed. *The Metropolitan Opera Encyclopedia: A Comprehensive Guide to the World of Opera*. New York: Simon and Schuster, 1987.

Holden, Amanda. *The Viking Opera Guide*. New York: Viking Press, 1993.

Internet Movie Database. "Ann Ronell." http://www.imdb.com/name/nm0740056/ (accessed November 30, 2004).

Jablonski, Edward. "Ann Ronell — Omaha's Musical Trailblazer." *Nebraska Life* (Fall 1997): 16–19.

_____. *Harold Arlen: Rhythm, Rainbows, and Blues*. Boston: Northeastern University Press, 1996.

Jacobs, Dick, and Harriet Jacobs. *Who Wrote That Song?*. 2nd ed. Cincinnati, OH: Writer's Digest Books, 1994.

Johnson, Alva. "Profiles: American Maestro." *The New Yorker* (October 20, 1943): 26–30, (October 27, 1943): 23–26.

Kael, Pauline. *5001 Nights at the Movies*. New York: Henry Holt, 1991.

Kinkle, Roger D., ed. *The Complete Encyclopedia of Popular Music and Jazz: 1900–1950*. New Rochelle, NY: Arlington House, 1974.

Kowalke, Kim H. and Lys Symonette, eds. *Speak Low (When You Speak Love): The Letters of Kurt Weill and Lotte Lenya*. Berkeley: University of California Press, 1995.

Larkin, Colin, ed. *The Encyclopedia of Popular Music*. 3rd ed. New York: Music Video Books, 1998.

_____, ed. *The Encyclopedia of Popular Music*. 4th ed. Oxford: Oxford University Press, 2006.

Lees, Gene. *The Musical Worlds of Lerner and Loewe*. Lincoln, NE: University of Nebraska Press, 1990.

"Little Lady of Song: An Interview with Composer Ann Ronell." *American Illustrated* (Story #335-63, draft copy, 1963).

Maher, Michael J. *John Charles Thomas: Beloved Baritone of American Opera and Popular Music*. Jefferson, NC: McFarland, 2006.

"Main Street to Broadway." *Theatre Arts* (July 1953).

Miller, Tice L., and Don B. Wilmeth, eds. *Cambridge Guide to American Theatre*. Cambridge: Cambridge University Press, 1993.

Murphy, Bruce, ed. *Benet's Reader's Encyclopedia*. New York: HarperCollins, 1996.

Nelson, Nels. "Composer Ronell's 'Willow' Will Weep Forever." *Philadelphia Daily News* (January 7, 1994).

Nicholson, Stuart. *Billie Holiday*. Boston: Northeastern University Press, 1995.

Nixon, Marni, with Stephen Cole. *I Could Have Sung All Night*. New York: Billboard Press, 2006.

Notable Names in the American Theatre. Clifton, NJ: James T. White, 1976.

Peale, Patricia. "Those Songwriter Blues." *The New Yorker* (January 27, 1951): 49, 55.

Pearsall, Judy, and Bill Trumble, eds. *Oxford English Reference Dictionary*. Revised 2nd ed. Oxford: Oxford University Press, 2002.

Peirce, Bill. "Biography of Ann Ronell." Hollywood: Cinema Productions, 1953.

Perrigo, Lucia. "Women Composer May Try Score of First American Film Opera." *Terre Haute (IN) Tribune and Star* (August 27, 1950).

Peyser, Joan. *The Memory of All That: The Life of George Gershwin*. New York: Simon and Schuster, 1993.

Picture Music, Inc. v. Bourne, Inc., 457 F.2d 1213, *cert. denied,* 93 S. Ct. 320, 409 U.S. 99 L. Ed. 2d 262. New York: Southern District New York, 1970.

Pittman, Jack. "With Joint U.S.–USSR Pic Still Pending, Cowan-Ronell Try TV Cold War Thaw." *Variety* (March 17, 1965).

Pollack, Howard. *George Gershwin: His Life and Work*. Berkeley, CA: University of California Press, 2006.

Randel, Don Michael, ed. *The Harvard Concise Dictionary of Music*. 4th ed. Cambridge, MA: Belknap Press of Harvard University, 2003.

Reis, Claire R. *Composers in America: Biographical Sketches of Contemporary Composers with a Record of Their Works*. New York: Macmillan, 1947.

Rica, J. Benito. "Who Says Women Can't Write Song." *Popular Songs* (October 1934): 17–33.

Ronell, Ann. "Account of Creative Work." Unpublished: Nebraska Jewish Historical Society, n.d.

_____. "Ann Ronell — Personal Notes." Unpublished: author's collection, 1941

_____. "Ann Ronell — Prestige Work." Unpublished: author's collection, 1961.

_____. "Document composed by Ann Ronell for Werner Janssen to be included in his book." Unpublished: author's collection, 1979.

_____. "Notes on Ann Ronell's Life." Unpublished: author's collection, 1985.

_____. "Notes on Tin Pan Alley Girl." Unpublished: author's collection, 1958.

_____. "Record of the Published and Performed Works of Ann Ronell: Popular and Classical." Grant application, John Simon Guggenheim Foundation: author's collection, 1941.

_____, and Alva Coil Denison. "The River." *Film Music* (January-February, 1952): 4–10.

_____, Harry Geller, and Paul Smith. "The Score of the Month — *Love Happy*." *Film Music Notes* (March-April, 1950):4–12.

Rosenblatt, Anne. "A Dissertation on What's It All About." *Radcliffe Magazine* (January 1927), 26–27.

Sackett, Susan. *Hollywood Sings! An Inside Look at 60 Years of Academy Award-nominated Songs*. New York: Billboard Books, 1995.

Sadie, Stanley, ed. *The New Grove Dictionary of Music and Musicians*. 2nd ed. London: Grove Press, 2001.

_____. *The New Grove Dictionary of Opera*. London: Macmillan Reference Limited, 1997.

Sanders, Ronald. *The Days Grow Short: The Life and Music of Kurt Weill*. New York: Holt, Rinehart and Winston, 1980.

Schebera, Jurgen. *Kurt Weill: An Illustrated Life*. New Haven, CT: Yale University Press, 1995.

Schwartz, Nancy Lynn. *The Hollywood Writers' Wars*. New York: Alfred A. Knopf, 1982.

Sears, Benjamin. "Ann Ronell." Unpublished: collection of E.A. Kral, 2005.

Sheed, Wilfrid. *The House That George Built*. New York: Random House, 2007.

Slonimsky, Nicolas, ed. *The Concise Edition of Baker's Biographical Dictionary of Musicians*. 8th ed. New York: Schirmer Books, 1994.

Stewart, John. *Broadway Musicals: 1943–2004*. Jefferson, NC: McFarland, 2006.

Stubblebine, Donald J. *Broadway Sheet Music: A Comprehensive Listing of Published Music from Broadway and Other Stage Shows, 1918–1993*. Jefferson, NC: McFarland, 1996.

_____. *Cinema Sheet Music: A Comprehensive Listing of Published Film Music from* Squaw Man *(1914) to* Batman *(1989)*. Jefferson, NC: McFarland, 1991.

Suskin, Steven. *Show Tunes: 1905–1985: The Songs, Shows and Careers of Broadway's Major Composers*. New York: Dodd, Mead, 1986.

_____. *Show Tunes: The Songs, Shows, and Careers of Broadway's Major Composers*. 3rd ed. New York: Oxford University Press, 2000.

Tamarin, Al. "Ann Ronell Biography." New York: United Artists Corporation, n.d.

Thomas, Tony. *Harry Warren and the Hollywood Musicals*. Secaucus, NJ: Citadel Press, 1975.

Tietyen, David. *The Musical World of Walt Disney*. Milwaukee: Hal Leonard Publishing Corporation, 1990.

"Tikhon Khrennikov." *The Voice of Russia*. http://www.vor.ru/VIS_A_VIS_new/TKhrennikov_arx.html (accessed October 7, 2006).

Trenkle, Tom. "Ann Ronell, A Triple-Threat Author and Composer." New York: author's collection, 1961.

Warrack, John, and Ewan West, eds. *The Oxford Dictionary of Opera*. Oxford: Oxford University Press, 1992.

Who Was Who in America: 1943–1950. Chicago: A.N. Marquis, 1950.

Wilder, Alec. *American Popular Song: The Great Innovators: 1900–1950*. New York: Oxford University Press, 1972.

World Book Encyclopedia, 2006.

Index